33

DATE DUE
Unless Recalled Earlier

ILL 4-14-93			

DEMCO 38-297

The Politics
of Penury

Frontispiece:
Casa de la Moneda, c. 1881.
Departamento de Antropología,
e Historia de Mexico.

The
Politics of Penury

Debts and Taxes in Mexico, 1821–1856

Barbara A. Tenenbaum

University of New Mexico Press
Albuquerque

Library of Congress Cataloging-in-Publication Data

Tenenbaum, Barbara, 1946–
  The politics of penury.

  Originally presented as the author's thesis
(doctoral—Harvard)
  Bibliography: p.
  Includes index.
  1. Finance, Public—Mexico—History—19th century.
2. Debts, Public—Mexico—History—19th century.
3. Taxation—Mexico—History—19th century.
4. Mexico—Politics and government—1821–1861. I. Title.
HJ802.T46   1986   336.72   86-16027
ISBN 0-8263-0890-2

In Memory of My Grandmother
Bessie Zifferblatt Kerner

Contents

List of Tables

Preface

The science of government is the science of numbers.

Manuel Payno, *El Siglo XIX*

In 1800 New Spain was the most prosperous colony in Spanish America, and Mexico City, the viceregal capital, was the most populous city in the Western Hemisphere. From 1821, when Mexico declared its independence from Spain, until 1856, when the national government declared the dissolution of clerical mortmain, Mexico suffered severe political instability, fiscal insolvency, and military weakness. During those years, the nation had four different constitutional arrangements, fifty-three separate governments, and several hundred ministers. It was unable to fulfill its financial commitments to British bondholders, uphold provisions of diplomatic agreements designed to satisfy creditors in France and Spain, or pay its expenses. Furthermore, it could not adequately defend itself against an invasion of troops from the United States and, as a result, had to relinquish over one-half of its territory to its northern neighbor.

The reasons behind Mexico's rapid fall from great wealth and stability to economic and political chaos after independence continue to fascinate scholars and politicians. Some thinkers circulated explanations at the time which formed the theoretical bases for political parties. The Liberals argued that republican governments were too weak to maintain order and foster development because of the continued power and privileges of two colonial institutions—the Church and the army. Their Conservative opponents asserted that Mexican leaders had rushed into independence before the country was ready to govern itself and that they had deviated from colonial patterns too drastically and too rapidly. As time passed and the political and economic problems worsened, some began to speculate that the political disputes themselves caused all the difficulties.

Since then scholars have focused on other explanations. Justo Sierra, in his apologia for the centralized state established by Porfirio Díaz in the 1880s, argued that empty treasuries produced political instability. Bernard Moses thought that Mexican political instability was caused by its ineffective and antiquated transportation system. He believed that once Mexico entered the railroad age, national order and centralization would soon follow. Wilfrid Callcott blamed the weaknesses of the republic on corrupt and dishonorable leadership, an analysis seconded by Charles Cumberland and more recently by Michael Meyer and William Sherman.[1]

This study posits yet another explanation, not completely new in its focus, but wholly different in its implications. I argue here that Mexico was politically unstable during the early republic because its leaders mistakenly believed they could finance the government mostly from the proceeds of taxes levied on foreign trade. Unfortunately such collections fell far below projections, in part because of the collapse of silver mining; officials then were unable to meet expenditures and satisfy the inevitable opposition. My advocacy of a basically fiscal explanation does not exclude other factors. As this study will demonstrate the colonial heritage posed considerable obstacles to the evolution of a sound national government. And the Mexican elites' unwillingness to confront the structural problems imbedded in the fiscal system and to accept greater taxation of its wealth revealed its political immaturity. The absence of a significant export trade also took its toll. So did regionalism and the lack of a generally accepted national identity. Finally, the eagerness of politicians to use factional disputes and partisan views of history to obscure real problems and the venality and ambition of some generals must also be acknowledged. Yet it is the fiscal explanation which I will consistently present and develop in these pages. It is based on a careful study of all official budget reports *(Memoria de Hacienda)* issued by the Mexican republic during this period. Although the series is incomplete because governments failed to issue reports during times of exceptional turmoil, the treasury ministries issued sufficient sets of figures to allow adequate observation of the Mexican fiscal system at work and to identify fraud when it occurred.

If studied by themselves, however, budget reports do not reveal everything and can be very misleading. For example, do low collections from poor states mean lack of response to national authority or do they simply reflect the meager resources being taxed? This study supplements the printed reports with eyewitness accounts and explanations as well as regional records.

This work fits into a growing body of literature concerning taxes and fiscal policy in Spanish America. It follows in the tradition of Miron Burgin, *The Economic Aspects of Argentine Federalism 1820–1852* and David Bushnell, *The Santander Regime in Gran Colombia* and more recent work on the same areas *Guerra y Finanzas en los Origenes del Estado Argentino (1791–1850)* by Tulio Halperin Donghi and the provocative article "The Fiscal Problems of Nineteenth Century Colombia" by Malcolm Deas. It has also benefited from the mammoth labor undertaken by John TePaske and Herbert Klein on the accounts of the viceregal treasuries in the late colonial period.

This subject has awakened new interest recently for a variety of reasons. Scholars have discovered that the study of the performance of certain taxes, such as the alcabala, tithe, tribute, and so forth can be useful in obtaining valuable social information. But the underlying motivation for the recent upsurge of interest in fiscal policy and performance, particularly in Latin America, is that it provides a wealth of knowledge about the evolution of the nation-state.

One way nations demonstrate the strength and geographical extent of their power is through their ability to impose and collect taxes. Most countries in Latin America developed strong central governments, partly in emulation of the colonial structure and partly to avoid much of the turmoil they associated with federal regimes that failed. The evolution of the state in Mexico to 1856 is shown in part through the colonial *cartas cuentas* and the *memorias* of republican treasury ministers. The portrait that emerges from these reams of paper depicts a state of considerable extent and more power than is commonly supposed.

That nation-state, however, was a far cry from its imperial forebear. Colonial legitimacy was based on clerical and elite loyalty, buttressed by military power, and sustained by the longevity of the Spanish monarchy. The republican version lacked tradition and could not depend on the undivided support of notables, clergy, or officers. Gradually, it developed strong ties with a new group—*agiotistas*—merchants who lent money at short-term at high rates of interest to the Treasury. They substituted for more customary types of support after 1827.

The moneylenders came to need the Mexican state as much as that state needed them. As they invested their profits from lending into other areas of the economy, they developed even greater ties with the national state. Also, they perceived threats to that state as synonymous with dangers to their own interests and profits. Although many analysts have assessed their contributions as "parasitic" or purely self-interested, the moneylenders performed a vital national service at considerable risk. Some were simply interested in profits; some also cared deeply about Mexico's future. Some went bankrupt. Nevertheless, they provided an underlying stability in the midst of apparently chaotic politics.

The republican fiscal system never collected amounts sufficient to pay expenses regardless of whether the administration was federalist or centralist. In the midst of constant revolt, frequent invasion, and ever-present uncertainty, governments, whether "Liberal" or "Conservative," federalist or centralist, relied on agiotistas to supply all-important funds. The speculators also were responsible for fixing roads, carrying mail, converting currency, and negotiating foreign debt schedules. In effect, some of them became not only a branch of the Treasury, but carried out several of the routine activities of government as well.

In the 1840s the agiotistas invested part of their profits in textile factories. These moneylenders, called *empresarios* in this study, discovered a decade later that they required better ways to get their increasing production to market. For the first time they needed a strong, centralized, efficient national government to negotiate, contract, and supervise large-scale projects designed to improve transportation. They also wanted a state which could guarantee the safety of goods on the move and protect the roads from habitual *bandidos*. In 1855, these empresarios and others turned away from Santa Anna and sided with the liberals in order to create free access to property by attacking clerical mortmain and communal holdings.

Historians have generally overlooked the vital connection between growing industrialization and the Reform. The Liberals are usually identified with physiocratic ideas about agriculture and mining and with a general opposition to the protectionism associated with the promotion of native industrialization.[2] The empresarios, who supported them, however, wanted new roads and strong governments to foster industrial growth. In exchange, they were willing to forego artificial tariff barriers.

The empresarios' perception of Mexico's future and their role in it helped lead the nation into the Reform. Their willingness to lend to empty treasuries gave coherence to a republic still in formation and their loyalty in times of crisis preserved nationality. The ten years of civil war that followed left some of them bankrupt and their dream of industrialization unfulfilled. Their vision would finally be realized several decades later financed almost exclusively by foreigners under the leadership of Porfirio Díaz.

Acknowledgments

The World is too much with us; late and soon,
Getting and Spending, we lay waste our powers.
William Wordsworth, *Miscellaneous*
Sonnets (1807)

I'm just a material girl,
living in a material world.
Madonna, "Material Girl" (1984)

Many scholars have helped me in the research and writing of this study since it first appeared as a doctoral dissertation at Harvard University. My advisor, Professor John Womack, Jr., consistently supported this work and provided thought-provoking insights. Silvia Arrom, Marvin Bernstein, John Coatsworth, Carlos Marichal, Michael Smith, and Donald Stevens all read earlier drafts of the complete manuscript and offered useful suggestions as did Jean-Christophe Agnew, Peter Stanley, and Michael Weisser, who each read chapters.

Librarians and archivists in Mexico and in the United States worked tirelessly to assist in the research of this study. Special thanks are due to the staffs of the Lafragua Collection of the Biblioteca Nacional, the Archivo General de la Nación, the Hemeroteca Nacional, the Biblioteca de México, the Centro de Estudios Mexicanos (Condumex), Widener Library of Harvard University, and the Bancroft Library of the University of California at Berkeley. I am particularly grateful to Laura Gutiérrez-Witt, director, Wanda Turnley of the Manuscript Division, and the entire staff of the Nettie Lee Benson Latin American Collection of the University of Texas, Austin for their many kindnesses and displays of bibliographic expertise. I am also indebted to Dr. Sara Castro-Klarén, Chief, and her staff at the Hispanic Division of the Library of Congress, who always managed to locate crucial volumes. Mary-Dave Blackman and Peggy Clark typed the manuscript, and Barbara Guth edited it for the University of New Mexico Press.

This study received financial support from several different sources. The dissertation research was funded by a Harvard Graduate Prize Fellowship, the writing from a Radcliffe Grant. Vassar College Faculty Research funds facilitated subsequent trips to the archives. Some of the material in this volume first appeared in *México en la época de los agiotistas (1821–1851)* (Mexico: Fondo de cultura económica, 1985).

Because of the September 1985 earthquakes which devastated Mexico City, some citations, particularly from the Lafragua Collection of the Biblioteca Nacional, could not be verified prior to publication. Despite the help acknowledged here, all errors of fact and judgment are mine alone.

Finally, I want to thank my friends and family for their constant support and love.

Introduction:
Conquest by Taxation

> The Spanish colonies struggle in vain to extirpate the deleterious effects which we [Spain] gave them in return for the payment of their treasures, and by which the very entrails of their society were destroyed.
>
> *El clamor público*, May 21, 1853

> The first plan of independence for Mexico occurred to the property owners who held capital usurped by the famous Consolidation.
>
> Lucas Alamán, *Documentos diversos*

On many occasions during the nineteenth century, Mexican statesmen looked back nostalgically at the glories of the colonial past. Those with an interest in fiscal matters often bemoaned the passing of the highly efficient viceregal tax system which had earned so much revenue for Spain.[1] None of the commentators, however, ever acknowledged that the colonial treasury too had its share of problems.

For example, no viceregal official publicly revealed that as early as the end of the eighteenth century, the royal treasury *(real hacienda)* consistently outspent its income and was seriously in debt year after year to the colonial elite.[2] Few noted how the Crown's ever escalating demands for funds stimulated the drive for independence in New Spain. Finally, although hacendados and mine owners vociferously denounced the wars which followed for damage to their property, they hardly noticed the parallel destruction of the entire fiscal structure. As this study will show, the general ignorance of, or reluctance to accept, these basic facts significantly biased common perceptions of the fiscal situation once independence was achieved.

During the first centuries of colonial rule, the Spanish Crown devised a tax structure to extract as much wealth as possible from its possessions. Taxes on mining provided substantially more revenue than any other category in the viceroyalty of New Spain. The Crown gathered still more funds from sales taxes on goods including food and liquor levied on the general population, and from Indian tribute. Receipts from port taxes, however, were small and with only one or two exceptions, the system included neither property nor income taxes.[3]

Spanish authorities created a diversified tax base in order to insure revenue production in the event of a decline in mining output or a disruption of trade. Throughout the colonial period, residents faced a herd of royal officials demanding tax payments and beginning in 1602, the Crown also enlisted the cooperation of wealthier colonists by farming out the tax collections in the capital to the merchant guild of Mexico City (the *consulado*).[4]

The Bourbon Reforms

After the British capture of Havana in 1762, King Charles III and his ministers devised a program to improve colonial administration and to protect the colonies against future British attacks. The Spanish, like the British in their colonies, levied new taxes so that their possessions in the Western Hemisphere could finance their own defenses without help from Europe. Specifically the Crown wanted to stimulate mining in New Spain and boost the general economy there to generate tax revenues sufficient to finance a colonial army.

Charles III planned to establish the military security of the empire as quickly as possible. In 1764 he ordered Lieutenant-General Juan de Villalba y Angulo and his men to New Spain to organize a creole army. The colonists violently opposed military recruitment until the Crown increased the special rights of the army *(fueros)* to make it more attractive. Creoles then began to volunteer. By 1800, New Spain had an army of 9,917 men and a militia of 22,277.[5]

After efforts had begun to set up an army, Charles III sent José de Gálvez to New Spain in 1765 as *visitador general* with orders to promote silver mining and devise ways to increase tax revenues. The Spanish Crown, well aware that Britain and France were much more powerful economically and politically, also refined its techniques of siphoning off colonial wealth and sending it to the royal treasury. Gálvez lowered the taxes mine owners had to pay in order to cut production costs. For example, the government reduced its price for mercury from 82 pesos which it had collected in 1750 to 41.25 pesos per *quintal* in 1778, a 50 percent decline in just twenty-eight years. The Crown also began to favor miners in New Spain more than their Peruvian counterparts by deliberately shipping them more mercury in order to increase production. It reduced the price of gunpowder, also a government monopoly, by 25 percent. In 1781 miners received an exemption from the hated sales tax *(alcabala)* on supplies necessary to continued work. According to Brading, these reforms amounted to a 15 percent reduction in the overall costs of mining.[6]

More important, the Bourbon "revolution in government" as Brading has described it, profoundly affected the colonial tax structure.[7] In 1760, citizens of New Spain paid thirty-nine different categories of taxes—thirty-two in Mexico City and seven more on trade levied at the port of Veracruz. By 1790, those residents had to pay eighty-four separate taxes, fifty-four in Mexico City and thirty in Veracruz. This represented an increase over a thirty-year period of 169 percent in the number of taxes collected in Mexico City and a 329 percent hike in those gathered in Veracruz.[8]

Later, after he had become Minister of the Indies in Spain in 1776, Gálvez also reorganized the Royal Treasury in New Spain. He ended the previous practice of tax farming, and royal officials regained control over revenue collections throughout the colony. Gálvez also replaced creoles not merely with Spanish-born *peninsulares* but with many from his home region of Malaga. These new officials were eager to curry favor with their superiors and win promotion by squeezing as much revenue as possible from the local population.[9] Even Viceroy Conde de Revillagigedo the Younger complained to his successor:

It is impossible for the taxpayer to have knowledge of every one of the contributions, to know clearly what he ought to pay, and how and why he ought to do so. Such ignorance makes payment more difficult, even among the better class of vassals, who are incapable of defrauding the royal treasury, being quite convinced that

they have the obligation of bearing the expenses of the crown, . . .
To such vassals, the arbitrary methods of subordinates under a multitude of complicated rules, added to the unjust or improper manner in which subordinates are wont to conduct themselves, are
for this reason alone repugnant.

All of this is extremely difficult to remedy when there are so
many exactions, some of them so complicated and so difficult to
determine that their collection has to be left to the discrimina-
tion of the collector.[10]

One of the most significant alterations in the Spanish tax structure was the imposition of the tobacco monopoly in 1766. In his
instructions to Gálvez, the King had specifically ordered him to
organize an office and regulate the purchase and sale of tobacco
in New Spain. The colonists opposed the monopoly; growers protested Crown decrees that tobacco could only be cultivated in
certain areas and only sold to the state at fixed prices, and the
general public bitterly resented a monopoly on an addictive com-
modity like tobacco. For example, citizens of Guanajuato revolted
on July 17, 1766, demanding that army recruitment be stopped,
that state tobacco shops be closed, and new taxes annulled. Gálvez
suppressed the uprising with Lieutenant-General Villalba's troops
and continued all the controversial programs. In 1769 the government opened a state factory to manufacture tobacco products.
The monopoly was so profitable that one of its administrators
Joaquín Maniau called it "the most precious jewel that the King
had in his American domains."[11]

The new taxes considerably enhanced royal revenue collections.
In 1760 the Crown collected revenues totaling $ 4,675,178; in
1790 it garnered $ 11,493,748—a 23.9 percent increase over a
thirty-year period. Most gains appeared in port taxes (up 1156.7
percent), miscellaneous collections (up 944.6 percent), and taxes
on salaries (up 514.4 percent), but all groups except Indian tribute increased substantially due to Bourbon promotion of mining
and improved fiscal administration.

After collection, the Crown divided its revenue into four separate categories according to its eventual use. The first and most
important group included funds derived from taxes on mining,
tribute, taxes on the sales of offices, general sales taxes, port taxes,
the lottery, and monopolies on ice, salt, cockfights, and gunpowder. The third and fourth divisions included those taxes set aside

Table 1.   Comparison of Tax Collection in 1760 and 1790

Category of Tax	1760 collections	1790 collections	1790 collections as % of 1760
Mining	$1,458,695	$ 2,560,195	175.5
Sales tax	1,305,107	2,622,206	200.9
Indian tribute	765,849	741,770	96.9
Taxes on salaries	178,248	916,820	514.4
Monopolies	860,442	2,463,005	286.2
Port taxes	72,457	838,079	1156.7
Miscellaneous	34,380	324,756*	944.6
Totals	4,675,178	10,466,831	223.9

*Proceeds from sales of Jesuit properties *(Temporalidades,* $ 702,161) have been excluded.

Source: John J. TePaske with the collaboration of José and Mari Luz Palomo, *La Real Hacienda de Nueva España: Le real caja de México (1576–1816)* and John T. TePaske, "Sumario General de Carta Cuenta de Veracruz."

for special purposes, usually for public welfare. The amounts gathered from taxes in these three categories stayed in the Viceroyalty of New Spain, although not necessarily in Mexico. But the second category—proceeds from the monopolies on cards, tobacco, and mercury—went directly to Spain. In 1790, the Crown collected $ 1,798,520 or 16 percent of total revenue from these three monopolies; state control of tobacco sales alone accounted for $ 986,559 or 55 percent of that amount.[12]

The Impact of the Bourbon Reforms on a Credit Economy

Tax collections combined with payments for imported goods contributed to a widespread shortage of cash throughout the viceroyalty of New Spain. During those times when specie was in short supply, business had to be transacted on credit. But loans were available only to those who possessed recognized collateral or who were connected to others who did. The need for credit dictated the formation of the elite-family enterprise upon which the dynamics of the economy of New Spain were based.

As depicted by Kicza for Mexico City and Lindley for Guadalajara, the elite-family enterprise combined the security and agricultural production of land ownership with the marketing operations and access to liquid capital of the merchant. Since land was the only security generally accepted as collateral for loans essential in a cash poor economy, merchants needed to ally with estate owners or *hacendados*. Because estates required imports and the sale of their products, the hacendados, in turn, had to join together with merchants. The two groups often cemented their alliances by marriages turning everyone concerned into kinfolk, indissolubly tied together into one all-encompassing elite-family enterprise. Such organizations overcame potential disputes between peninsulares and creoles and between landowners and merchants. Consequently, some have argued these marriages and family businesses rendered those divisions meaningless throughout much of the colonial period.[13]

The new taxes and monopolies of the Bourbon Reforms aggravated the cash shortage for all but the few with connections to the mining industry. Yet the Crown even struck at them when it debased the coinage in 1772 and in 1786 and forced the mining guilds to lend it $ 2,500,000. Not content with that, Spanish officials also ordered guilds to take their money out of clerical control and form their own credit associations under royal supervision. Despite the new exactions, the colonial treasury began to borrow heavily and consistently from the elite beginning in 1795.[14]

When the Napoleonic Wars (1798–1815) cut Spain off from its colonies and emptied its coffers, conditions became more desperate. In 1798 in response to severe financial need and to those who claimed that clerical landholding retarded progress, the Crown ordered the Church to sell all property belonging to welfare institutions, brotherhoods, pious works, and church officials. The Church was then forced to lend the proceeds to the Crown at 3 percent yearly interest. The law netted very little in revenue and money was still needed to redeem war bonds *(vales reales)* sold to patriotic citizens in Spain.[15] Therefore on December 26, 1804, Viceroy José Iturrigaray promulgated the Consolidation Law, the culmination of a Bourbon attack on clerical power and wealth which had begun with the expulsion of the Jesuits in 1767.

The Consolidation Law was supposed to extend the peninsular expropriation of Church property begun in 1798 to New Spain, but it affected the society and economy in the colony very differently than in the mother country. In Spain, clerical capital was indeed invested in land which could subsequently be sold; in New Spain it was held in loans and mortgages used to operate an economy starved for cash. In fact this difference merely reflected a much more fundamental divergence between the Church as an institution in Spain and its colonial counterpart. Whereas the Spanish Crown and its servitors at home might justifiably have looked upon the clerical establishment as a competitor and a threat, in the New World the Church served as a firm supporter of Crown authority.

The Church provided a continuation of Spanish Christian culture and a sense of stability in the unfamiliar and challenging conditions of the New World. It did so by converting indigenous populations not only to the mysteries of a new faith, but also to the values of the Hispanic world. In addition, it controlled all formal education available in the Spanish colonies, essential to the pursuit of respectable careers and the maintenance of control over a numerically superior conquered population. Finally, the Church provided low-interest, long-term loans for the landed families.

Since the time when New Spain was established, many conquistadores and their heirs had willed part of their wealth to the Church. They did so not only to ease guilty consciences, but also because the Church, unlike secular property holders, was forbidden to sell its possessions, which it held in trust and in perpetuity as God's steward on earth. This aspect of Catholicism, known as clerical mortmain, gave the creole elite a sense of security and permanence. It also gave the Church access to immense wealth, which in times of financial hardship it customarily supplied to landowners.[16] As a result, stability and liquidity were assured and the aristocratic-clerical alliance firmly cemented, adding support to the elite-family enterprise.

It is impossible to determine precisely the impact of clerical credit on the economy of New Spain. In 1805, the Bishop of Michoacán, Miguel Abad y Queipo, figured that clerical coffers provided 1,999 of every 2,000 pesos on loan in the colony. The creole population regarded this system as a kind of tax shelter for its money. As Viceroy Conde de Revillagigedo the Younger noted,

Fortunes . . . would seldom remain in the soil where they were created. Sooner or later they would go to be consumed in Spain if they had not been invested in opulent foundations of convents, schools, chantries, and the many kinds of pious works which abound in this kingdom.[17]

The union of elite-family enterprise and the Church formed the foundation for Spanish authority in the New World and the basis of the colonial tax structure. Although the wealthy paid no income or property taxes as such, they supplied large amounts of revenue to the Crown from their mines. During the forty years from 1741 to 1781, the Conde de Regla paid $ 2,500,000 to the Crown for purchases of mercury, explosives, and for payment of taxes ($ 62,300 per year); the Conde de Valenciana had paid $ 2,800,000 in taxes by 1804.[18]

According to Doris Ladd, the notables of New Spain also gave the Crown voluntary low-interest loans *(donativos)* in exchange for the right to establish entails and preserve family fortunes. In this way the wealthy avoided the imposition of property and income taxes and provided moral and financial support for the political status quo.[19] However, the entire edifice rested on the continued availability of loans from the Church.

The Consolidation Law ended this happy arrangement by ordering that all mortgages be paid up. Each diocese had to draw up lists of loans and borrowers had to supply documentation of their obligations. Bishop Abad y Queipo complained that such paperwork would cost the colonists more than one million pesos. According to a table compiled by Ladd, twenty-six men of property alone owed a total of 1,754,878 pesos. This figure included a debt of $ 462,409 owed by the Marqués de Aguayo, $ 184,700 owed by the merchant and sugar grower Gabriel Yermo, and $ 7,000 owed by the parish priest Miguel Hidalgo.

Prominent landowners and creole officials vehemently protested against the law. The Marqués de Aguayo noted that if it were executed, no one would have the money to buy the property on sale and it would lay untilled and the people would be unemployed. He warned that widespread famine and crime would inevitably follow. The Crown, however, refused to rescind the order and its subjects dutifully went about obeying it. By 1809, the Church had sent over ten million pesos to Spain in exchange for the vales reales, one-fourth of which had come from the archdiocese of Mexico. Within the colony itself 218,000 pesos had been disbursed in payoffs to the Viceroy, the Archbishop, and other officials.[20] Yet these hard-won funds were still not enough to save Spain. In May 1808 the agents acting on behalf of the favorite of King Charles IV, Manuel Godoy, presented five million pesos of Consolidation collections to Napoleon.

By the eve of the Hidalgo revolt in 1810, many creoles had become deeply resentful of colonial taxation which shipped their wealth to Spain. Indeed residents of the provinces were equally annoyed at shipping their profits to Mexico City.[21] Further, irrespective of the impact of the Enlightenment ideas about economics and free markets, the creoles instinctively opposed monopolies of trade and commodities.[22] The success of the commercial reforms of the 1780s and 1790s *(comercio libre)* which opened twelve new ports in Spain and additional colonial harbors to trade had only confirmed their opinion. It also whetted their appetite for unrestricted exchanges with all nations. Similarly they agreed with the Prussian mining engineer Baron Alexander von Humboldt that mining would boom once under local control.[23] The subsequent fiasco of the Consolidation Law and the Napoleonic takeover of Spain served merely to reinforce their growing certainty of and opposition to peninsular weakness and ineptitude.

The Struggle for Independence

The Napoleonic takeover of Spain in 1808 inaugurated a period of great transition for its colonies. At first the Spanish merchants in New Spain simply feared retaliation in a nation controlled by creoles, and both the Spaniards and the creoles living in Mexico City wanted to protect their predominance over rivals in Guadalajara, Veracruz, Guanajuato, and elsewhere. As a result, fearful Spaniards led a pre-emptive coup against Viceroy José Iturrigaray which seriously weakened traditional colonial society and its assumptions.

Two years later, Father Miguel Hidalgo and army officer Ignacio Allende led between thirty and sixty thousand Indians in revolt against the Spanish Crown. Afterwards creole landowners were quick to associate images of Hidalgo's uncontrolled Indians with stories of guillotines in France and tales of large-scale massacres of whites in Haiti after independence. Mexican nationalists were shocked by such altered circumstances into a new loyalty to Spain and put aside deeply held grievances against taxation. They willingly shipped whatever wealth remained in New Spain in hopes that an authoritarian government could protect them from their social inferiors. The elites and the Church still felt themselves valued partners of the state and gladly contributed to its maintenance and stability. From 1808–1810 the landowners supplied the Crown with eight million pesos and, until 1812, voluntarily lent additional sums to the colonial government.[24]

The battle between those who sought to retain the colonial structure and those who desired complete independence continued for eleven years. In the Bajío and Western Mexico, rebel activities continued to threaten the status quo well after the execution of Hidalgo and his successors. The insurgency atomized into a series of localized battlegrounds where those with men under command, either guerrilla or royalist, could exact payment in exchange for the promise to protect lives, property, and/or crops.[25] The new environment fostered the development of caudillos of either stripe who came to replace royal intendants as the representatives of order.

But even as unrest upset the security of the countryside, new economic patterns promised to do equal violence to customary ways of transacting business. As Lindley has documented for Guadalajara, the Crown encouraged new settlers to come to the region, particularly after the Hidalgo revolt had led to a mass exodus of Spanish merchants. These colonists, some of whom claimed Panamanian origin, soon bought into important commercial ventures in the Bajío region and, once independence had been declared, quickly and openly affiliated themselves with British capital.

The newcomers insinuated themselves into Guadalajara with large sums in cash and took advantage of the customary shortage of specie intensified by the Consolidation, the ravages of the insurgency, and the government's demands for loans. As a result, they made strong inroads on the traditional credit economy and the elite-family enterprise, which for over three centuries had been the underpinning of Spanish rule in New Spain.[26] And the recent intrusion of cash transactions made propertied elite families even more reluctant to lend money to a government increasingly unable to repay them.

After 1798, 20 percent of yearly income for New Spain came from outright loans. Beginning in 1795 other categories such as "imposición de capitales" and "suplementos" appear that included groups of loans from clerical and other organizations. Together with acknowledged loans, these items produced 55.4 percent of royal revenue from 1809 to 1816.[27] In 1794, the Spanish Crown claimed an internal debt in New Spain of $ 8,532,324; by 1810 it had risen to $ 31,000,000, and two years later the official total read $ 35,489,020 although the Junta Superior de Real Hacienda claimed it was closer to $ 41,751,507.[28]

Some Mexicans quickly recognized the nature of the problem and offered solutions. For example, Bishop Miguel Abad y Queipo proposed in 1812 that all parties—borrowers and lenders alike—should share the debt and that the Church continue to apply flexible terms for loans. He predicted that unless credit was restored, the economy would disintegrate into a "new anarchy."[29]

The Crown reacted somewhat differently; it declared forced loans and demanded that colonists surrender their worked gold and silver as coins. In response, merchants began to refuse solicitations for funds unless their interests were guaranteed and started to speculate with mortgages on future tax collections. Viceroy Félix Calleja complained as early as 1813 that the government had fallen completely into the hands of its creditors and by April of that year, he calculated a monthly deficit of $ 260,000.

When he approached the elites for a loan, they demanded a mortgage on all the sales tax receipts for Mexico City and surrounding areas, on the pulque revenue, the two mill tax on road usage, and the war tax on food. Calleja had to pledge one half of the tax collections from Mexico City to obtain enough money to keep the tobacco monopoly, the gunpowder factory, and the mint in operation.[30]

Spain, too, was in financial difficulties and on September 13, 1813, the Cortes issued a *Nuevo Plan de Contribuciones Públicas*. This new scheme replaced sales taxes and monopolies with port taxes and *contribuciones directas* (head taxes) based on estimates of the size and wealth of each city, town, or village. Starting on November 15, 1813, the Junta Superior began to implement the plan augmented by a new 10 percent tax on urban property,

1 percent on coined silver, and, flying in the face of the Cortes's recommendations, a 50 percent increase in the price of tobacco and similar ones for other consumer items. In order to placate Spanish merchants the Junta exempted all capital from taxation.

Calleja was well aware of the defects of such a plan and wrote to his superiors at court:

> My government will inevitably be detested. Not only will the known enemies of the State abhor it and will do everything in their power to present it in a bad light to the people, but also the so-called Spaniards who are indifferent and egotistical and are not inclined to sacrifice what they have to save the country or perish with it heroically or with generosity.[31]

On July 21, 1814, Calleja established new principles for improving tax collections which included committees throughout the kingdom to assess rates and draw up lists for monthly regional collections. After the fall of the Spanish Cortes in 1814, Calleja renamed the new taxes "temporary war levies" *(subvención temporal de guerra)*. Meanwhile the viceroy experienced considerable difficulty in getting inhabitants to ante up for his forced loan and was obliged to resort to threats. The colonists' unwillingness to lend still more money stemmed from their pessimistic assessment of the future of New Spain. They believed that royal control would soon end and that the independent government would not be inclined to honor its debts. These assumptions helped the insurgency since wealthy residents gradually preferred to send their money out of the country rather than lend it to the government. The necessary new taxes further eroded the regime's base of popular support. At the close of 1815, the situation grew so serious that Viceroy Calleja even established a forced lottery.[32]

These additional levies show that the insurgency seriously affected collections of the standard taxes. In fact, the fiscal structure of 1785–1789 outlined by Fonseca and de Urrutia and subsequently used as a model by republican treasury ministers was already in decline in 1808 and hardly functioned in 1816 (Table 2). In that year the revenue gained from mining dwindled into insignificance and the viceregal government lacked the power to extract more money in any other category; increases in taxes on salaries resulted more from vacancies than loyalty. Although Ladd

Table 2. Comparison of colonial tax collections
            in selected years[34]

	Average 1785–89	1808	1816
Mining	3,691,038	1,981,623	258,521
Sales Taxes	4,533,237	1,832,269	542,592
Indian Tribute	825,697	336,985	1,417
Taxes on Salaries	827,279	1,663,610	1,758,340
Monopolies	8,088,700	721,244	318,008
Port Taxes	650,339	Not available	Not available
Loans, "Suplementos," etc.	0	21,154,001	29,678,563
Other	1,459,072	31,140,008	15,362,629
Total	20,075,362	58,829,740	47,920,070

Source: *Memoria de Hacienda 1870*, pp. 61–66; TePaske and Hernández Palomo,
La Real Hacienda de Nueva España for 1808, 1816.

presents a convincing case that the economy improved after this
date, we have little evidence to indicate that such improvements
were reflected in the revenues reaching the royal treasury.[33]

Credit became less and less available. In 1816 the administra-
tor of the estates of the Marqués de Vivanco complained that "the
most opulent capitals, the most lucrative trades, the largest and
most productive fincas, the best investments, the best-established
individuals—all have stopped paying their debts punctually. There
is no security for investment." In 1818, José María Quíros, a member of the Veracruz consulado, estimated that since 1810 some
786 million pesos in specie had disappeared from the economy.
Consequently, those few who still had cash refused to lend it,
and those who owed money refused to pay it back.[35]

In addition, the independence wars caused untold property damage, particularly in the silver-rich Bajío. Quíros calculated that
the colony had suffered losses of at least seventy million in agriculture, twelve million in industry, and twenty million more in
mining. From 1803–1810 the mints of New Spain coined a yearly
average of $ 24,016,182 pesos, but from 1811 to 1825 mining pro-
duction declined by one third. Not until the 1850s would the min-

ing of silver regain the levels typical of the years prior to 1810.[36] Nevertheless, up until the last moments before Iturbide's victory in 1821, royal officials tried to raise increasing amounts through loans and taxation despite salary reductions for civil, military, and clerical personnel.[37]

The Legacy of Insurgency

No one in 1821, no matter how prescient, could have assessed how much and in what ways the new republic of Mexico had diverged from its colonial past since 1808. In many respects, everything seemed much as before. This was particularly true since the Army of the Three Guarantees under the leadership of Agustín de Iturbide had triumphed because conservative interests wanted not independence but an autonomous status which would allow them to disassociate Mexico from a Spain controlled by liberals.

Nevertheless, the fighting itself produced significant changes in the country and sharp divisions on how to solve the political, social, and economic problems inherited from the colonial regime. In addition to the different viewpoints of insurgent and royalist and the legacy of flooded mines, enormous debts, and widespread property damage, the Mexican republic faced three unacknowledged challenges to its becoming a viable nation.

First, it would have to reestablish control over its territory. By 1821, the last viceroy Juan O'Donojú could not simply arrange an orderly transition from colonial to republican authority because many areas, such as the western coast later to be part of the state of Guerrero, were ruled not by a royal subordinate but by an insurgent in that area, Juan Álvarez.[38] Army commanders under Iturbide also laid claim to their own jurisdictions. Thus, the area that the republic inherited was not quite the same as the one Spain lost, but rather resembled a collection of petty fiefdoms ruled by suspicious leaders.

Second, it had to reclaim the loyalty of a population disaffected by frequent exactions and constant insecurity. The new national leaders had to convince the elites that they could control local chieftains and reestablish and maintain order and public safety throughout the republic. Further they had to do so quickly and convincingly in order to reverse a long-standing trend toward alienation and atomization. That done, the new republic could look forward to easy access to loans and public confidence.

Third, it would have to create a new and workable tax structure out of the ruins of the colonial system in order to support itself and maintain the troop strength necessary to the stability so urgently required. At the time of independence, the only source of revenue left to the government came from the universally detested tobacco monopoly. Thus, the republican government would have to design a new system which could satisfy its needs without sacrificing too much of its popularity. It had several models on which to draw—the prereform structure, the additions designed by the Bourbon monarchs, and the new proposals suggested by the Cortes at Cádiz—but it would have to settle on a plan and force the officials left over from colonial days to implement it.

The analysis of the period from independence to the forced sales of church property in 1856 depicted in these pages focuses mainly on the problems involved in meeting the third set of challenges. But it is the struggle to overcome all three and maintain the Mexican republic sovereign and whole which defines those years and determines their success and failure. What follows, then, is a case study of how well-meaning, intelligent, and often patriotic leaders tried to master the normal obstacles involved in transforming a colonial possession into a viable nation and may have as much relevance to problems in newly emerging states in the twentieth century as for those of Mexico in the nineteenth.

1

Independent Financing
1821–1834

Among the various errors we made upon becoming independent, the biggest perhaps was
our desire to be considered as one of the most
powerful nations: the resources of a colony, no
matter how wealthy, could not pay the expenses
of an independent nation.

Manuel Gómez Pedraza in his speech
against Piña y Cuevas's request for an
advance on the U.S. indemnity payment,
March 22, 1849.

Iturbide's Financial Strategy

Mexicans won their independence by uniting behind Agustín de
Iturbide and his *Plan of Iguala* issued in February 1821. His proclamation with its guarantees of Roman Catholicism as the state
religion, the equality of creoles and peninsulares, and the abolition of the caste system defined independence as separation from
Spain governed by a liberal cortes. On August 24, 1821, Viceroy
Juan O'Donojú and Agustín de Iturbide signed the Treaty of
Córdoba which recognized Mexico as separate from Spain and to
be governed by a junta including Iturbide and O'Donojú until the
treaty could be ratified by the Cortes.

Wealthy Mexicans supported the *Plan of Iguala* because they
saw it as their best chance to maintain a hierarchical social structure, get their credits acknowledged, and still be free of "the re-
strictions Spain had imposed on the Mexican economy."[1] The
insurgents accepted Iturbide's leadership as the only way to
achieve independence from Spain.

After he signed the Treaty of Córdoba, Iturbide consistently upheld his pledge of creole-peninsular equality and protection for the Church. When the Spanish Cortes rejected the Treaty of Córdoba on February 12, 1822, and their country became independent, most Mexicans revered Iturbide as a hero. There were few significant complaints when, on May 18, 1822, he declared himself Emperor Agustín I.

The elites now looked to their emperor to restore the economy and establish political stability. In the euphoria of the newly won independence, they seriously underestimated the difficulties of revitalizing the mining industry and restoring a severely damaged fiscal structure. Iturbide had made Mexico independent, but he was quite incapable of producing what only time and changing economic circumstance could accomplish.

Nevertheless he made a valiant attempt to tailor the remnants of the colonial tax system to provide revenue once more, to encourage foreign investment, and to preserve political consensus. He and the governing junta acted quickly to make mining more attractive, to boost trade, and to reestablish confidence. In a manner reminiscent of the Bourbon Reforms, the new nation lowered the costs of mining by abolishing the "royal tenth," consolidating nine separate taxes on precious metals into a simple 3 percent ad valorem tax, and ending the gunpowder and mercury monopolies. Trade became cheaper as import duties fell from 36.5 percent to 25 percent ad valorem; the alcabala dropped 10 percent to its prewar level of 6 percent and the 10 percent surcharge on goods leaving the capital was eliminated altogether. At the same time, the junta organized a committee to prepare lists of all preindependence debts so that the government could decide how to recognize and redeem them. Iturbide even tried to cultivate Indian support by officially sanctioning the de facto elimination of tribute payments. He retained the tithe, not only to help the Church but because it was one of the few taxes which had successfully generated income during the insurgency.[2]

Modern economists would praise Iturbide for his sound strategy for promoting national recovery. His efforts, however, required time and patience and those were in short supply given the overheated expectations independence had generated. It was inevitable that on every occasion when the empire fell short of some unrealistic goal, discontent would increase. But as the fiscal system refused to regenerate itself quickly, there was no money to placate grumbling or to buy support.

From the very beginning, the elites refused to rally round and lend money to the new government, even for short periods. For example, the merchant consulados rebuffed Iturbide's request for a $ 900,000 loan. The junta then demanded a forced loan for that amount guaranteed by properties of the Inquisition and a mortgage on the Pious Fund of the Californias, and half of the customs duties of Mexico City. But the difficulties continued. At the close of 1821, the Treasury contained a mere $ 6,647.[3]

As deficits increased, Iturbide's consensus began to deteriorate. Contemporary observers complained that the army was not receiving its due, while the emperor retained a court of 134 people costing $ 255,400 for household expenses for nine months, five times as much as the last Spanish viceroys. They also decried the significant drop in public services after independence and a concomitant rise in street crime in Mexico City.

These protests against "wasteful" expenditures and inefficient performance introduced the major theme of discussions of fiscal issues in Mexico during the years from independence to "the Reform." Since the elites refused to invest in the new government, it had no money to provide services or reward its supporters. In such an atmosphere, any expenditure looks excessive, and public welfare is certain to be neglected. But these were merely the visible effects of a far more important cause—the inadequacies of the fiscal system. Until the tax structure generated adequate revenues, Mexico would continue to suffer from severe political instability, ineffective government, and mounting deficits.

Yet the politicians continued to focus on the problems rather than the solution because the elites had no intention of paying more of their money to the government either in the form of loans or new taxes. When the fiscal situation grew untenable and leaders were forced to devise measures to increase revenue, the elites simply took advantage of long-simmering discontent in the army bred by inadequate pay and overthrew the offending government. This pattern was poignantly inaugurated with the fall of the first Mexican empire.[4]

The Constituent Congress which succeeded the governing junta on February 24, 1822, had to ask for gifts, loans, and then to exact funds and confiscate monies reserved for the Philippine missions and pious works. It was also forced to reduce employee salaries by 20 percent. In the meantime, the Congress authorized representatives to solicit a foreign loan for twenty-five to thirty million pesos with the entire national treasury as collateral.

By this time various opponents of Iturbide suggested that Mexico needed a federal republic rather than a greedy empire. On August 26, 1822, after he had rescinded pay cuts for the military, Emperor Agustín I ordered members of Congress arrested and suspended sessions. Nevertheless, his elite supporters still refused to lend to him despite promises to repay the debt and abolish the tobacco monopoly by 1825. At year's end, the deficit had risen to $ 2,826,637.[5]

The government had to levy new taxes and suggested an individual contribution of four reales from every person fourteen to seventy (derecho auxiliar nacional) and a housing duty (derecho de consumo) of 40 percent of the value of property or annual rent. In addition, the government printed four million pesos in paper money, which in an atmosphere of growing instability, quickly lost its value.[6]

On February 1, 1823, many important civilian and military leaders revolted in favor of a new Congress, provincial autonomy, and the establishment of a republic under the Plan of Casa Mata. On March 19, 1823, Iturbide abdicated and the paper money he had established was withdrawn from circulation. The first Mexican empire had ended.[7]

Loans from British Banking Houses

The leaders of the revolt against Iturbide expected deficits for the first few years. However, they were confronted by the same resistance to internal loans which had plagued their predecessor. The elites continued to view the government not as a partner, but as a greedy and indifferent consumer of their wealth.[8] Land and mine owners refused to risk their money by lending it to the government. Instead, they preferred to protect what they had left and try to recover their losses.[9] It would take years to renew their much abused confidence and regain their trust. In the interim, the elites decided to bide their time and solicit the urgently needed funds for recovery from abroad. As in many newly independent parts of the world, the merchants and landowners of Mexico believed that freedom and foreign investment would fulfill their dreams of peace, progress, and prosperity.[10] And, as elsewhere, reality fell far short of such overheated expectations.

Given the elites' reluctance to lend to any government, the new leaders decided to supplement tax receipts by negotiating a loan from British banking houses and by appointing Francisco de Borja Migoni Minister Plenipotentiary to Great Britain in May 1823.[11] They selected Great Britain as an appropriate source of funds in recognition of its preeminent status in capital markets following the Battle of Waterloo. During the eighteenth century Britain had accumulated substantial cash reserves because it could sell large quantities of manufactured goods to gold-rich Brazil. After the conclusion of the Napoleonic Wars, Baring Brothers and other banking houses lent large sums to the restored French monarchy, to other European countries, and eventually to the newly independent nations of Spanish and Portuguese America.[12]

The British held long-standing interests in Latin America dating from colonial times when they smuggled their goods into every port from Buenos Aires to Veracruz. In 1762 they captured Havana; in 1806 they invaded Buenos Aires and Montevideo and seized treasure there. These events stimulated the British desire for the wealth of Spanish America and the belief that flooded and abandoned Mexican mines would surrender their precious ore when confronted by British tenacity and know-how.[13] In fact Baring Brothers and Barclay, Herring, Richardson and Company were so anxious that the United States not reap this bonanza first that they petitioned Foreign Secretary George Canning to recognize the new republics of Spanish America without delay.[14]

Mexico received two large loans from British commercial houses. In the first, Borja Migoni concluded a deal with B. A. Goldschmidt and Company on February 7, 1824, in which Mexico received $ 8,000,000 in cash in exchange for bonds worth $ 16,000,000 bearing an interest rate of 5 percent and set to mature in thirty years. The Mexican government pledged to set aside one-third of its tariff collections after April 1825 as security. Although Borja Migoni swore that those were the best terms available at a time when the Holy Alliance had indicated an interest in reconquering Mexico, it is now known that his was the most disadvantageous agreement made during that period, providing a net amount of only $ 5,686,157.

Mexico fared better with its second loan concluded on February 7, 1825, with Barclay, Herring, Richardson, and Company which netted $ 11,992,910 cash in exchange for bonds worth $ 16,000,000 paying 6 percent interest. To secure this loan, Mexico pledged a second third of its customs receipts. Mexico only received a total of $ 17,019,455 from the two loans, but was obliged to repay $ 32,000,000 plus interest.[15] The Mexican government used over 60 percent of these funds to pay general operating expenses; the rest paid outstanding debts and won army loyalty by purchasing new equipment.[16]

The Fiscal System under Federalism

Once the empire had been dismantled, the new Constituent Congress governed Mexico as a federal republic. Mexico adopted the federalist system in response to the decentralization of New Spain which had begun in 1808. In fact, many areas had broken free from Mexico City during the insurgency and had not as yet been reconquered. Regional leaders were reluctant to pledge allegiance and revenue to an empire headquartered in the capital and ruled by a former Spanish army officer. They preferred to remit some revenue in exchange for as much autonomy as distance, inefficiency, and geography would allow.

The Congress of 1824 paid very serious attention to the development of the federalist fiscal structure. Every proposal received full and thorough discussion. For example, Deputies Manuel Crescencío Rejón (Yucatán) and Bernardo González Angulo (Mexico State) argued that the national government could not institute new taxes because it conflicted with states' rights and amounted to double taxation. They withdrew their objection once satisfied that the law applied only to emergencies. González Angulo himself advocated that states collect all revenues (including tariffs) and then remit 80 percent of the proceeds to Mexico City. Other deputies eventually rejected the idea because they feared that national governments would claim fraud and intervene in state treasuries at will.[17]

Congress finally decreed that the federal government could re-

tain all of its urban and rural properties including those confiscated from religious groups and receive all port taxes, revenues
from the mints, the gunpowder, tobacco, and salt monopolies,
the post office, the lottery, taxes on national property, and those
established in the territories. All other revenues—from sales taxes
(alcabalas), duties on gold and silver, individual contributions of
the equivalent of three days' work *(contribución directa)*, two-
ninths of one-half of Church tithes *(novenos)*, income taxes levied on specific civil and ecclesiastical officials, and taxes on pulque
and fighting cocks—belonged to the individual states.

As Josefina Vázquez has observed, the adoption of federalism
in 1824 kept the Mexican nation together.[18] But it was highly
expensive. Federalism cost the national government approximately 46 percent of colonial tax collections when the system
was in good working order (Table 3) and required that each state
have its own set of offices and taxes in addition to those on the
national level.

To compensate for the loss of almost one-half of national
income, Congress created a new tariff to go into the national
treasury—the *internación* or 15 percent ad valorem—as a substitute for the 12 percent sales tax previously levied at the ports on
some items. Congress also added a payment from each of the nine-
teen states to the nation *(contingente)* which totalled $ 3,148,500
and ranged from a $ 975,000 assessment for Mexico State (six
reales for each of its 1,300,000 residents) to $ 18,750 for Tabasco.
According to the Treasury Ministry, this division of revenue gave
the national government $ 10,663,500 to cover expenses totaling
$ 9,481,738 and provided $ 7,419,245 for the states with which
to pay the $ 3,148,500 assessment and $ 1,500,000 for expenses.[19]

The republican fiscal system was based on several generally
accepted assumptions about Mexico's future prosperity. Most
Mexicans confidently expected that taxes on international trade
would more than make up for any losses in the colonial fiscal
system, and Congress predicted that 44 percent of the 10,663,500
peso projection for national revenue collections would come from
the new taxes collected at the ports.[20] They also assumed not only
that foreign trade would be substantial, but that it would continue to increase. Further, they expected that once they had abolished the taxes hindering internal trade, it too would soon flourish,
enabling the states to pay their fair share to the national govern-

Table 3. Federalist Division of the Colonial Fiscal
Structure in 1824

Type of tax	Yearly average 1785–89	Division after 1824 National Treasury	State Treasury
Port	650,339	650,339	
Mint	0		
Gunpowder monopoly	451,909	451,909	
Tobacco monopoly	6,147,341	6,147,341	
Salt	201,033	201,033	
Post Office	0		
Lottery	134,096	134,096	
National Property	1,540	1,540	
Alcabala	3,546,715		3,546,715
Gold and silver	1,813,860		1,813,860
Government tax on tithe	178,111		178,111
Pulque	816,820		816,820
Cockfights	42,489		42,489
Taxes on jobs	46,396		46,396
	14,030,649	7,586,258 (54%)	6,444,391 (46%)

Source: *Memoria de Hacienda 1870*, pp. 61–66; Macune, *México y la federación*, pp. 75–76.

ment. They also had faith that foreign investment would make the mines productive again. Finally, they believed that these conditions would revive the confidence of the wealthy in their government and that they would begin to lend and invest once more. None of these assumptions proved correct.

The government considerably underestimated the difficulties of collecting port taxes. Bona fide customshouses existed only in Veracruz, Acapulco, and San Blas; otherwise merchants brought their goods in duty free. José Ignacio Esteva reported of Mazatlán in 1827 that

[In 1824] there was one Custom House officer at this port and he was blind. In January 1825, the Port was composed of 2 huts of mud and 4 of straw; now a Commissary's Office has been established here and the number of houses exceeds 200.[21]

Smuggling and corruption became commonplace. Guaymas and Mazatlán handled illegal imports of metals and Tampico serviced the Mexican need for cheap flour from the United States. In ports with established installations, officials still in place from the colonial days harassed honest merchants. Yet it was these men, underpaid, and that often belatedly, and making do with inadequate harbor troops, who bore the responsibility of supplying most of the nation's revenue.

Treasury officials were unable to translate the new 25 percent ad valorem tariff into a uniform rate schedule and exceptions multiplied. In the end brandy carried a 40 percent tax, wines 35 percent in addition to import duties, gold coins 2 percent, silver 3½ percent, and metal for jewelry 6 percent. Mexicans, accustomed to high Spanish taxes, thought the new tariff rates very low, but the English considered them usurious.

As the demands on the treasury grew, tariff rates increased. Customs officials could not keep up with the multiplication of tariffs, schedules, and rates pouring in from Mexico City and the complexity of the situation even forced honest traders into bribery. One merchant claimed that he paid each official *not* to open and examine each crate in order to avoid theft and damage to the shipment. On the Pacific coast merchants sent only the cargo which would not fit aboard smuggling vessels to the customshouse. One American businessman revealed that he paid the commandant $ 1,000 and the customs inspector and the harbor patrol $ 500 each in order to land $ 15,000 worth of prohibited goods.[22] Each time the government tried to end smuggling by making new regulations, illicit trade increased.

But worse still, the Mexican government had to survive without collections from Veracruz, its major port. When Iturbide and his army had proclaimed Mexican independence in September 1821, Spanish troops seized the fort of San Juan de Ulúa at the entrance to a channel which led to the Veracruz harbor. Thereafter they stopped boats seeking to enter the port and ordered passengers to the fort to pay a series of duties on their cargo. Some traders reported that the fort smuggled in many goods in order to help their compatriots on the mainland. In September 1823, the Spanish troops opened fire on the port and refused to surrender until November 17, 1825. Veracruz was closed for over two years.[23]

These difficulties reduced vitally needed customs revenue tem-

Table 4. Customs collections during the Federal
Republic 1823–1835

Year	Veracruz Customs	Customs Totals	Total Collections	Veracruz Customs as % of Total Collections
April/Sept 1823	$ 725,604	$ 971,346	$ 6,418,814	11.3
Jan/Aug 1825	310,764	4,593,545	8,384,863	3.7
Sept/June 1826	1,769,384	6,571,491	11,921,863	14.8
1826/1827	5,388,872	8,049,399	15,137,981	35.6
1827/1828	3,895,630	5,912,126	12,446,893	31.3
1828/1829	4,350,544	6,684,157	12,787,994	34.0
1829/1830	2,626,169	4,986,157	11,656,479	22.5
1830/1831	5,284,538	9,483,006	14,521,690	36.4
1831/1832	3,577,116	7,550,253	13,033,698	27.4
1832/1833	4,873,689	7,764,315	11,891,909	41.0
1833/1834	6,006,192	9,051,789	12,838,721	46.8
1834/1835	3,881,803	9,241,054	not available	

Source: Miguel Lerdo de Tejada, *Comercio exterior de México desde la Conquista
hasta hoy*, chart number 43, no page number; *Memoria de Hacienda 1870*, pp.
75, 81–82, 84–89, 94–95, 98–100, 106–107, 113–14, 118–19, 124–25, 139.

porarily. Other flaws, intrinsic to the system, could not be reme-
died so easily. The treasury's reliance on trade taxes made it
dependent on foreign desires to deal with Mexico. Although Mexican planners never imagined that possibility, foreign trade declined
in 1827–1828, 1829–1830, and 1831–1832 (Table 4).

Finally, the new structure created logistical and subsequently
political problems for the new republic. Because the ports were
located far from the capital, Mexico City inadequately supervised
collections and failed to stop smuggling. The national government
could not always protect shipments from bandits as they jour-
neyed from the coast to the interior.[24] And worse, port cities—
Veracruz for one—often decided to retain their collections in order
to finance a revolt against the national government. Indeed Veracruz could force the government in Mexico City into submis-
sion or topple it because, at this time, it controlled between 22.5
percent and 46.8 percent of national revenue (Table 5).

These problems made port taxes difficult to predict, collect,
and control. Nevertheless, they were more reliable and substantial than the portion of the colonial fiscal structure reserved for

Table 5. Revenue Predictions of 1824 Congressional
Finance Committee

Type of Tax	1785–1789 average	1816	Congressional prediction
Income tax equal to 3 days salary (contribución directa)	0	0	3,000,000
Sales tax (alcabala)	3,546,715	461,075	1,572,531
Tobacco monopoly	6,147,341	not available	1,500,000
3% on mining	500,625	18,097	360,000
Two-ninths of one half of tithe (noveno)	178,111	738,742	450,000
pulque	816,820	68,083	155,006
official paper (papel sellado)	59,765	16,296	130,000
Total	11,249,377	1,302,293	7,167,507

Sources: *Memoria de Hacienda 1870*, pp. 61–66; TePaske and Hernández Palomo,
La Real Hacienda de Nueva España for 1816; Macune, *México y la federación*,
p. 76.

the states. The Congressional Finance Committee had predicted
that states should gather $ 7,419,245 from their share of the tax
system from which they could easily pay the $ 3,148,500 due to
the national government.

These estimates were based more on the collections in 1785–
1789 than on those made in 1816, and the committee assumed
that almost one-half of predicted state revenue would come from
a newly established direct income tax! The result was disaster.

The tobacco monopoly, once the crowning achievement of Bourbon finance, proved to be a great disappointment. In 1824, the
Congressional Finance Committee predicted that the monopoly
would produce $ 2,500,000 annually, but in the nine years which
followed, it never yielded more than 1,356,127 pesos. Often, the
states were unable to pay for their tobacco allotments from the
national government. In 1827, they collected 914,947 pesos, but
owed Mexico City $ 1,883,888.[25]

The decline of the once flourishing monopoly reflected the general economic malaise, but it was also a result of incompetent
administration. Treasury officials frequently delayed purchases

for so long that tobacco growers preferred to sell their leaves to contrabandists who paid cash rather than risk their becoming stale. The government purchased leaf was often stored for as long as a year giving it ample opportunity to go bad and thus making it uncompetitive against fine domestic tobacco or the imported varieties smuggled in. British Consul O'Gorman wrote to his superiors that the upper classes in Mexico were openly smoking cigars made in Havana.[26]

The poor performance of the tobacco monopoly helps to explain why the states never managed to pay their yearly assessment in full and often had to borrow themselves. During the period, the states never paid more than 1,435,970 pesos, barely 10 percent of the national income and only 45.6 percent of the 3,148,500 peso assessment. The Mexican federal system was unable to pay for itself in the 1820s and 1830s.

The British loans, as planned, effectively compensated for the inadequacies of the new fiscal system and the delay in economic recovery. Without the extra money, Mexico would have had to experience deficits of over one million pesos for four out of five years. The loans cushioned the Mexican fiscal system and kept Mexico peaceful for three years. But once the loan money had been exhausted, deficits mounted unchecked and factionalist wrangling escalated once more. The economy needed more time to right itself, and politicians disagreed about what should be done next.

The fiscal system established in 1824 was based on over-optimistic predictions and expectations. Although taxes on international trade produced substantial amounts of revenue in good years, they failed to offset the small amounts gathered by the states because economic conditions had not improved as rapidly as expected. Mexican planners counted on establishing and implementing an almost entirely new system within a few years using the British loans as a stopgap until it was running smoothly. No one could have foreseen that the process would require decades rather than the few years allotted to it. As expenses consistently outstripped revenue collections, Mexican leaders began to disagree sharply about how the system should be changed. Deficits and arguments about how to remedy them hardly helped to restore elite confidence; indeed they fostered new tensions in a society with a three-hundred-year history of silence on political matters.

Mexican citizens, unused to such debate, quickly decided that factionalism fostered by unrestrained public expression, not the fiscal structure, was the cause of their problems. Most politicians avoided discussing crucial revenue problems and diverted all dispute into the political arena which served to confirm the politicians' own suspicions of politics.

Mexican leaders concluded that political patronage had sparked excessive expenditures and that domestic loans would fill the gap temporarily until the government reduced the number of employees. They solidly opposed new taxes, and preferred to seek another foreign loan. However, the British were no longer willing to lend. By 1825–1826 England faced a financial crisis of its own caused in part by its eagerness to furnish capital to Spanish America. Many commercial houses failed including Goldschmidt and Company and Barclay, Herring, Richardson and Company, whose collapse cost Mexico its $ 1,517,644 on deposit. Fortunately Vicente Rocafuerte, Mexico's London agent, persuaded Baring Brothers to cover the dividend due bondholders in September 1826.[27]

As the British financial depression deepened, interest in Mexican ventures declined and credit disappeared. British manufacturers who had supposed Mexico a large consumer market for their goods in the boom years of 1824 and 1825, became disillusioned when the elites' hunger for their wares was sated by 1827. As a result, legal trade fell abruptly.[28] In 1828 the value of imports declined $ 4,941,189 or 33.2 percent. This loss was not offset by a rise in the value of exports since they paid much lower duties. Revenues from customs collections fell precipitously to $ 5,912,126, down from $ 8,049,399 gathered in the previous year—a loss of $ 2,137,273 or 26.6 percent. That decline was reflected in the treasury receipts for 1827/1828 which dropped 21.6 percent to $ 12,446,893 ($ 2,691,088 less than those for 1826/1827).[29]

Reduced imports cut tax revenues so greatly that Mexico failed to pay its bondholders their August 1827 divided and defaulted on its loan obligations. When in October 1827 President Guadalupe Victoria instructed the Treasury Minister to renegotiate the British debt, Alexander Baring of Baring Brothers advised that Mexico first alter its fiscal system substantively before it promised to honor commitments previously broken.[30]

Three Remedies to the Problem

When Mexico defaulted on its payments to British bondholders, political leaders had to face the fiscal problem and try to find solutions for it. Despite the shock and shame of default, however, they refused to acknowledge that foreign trade and the internal economy had failed to produce sufficient revenue. Rather than reform the tax structure, they searched for ways to buy time until the system began to work as planned. The solutions that leaders proposed to meet this crisis ranged from the short-term expedient of internal borrowing to attempts to increase income and reduce expenses through foreign investment and better management to the more radical step of expropriating Church property.

Mexican political leaders decided to borrow funds from individual lenders, usually merchants, living in Mexico as a short-term solution to the problem of the deficit. Governments in Mexico had solicited loans during the colonial period and Iturbide had asked for first voluntary, and then forced, loans almost as soon as independence had been declared. These obligations had never been repaid, and in the years since 1821 the wealthy were too preoccupied with restoring their fortunes, in some cases by long litigations to break entails upon their estates, to consider lending to the new government.[31] Simply put, they lacked confidence in Mexico's future.

As Lindley has noted in his study of Guadalajara during the same period, the credit economy based on kinship, loyalty, and trust was giving way to more capitalist relations where the major considerations were risk versus profit.[32] Loans to the national government after Mexico's default in August 1827 had a different character from those made during the colonial period and in the first years of independence. They were designed to appeal to the lenders on the basis of profit, rather than patriotism, preservation, or partnership. They were also arranged so that lenders to previous governments and to the colony could use their debt certificates to form part of the total amount of the new loan. Through this mechanism, the government increased profit possibilities (since these credits were rarely sold at face value), enlarged the number of potential lenders, and reassured creditors that their paper could be used for something worthwhile while they waited for full payment.

The government authorized its first major internal loan in the amount of $ 8,000,000, half in cash and half in credits (accepted at 50–60 percent of face value) on November 21, 1827, just seven weeks after its default on the British debt. Five days later on November 26, several deputies introduced a bill in Congress calling for the expulsion of all Spanish-born residents from Mexico.[38] Although Mexican hostility against the peninsulares was at a fever pitch, the timing of the expulsion legislation was extremely suggestive. Many peninsulares who subsequently lent money to the government were exempted from its provisions.

Wealthy Spaniards like Antonio Alonso Terán and his nephew Gregorio Mier y Terán demonstrated their loyalty to the republic in cash in order to continue transacting business within its borders. The elder Terán had come to Mexico sometime before 1813 and founded a chain of silk shops with connections from Manila to Burgos. Mier y Terán arrived in 1818 and, when his uncle died in 1835, inherited a brigantine, haciendas, and ranches as well as property in Mexico City.[34] Neither entrepreneur wished to abandon his financial empire in 1827 and return to Spain so they managed to find a way to stay in Mexico. Indeed as *El Correo de la Federación* complained, exemptions were given to "people like Antonio Terán [who] had done nothing for the country but lend money to the established government without ever becoming its supporters."[35]

Many other Spaniards including Antonio Olarte, Ramón Martínez Arellano, Francisco Gámez, José García, Ramón Pardo, Esteban Vélez Escalante, Francisco Escalera, Manuel Gargallo, Florentino Martínez, Venecio and Juan Estanillo, Juan Monasterio, Antonio Ramon Landa, José María Rico (Terán's partner in the silk business), José Miguel Garibay, Pedro Jorrín, Ignacio Cortina Chávez, and Francisco Ondovilla also "won" protection from expulsion by virtue of their status as lenders to the government. The group also contained José María Fagoaga, one of the most vociferous supporters of Mexican independence, and Francisco Arrillaga, a former Treasury Minister.[36]

Non-Spanish merchants and entrepreneurs lent money because "they saw that they could gain 300 percent in a few days." This group included Robert Staples who had helped negotiate the foreign loans; Manning and Marshall, the agents of Barclay, Herring; Edward Wilson who later became involved in the tobacco monopoly, Levenger and Company; the German India Company; Gustavo Schneider, Adouc and Plantevigne; and Gustavo Sehenenheyda and Charles Uhde.[37]

As its demand for resources increased, the government offered lenders better and better terms. On December 24, 1827, it agreed to accept credits at more than 60 percent of their face value, and by the end of the year it had to enact a law prohibiting loans of less than 20 percent in cash.[38] Soon it began to settle such debts with letters payable directly from tariff receipts for the total face value of the loan plus a monthly rate of interest regardless of how much of the loan had been supplied in cash. By the end of 1827, lending money to the government usually at high rates for short periods *(agiotaje)* became an established and highly profitable business in Mexico. This activity began in earnest *before* any revolt had overthrown an elected government of the Mexican republic. At the close of the 1827–1828 fiscal year the amount borrowed within the country had grown by $ 755,936 or 1,633 percent over the previous year; the amounts steadily increased in the years which followed.

Historians may never determine precisely what percentage of "income" was really derived from loans since for each loan recorded there may have been two or three which disappeared into "general income." The money gathered from loans paid the army and bureaucracy but did nothing to solve the problem of fiscal insufficiency. The government paid exorbitant interest rates sometimes exceeding 300 percent from its only consistent source of revenue—the customs receipts—from which it also expected to pay more than half of its operating expenses. The treasury received even less money because it soon permitted lenders to receive payment directly at ports leaving open vast opportunities for fraud which guaranteed even lower collections. Administrations in power spent the treasury of their successors forcing them in turn to borrow still more in order to pay the bureaucracy and the army and remain in power. By 1830 the pattern was well established as internal borrowing became a way of life, necessitated by the inadequate and inefficient revenue structure.

Desperate financial need prompted governments incapable of bargaining into all sorts of deals with the agiotistas. According to Treasury Minister Lorenzo Zavala, on June 1, 1828, Manuel Lizardi lent money to the government at an effective annual rate of 536 percent and on July 23, 1828, Ángel González settled for a loan at a mere 232 percent annual interest.[39] In 1831 Treasury Minister Rafael Mangino boasted that the capitalist backers of the Bustamante regime willingly supplied it funds at 1 to 2 percent interest while at the same time listing an obligation of $ 2,570,324 for loans totaling $ 832,350 made in 1829/1830, an effective rate of return of 308 percent.[40]

Fortunately for historians, Treasury Minister José María de Bocanegra had to justify one such transaction to a hostile Congress and so wrote a description of it in the *Memoria de Hacienda* for 1832. At that time the treasury was so pressed for funds it sold a 4 1/8 percent share in the tobacco monopoly to Agüero, González and Company for $ 309,375 in credits and only $ 30,000 in cash. As Bocanegra explained:

> The $ 30,000 in cash . . . could not have come at a better time because the day it arrived in the treasury, we had no cash on hand and the need for funds was urgent and of high priority, such as giving $ 18,000 to the troops of General Mejía about to march South, and $ 10,000 to help out General Valencia's troops ordered to put down the rebels of Zacapoaxtla; and that was then one more, and if you will, the strongest reason for entering into the contract.[41]

In 1834 a former chief clerk of the Treasury Ministry, Juan José del Corral wrote an exposé of such loans, "Exposition on the harm moneylending has wrought on the funds of the treasury of the Republic and its administration and reflection on ways to remedy such damage." Corral argued that revenue had declined because Mexican leaders only addressed political problems. He complained that they had not bothered to examine the colonial attitude about taxes and had, instead, worshipped foreign models which hurt tax collection. Such indifference to the problem led Corral to denounce "the cabals and sordid maneuvers that more than a half dozen unpatriotic men have put into practice in order to ensnare the government."[42]

The agiotistas proposed to provide the specified sum in cash if the government would exchange $ 5,000,000 worth of debt paper for an equivalent amount in letters payable at the customs. Corral vehemently opposed the plan and soon resigned; a few days later Gómez Farías named Antonio Garay, the agiotista from Veracruz, to be Treasury Minister. Thus Garay, partly because of his probable friendship with another Veracruzano, President Santa Anna, became the first moneylender to serve in that post. During his short tenure in office (January 2 – April 24, 1834) he managed to expand the role of the agiotistas in Mexican life.[43]

Less than a year before, on June 1, 1833, Garay along with Francisco Gámes and Anselmo Zurutuza had become partners in a stagecoach line which had been purchased by Manuel Escandón the month before from an American firm. On June 10, 1834, after Garay had left the ministry yet undoubtedly instigated by him, the government contracted with that firm to repair roads running from Mexico City to Cuernavaca and in the Bajío. In exchange, the company would receive rights to all tolls collected in Jalapa, Veracruz, and Puebla, and permission to station its employees in the appropriate toll booths for the next fifteen years (1834–1849). The government also pledged to indemnify the company during periods when warfare disrupted normal collections. The pact was the first in which a moneylending firm took over the functions of the defunct consulados, and it began their official connections to the government outside of the lending business.[44]

Garay had been in office one day when the government agreed to accept any type of credit at 60 percent of face value in exchange for up to 60 percent of required customs payments; orders issued in 1834 could cover 50 percent of assessed customs duties. In addition, the government pledged to set aside 30 percent of the customs receipts to pay outstanding debts. In return the agiotistas quickly supplied the administration with loans of $ 500,000 and $ 1,500,000, reportedly in cash. According to Corral merchants made no contribution to these loans because "these very usurers by themselves supplied the money urgently needed for army expenses at good rates and terms: from then on there were always two brokers from the houses of Zurutuza and Garay on hand . . . because the usurers governed the Treasury Ministry."[45]

Mexican political leaders saw agiotista loans as a short-term remedy to the deficit problem. They believed that such infusions of revenue were needed to fill in the gap left by the exhaustion of the British loans until the fiscal system began to work properly. In the meantime, the politicians tried to find a way to increase revenue and decrease spending.

The process began on May 22, 1829, when Treasury Minister

Lorenzo Zavala levied new taxes to pay for the expenses of defending Mexico against the forthcoming invasion by Spanish troops led by General Barradas. He struck hard at the wealthy by imposing a 5 percent tax on yearly incomes exceeding $ 1,000 and 10 percent on those over $ 10,000; a business tax on capital investment in Federal District shops, and a 5 percent surcharge on property owned by nonresidents of Mexico. In exchange, he abolished the tobacco monopoly. In August 1829 Congress reduced salaries and pensions for all civil and military employees and demanded a forced loan from the states of $ 2,818,313. Finally on September 15, Zavala levied a 10 percent tax on rent for property worth over $ 500, a 5 percent addition to the import tax for foreign goods traveling to the interior, the extension of the Federal District business taxes to the rest of the republic, and a $ 12 per wheel tax on carriages.[46]

Despite the patriotic purpose for the levy, citizens were outraged. Within six weeks Zavala was forced to resign and the laws of September 15 were repealed. To replace the radical taxation, the government decreed a monthly state contribution of $ 265,000 most of which would come from the regressive state alcabala until a new fiscal system was designed. In the meantime the states and territories could appropriate the 10 percent tax on rents, a six peso tax on carriages, a 6 percent *consumo* tax on foreign products and 10 percent for foreign liquor, and the taxes on salaries. All these taxes, however, were repealed on February 9, 1831, retroactive to January 1, 1830.[47]

The wealthy took action against these threats to their possessions and supported a successful coup on December 4, 1829 led by General Anastasio Bustamante and fashioned by Lucas Alamán. Alamán hoped to create a republic in the image of Bourbon New Spain with a strong army and government aid to industry. He differed from Charles III only on matters of religion for Alamán believed that a strong Church buttressed social order.

The new administration planned a dual approach to fiscal problems. Treasury Minister Mangino sought to cut deficits through the efficient management of collections and disbursements rather than through the introduction of new taxes. As he explained:

> Since the deep wounds which we have received because of the emigration of capitalists are still fresh and because of the inevitable

upset caused by internal disturbances we have experienced, and
finally since neither credit nor public confidence has yet to be to-
tally restored, it would appear that in these critical moments it
would not be prudent nor even fruitful to create new taxes.[48]

At the same time Mangino and Alamán, as Minister of Relations,
encouraged additional foreign investment in Mexican enterprises
and industries. They believed that they could best inspire confidence by renegotiating the foreign debt and beginning payments
anew.

On September 28, 1831, the British bondholders ratified a new
arrangement with Mexico stipulating that the $ 7,922,100 in in-
terest owed since October 1827 would become $ 5,542,105 added
to the principal of the debt. They further agreed that interest due
from 1832–36 would not be payable until 1836. The Mexican government agreed that one-sixth of the revenue produced by customs collections at Veracruz and Tampico be set aside for debt
payments and the British consuls could be present to receive the
funds and report to the bondholders' representative.[49]

Their conciliatory attitude demonstrated a sad misreading of
international economic events of the time and had serious consequences for the republic. As Randall, Liehr, Platt and others
have noted, substantial British investments in Mexican mining
and other ventures made in the euphoria of the British boom of
1824–1825 had proven decidedly unprofitable.[50] By 1830, British
capitalists turned their attention to less speculative ventures primarily in Europe and less so in the United States. In the period
from 1830 to 1854, British investment in Latin America actually
declined from 23 to 15 percent of the total amount, and most of
the new monies went to Brazil. Mexico received little at all.[51] In
this atmosphere Alamán and Mangino's plans to stimulate investment had scant hope of success. Their insistence on paying
Mexican obligations in a futile effort to win foreign investment,
spent resources better used for other items. Also, the 1831 renegotiation called for consuls and bondholder representatives to be
stationed at the ports giving them legitimate access to customs
agents and ample opportunity for bribery and smuggling. Finally,
the Mexican inability to pay the debt owed to British bondholders intensified the reluctance to invest among the national elite
and weakened their faith in the nation. Such feelings were inten-

sified when, despite Alamán's establishment of the Banco de Avío for industrial development, foreign investors did not put their funds in Mexican projects. Thus the mistaken emphasis upon stimulating foreign investment at a time when none would be forthcoming hardly restored domestic willingness to risk venture capital at home.[52]

The Bustamante government promised to cut deficits through more effective management. During its lifetime (January 1830–August 14, 1832) income increased because of a spectacular 70.1 percent leap in customs collections from a low of $ 4,986,575 (1829/30) to $ 8,483,006 (1830/31).[53] However, this gain was offset by dramatic surges in both military and treasury expenditures. The growth in military expenses came from the administration's decision to win army support through preferential payment, the purchase of new equipment, and improved recruitment and organization. It spent $ 10,450,251 just on the army, the largest amount recorded in the history of the republic thus far. Since the years 1830–1832 were a period of relative "calm," these expenditures demonstrated the extent of the government's campaign to buy military loyalty, repress the population, and collect revenues.[54]

Despite claims of a $ 645,544 surplus for 1831–32 and notwithstanding phenomenal customs collections, the Bustamante administration borrowed $ 2,356,997 from moneylenders in 1830/31 and $ 3,734,566 more in 1831/32.[55]

While the Bustamante administration did not increase taxes, it made enemies by jailing political opponents and refusing to compromise with other points of view.[56] In 1832 General Antonio López de Santa Anna seized the Veracruz customs receipts totaling $ 279,000 and declared himself in revolt. The battles between Santa Anna and government forces are said to have been the bloodiest since the independence wars. By June 1832, Santa Anna had been so successful that the cabinet resigned and all parties drew up a convention pledging army support for the federal Constitution of 1824 and new elections, which Santa Anna won easily.[57] After he became President, he retired to his hacienda leaving his Vice President, Valentín Gómez Farías to fill the empty treasury and pay the $ 11,244,567 debt left by the Bustamante administration.[58]

Gómez Farías realized that he could not save federalism by cutting expenses. Many of his supporters were new to Mexico City and were eager to experience the pleasures of a government job in the capital. As Francisco Arrangoiz described them:

> The majority of the members of the Congress were new to the political theatre, absolutely unknown in good society . . . and some put on a dress coat or a Prince Albert and gloves for the first time in their lives when they attended the opening of the session.[59]

Nor, as Santa Anna's vice president, could he consider scaling down the army. Instead, he reintroduced Bourbon-style anticlericalism in the hopes of enlarging the tax base.

The Spanish Crown had begun using Church monies for secular ends in 1767 when it had shown little hesitation in expelling the Jesuit order from the New World, seizing its properties and pocketing the proceeds. The new rulers of the republic quickly followed their example with respect to the estates of the Inquisition. This behavior elicited much less protest in Mexico than actions against the Jesuits had earlier. The Church had lost considerable popularity in Mexico after the Pope ordered the Spanish-American clergy to support King Ferdinand VII of Spain in preference to the new republican governments and refused to appoint bishops to sees vacant since Independence.[60]

Francisco García, the anticlerical governor of Zacatecas, continued the attack in 1829 by trying to use Church property and capital in his state to fund an agricultural bank. After the Congress of the Bustamante administration had declared such action illegal in 1831, García offered a 2,000 peso prize and a gold medal for the best essay on the extent of civil authority over the clergy. The winner was Father José María Luis Mora, a genuine ideologue who believed that selling Church property could transform Mexico into a liberal, progressive nation of small landowners.

Gómez Farías and his allies, resentful of the support given by the Church to the Bustamante regime and determined to limit its power in republican Mexico, welcomed the ideas of the anticlerical priest. After Gómez Farías's government reduced the clergy's role in education and ended tithe collection, it sought to transform land owned by the Church into cash for the treasury.[61] Father Mora proposed that the government pledge to pay all operating expenses of the Church from the proceeds of the sale of its nonessential property to be valued at twenty times its yearly rental income. The government would then levy a 4 percent sales tax to be divided equally with the states.[62]

Former Treasury Minister Lorenzo Zavala proposed an alternative plan to fill the empty treasury. Zavala suggested that the government seize church property, sell it rapidly at public auctions, and use those funds to pay its creditors—a plan very similar to that used in France after 1791.[63] Gómez Farías opposed this proposal because it would have sold Church land to speculators in order to pay debts owed to the same speculators and strengthened their position in Mexican society. He urged Congress to adopt Mora's more moderate plan instead.[64]

Although Congressional committees approved Mora's proposal in February 1834, it never became law. The Church represented a conservative hierarchy to those still very powerful groups—the army, the clergy, the wealthy, and the traditional landowners—who hoped to maintain the colonial order under the aegis of a republic. They succeeded in recalling Santa Anna from his estate and by April 29, 1834, he ended the government's attempt to reform Mexican society. A beaten Gómez Farías officially resigned a few days later.[65] The flurry of reform was over.

The federalist fiscal system collapsed in Mexico for many reasons, not the least of which was its failure to generate revenue as expected. But it was also politically unnecessary. Fears of a strong central government and its fiscal system had prompted the federalist surge for regional autonomy. When it became apparent that the central government and fiscal authority had fallen permanent victim to the insurgency and could not be easily resuscitated, such protective devices became dispensable. Federalism in the 1820s and 1830s accurately described political reality and not merely a constitutional system. There was no need to sacrifice the Church to save something in no danger of extinction.

But even the vast wealth of the Church could not have saved Mexico from deficits. *El Fénix*, the forum for the most progressive viewpoint, argued that the radical step of selling Church property would not yield enough to help pay the debt. It claimed that if the Church owned $ 49,000,000 worth of land, even at an interest rate of 5 percent, the state could gain a mere $ 1,283,300 after paying clerical expenses to put toward the $ 2,400,000 annual interest payment on the foreign debt.[66] Indeed, it turned out to be even less effective in 1856 when the forced sale of Church property prompted a civil war and later a foreign intervention.

Furthermore, the Church was still irreplaceable in Mexican society in the 1830s. By that time, there was still no group as yet capable of lending money to both the government and the clients of the Church at the same time. The moneylender community was still forming in 1833–34 and was just beginning to win large-scale government contracts and no foreign bank had offered to assume the risks of lending money in Mexico.

Although the anticlericals failed in 1833–34, their attempt to end clerical mortmain to provide money for the nation had serious repercussions. In response to the attack, the Church decided that its future in Mexico depended on the preservation of centralists in power, thus creating a new strong clerical-centralist and later conservative political alliance. This army-clerical-aristocratic coalition demanded more from Santa Anna than a mere declaration of support for the status quo. It insisted that the President dismantle the federalist system and replace it with centralism. Various cities and states revolted in favor of centralism and by May 25, 1834, agreed on a formula known as the *Plan of Cuernavaca* which called upon Santa Anna to dismiss Congress and repeal all its anticlerical measures as a prelude to more substantive changes.

The Church recognized that centralism could only survive if it succeeded in generating enough revenue to support a government. Accordingly on June 3, 1834, nine days after the *Plan of Cuernavaca* was proclaimed, the Church pledged $ 30,000–40,000 to Santa Anna each month for the next six months and accepted the abolition of the tithe. In exchange the government pledged that it would not allow even the suggestion that Church property be expropriated.[67]

Although the Mexican republic did not proclaim a new Constitution until December 1836, the bargain between centralists, clerics, generals, and Santa Anna was sealed when the national government announced on December 8, 1834, its right to "confiscate the treasuries of the states in order to make sure the contribution was paid."[68] Its willingness to send troops to seize state coffers represents the true end of federalism and the introduction of centralism with its use of the army as tax collector. Yet even as Mexico's official fiscal structure changed, the moneylenders and their employees continued to prowl treasury corridors plying their trade.

2

The Invisible Stability
1834–1848

What would become of us if there was a well-
established government swimming in money?
For us there would remain no recourse except
to give up our accounts and become farmers or
mortgage our Capital like the nuns and friars to
live vegetating on our revenue.
Pedro Ansoateguí to Gregorio José Martínez
del Río, partners in Martínez del Río
Hermanos, June 15, 1839[1]

Santa Anna's statue was erected in the plaza,
with one hand pointing toward Texas, which he
was still promising to reconquer—though it was
remarked that it also appeared to be pointing to-
wards the mint.
Henry Bamford Parkes, *A History of Mexico*

Historians have not yet devoted sufficient attention to the nature of centralism in nineteenth century Mexico. While de facto
centralism began in December 1834 when the government decreed
that its troops could confiscate state coffers if the contingente
(state contribution) were unpaid, the transformation of Mexico
from a federalist to a centralist republic proceeded slowly. In May
1835 Congress assumed the right to modify the constitution at
will. It was not until October 3 that the government officially
declared itself to be centralist; thereafter states would be redrawn
into departments. This law also proclaimed that all state employees were forthwith at the disposition of the national government
through their respective governors. State treasury accounts were
closed and turned over to the officials of the new departments.

On October 10, 1835 the government ordered departments to give one-half of their incomes to the *subcomisarías* (local branches of the national treasury) to be used to pay the troops in each area, instead of the federalist contingente. Finally, on December 15 the national government ordered departments to stop paying salaries and bills and employees to prepare to turn over all payments to the *comisarías* and subcomisarías. The law specifically noted that payments to the army took precedence, leaving whatever monies remained to cover civil salaries and legal credits.[2] The centralist era had begun.

Centralism as a Political Organization

Centralism, as defined by the above legislation, resembled the political organization of Bourbon New Spain with the governor serving as the republican equivalent of Bourbon intendants. This arrangement in the Mexico of the 1830s and 1840s promoted regional autonomy even more than federalism had. The only link between the departments and the national administration in Mexico City was to be the governor and the comisaría officials. National supervision stopped at the governor's office, leaving him to direct internal events within the department. As Voss noted in his study of Sonora and Sinaloa in this period, "the centralist system, in the peripheral areas of the country at least, stripped away the powers of the states but was largely inattentive to their effective governance." Further, under centralism, the wealthy and powerful could mobilize their networks in Mexico City to help their interests within a department, a practice unthinkable under federalism.[3]

The paradox of centralism became even more profound when peripheral departments like Sonora had to contend with problems unique to their area. National leaders in Mexico City had favored centralism in order to draw on the departments to serve their interests, but centralism could only function successfully with a strong power in control in Mexico City. Mexico City's weakness led to great frustration in the departments which lost their autonomy but received nothing in return.

The Sonoran case was but an exaggeration of the typical. Ignacio Zúñiga, auditor of the Guaymas customs and later deputy to the national Congress, eloquently expressed the problem. Sonora, he explained, needed Mexico City's help to shore up the frontier and develop its territory, not the attentions of "a commander general removable at every turn, preoccupied solely with the [revenue] from the port of Guaymas." He noted that he had "heard persons very close to the government speak with more ignorance when discussing remote Sonora than they do when speaking of Tunkin or Bidedulgerid."[4] The government in Mexico City was unable to help faraway states and left the population there to the mercy of the rich who dominated local government through their wealth and connections.

And, there was the army. By ordering departmental comisarías to pay military expenses preferentially, centralism decentralized the army into regional units with their very own equivalent of a customshouse on which to draw. This system reinforced the disintegration created by the insurgency and left generals in place forever primed to revolt. Centralism, then, only managed to reinforce regional autonomy and national disintegration. During the centralist period (1834–1846), Texas, Sonora, and Yucatán all mounted revolts against the national government demanding separation from the Mexican republic. The success of Texas seriously affected Mexico's future under centralism.

After Santa Anna deposed Gómez Farías in 1834 and made clear his plans to end federalism, several regional leaders "pronounced" against him. The revolts in Southern Mexico led by Juan Álvarez, in Guanajuato and Querétaro led by José Antonio Mejía, in Zacatecas led by its state militia were all ended easily.[5] The revolt in Texas was much more serious and was the first of those which threatened to dissolve Mexico. It also destabilized centralism before it had begun to take hold.

On March 2, 1836 the Texas settlers issued their declaration of independence from Mexico to sanction a war already in progress. Santa Anna, named Commander in Chief of the Mexican forces in November 1835, assembled 6,000 men and headed to San Antonio de Béjar. After suffering defeats at the Alamo and Goliad, the rebels subsequently routed Mexican troops at the Battle of San Jacinto where Santa Anna was taken prisoner. To save himself and his men, the General agreed to an armistice and ordered his second in command, General Vicente Filisola, to retreat. On May 14, 1836, the President of Mexico signed a treaty with the President of Texas, David G. Burnet, preliminary to an official recognition of Texas independence. Andrew Jackson, President of the United States, finally managed to get Santa Anna released from custody and the famous prisoner made his way back to Veracruz, via the United States in mid-February 1837.[6]

The Texas War seriously crippled Mexican centralism, and Santa Anna's political career. The Commander in Chief planned that after a triumphal return from Texas, he would install himself as some sort of "wise and virtuous despot," but his ludicrous defeat and capture postponed his elevation. His prestige was so damaged that he resigned from the presidency.

The failure to reconquer Texas both encouraged military revolts within the country and probably prompted another invasion from without. Throughout 1837 regions rose in favor of federalism and in December General Urrea led a serious uprising in Sonora which the army could not crush quickly.[7] These revolts meant a decline in revenue and an increase in expenses. Almost before it had any chance to prove its effectiveness, centralism as originally conceived ended because abnormally high expenses made efficient fiscal management impossible. Mexico had entered a period of pretorianism characterized by crisis finance.

An example of the military crises that continued to multiply was the action known as the Pastry War. In March 1838 a French squadron entered Veracruz harbor and began a blockade there the next month. Although Barker claims the invasion was the result of blunders, misunderstandings, and time lags, the French simultaneously harrassed Veracruz and Buenos Aires in 1838 in what appears to have been a conscious policy. In order to raise sufficient revenue to mount a defense, President Bustamante neglected to tell the Mexican people that the leaders of the invasion force had stated their determination not to press forward into the interior of the nation in order to make their claims.

The Pastry War, and the taxes it required, unleashed more domestic unrest. Michoacán, Puebla, Tampico, Sonora, Chiapas, and San Luis Potosí all revolted in favor of federalism which put additional strain on the customarily overburdened fiscal system.[9] Yet at the same time it produced a hero; during a December 1838 skirmish in Veracruz, Santa Anna lost a leg but recovered the prestige and charisma he had squandered in Texas. In January 1839 he once again took power, although this time as a substitute President for Bustamante.

The federalists continued their struggle for power and almost overthrew Bustamante in July 1840. By that year, some members of the elite had already deserted the centralist camp. In 1840 one of their group, José María Gutiérrez de Estrada, published a pamphlet which proposed an alternative to Bustamante—a foreign monarchy.[10] The mere suggestion unleashed such an outcry that its political backers quietly shelved their plan and bided their time. In August 1841 Nicolas Bravo, Santa Anna, and General Mariano Paredes y Arrillaga revolted in favor of a new constitution and an end to high taxes. The group unseated President Bustamante and Santa Anna became President once more.

The new President wanted to transform chaos into order by joining forces with the traditional elites who wanted a monarchy with its trappings. Santa Anna satisfied these groups by creating a personalistic dictatorship complete with a public burial of the leg he had lost during the Pastry War, a statue of himself, and lavish displays of pomp and pageantry. In addition, the new constitution *The Organic Bases* proclaimed on June 12, 1843, reflected elite notions of a popular government. The three-tiered indirect electoral system had income requirements for deputies and senators of $ 1,200 and $ 2,000 respectively and gave the national government almost total control over the states. It specifically reaffirmed Catholicism as the official religion of Mexico and pledged to maintain the privileges of clergy, army, and mining corporations.[11]

Santa Anna also strengthened his control over the army. After first placating Generals Álvarez, Bravo, and Urrea and authorizing the purchase of war materiel in Europe, he created new troop units, which would provide promotions for the officer corps. He added two active squadrons in Jalapa and Orizaba, a regiment of cavalry in Michoacán, two squadrons in the department of Mexico, a regiment of cavalry in Jalisco, a battalion of grenadiers in Mexico City, a battalion, and two companies of coast guard units in Mazatlán, and a squadron in Baja California.[12]

Yet 1842 was hardly a quiet year. Indian revolts affected many of the peripheral areas, Sonora was in the midst of a civil war as was Baja California, and Puebla and Oaxaca continued in federalist revolt. Yucatán had declared itself independent in March

1841. Troops from Mexico City capitulated in 1843, but reinforcements besieged Campeche and helped foster an armistice which virtually made Yucatán a sovereign nation. The national army went on to subdue a rebellious Tabasco.[13] And of course plans were made and funds collected yet again to reconquer Texas, which, for its part, stirred up trouble with frequent incursions into New Mexico. In 1844, the government's plan for a public contribution of 10 million pesos, in addition to steadily elevated taxes and previous forced contributions encouraged General Paredes to launch a revolt. Santa Anna arrived in Querétaro on November 25, 1844 ready to battle Paredes and the other rebels. Meanwhile on December 5, the Mexico City garrison proclaimed José Joaquín de Herrera president. Santa Anna was captured at Perote and later put on a boat headed for what seemed like permanent exile.[14] Centralism had proved incapable of creating and maintaining as stable a political union as federalism and, in fact, had seriously weakened what unity there had been.

The Centralist Revenue System

Although centralism changed the fiscal relationship between the national treasury and those of the departments, it retained the original federalist division of revenue. As stated in chapter 1, the national government received all port taxes; revenues from the mints; the gunpowder, tobacco, and salt monopolies; the post office revenues; the lottery; and taxes on national property. In the years after 1824, the states as a rule collected revenue from alcabalas, taxes on pulque, the consumo tax (3 percent of the value of imported goods), official paper, cockfights, tobacco monopoly, clerical tithes, *contribuciones directas* (three days' salary) and duties on gold and silver. They were, of course, completely free to levy whatever taxes appeared necessary. In 1828 Michoacán collected six different alcabalas, and paid $ 107,535 to the national government (its scheduled payment was $ 175,000).

Under federalism, the states were connected to the national government and treasury by means of the contingente which was proportional to estimated state population. On February 11, 1832 that was changed to 30 percent of revenue collections.[15] The following year, the states gave the federal government a total of

$ 624,969, far short of the $ 3,148,500 envisioned in 1823. The system was in definite need of reform.

The centralists moved very slowly in restructuring the relationship between the states and the nation. On March 4, 1835, they decreed that the national treasury would only insist on collecting 25 percent of the amount owed for back contingente payments due since April 1, 1832 and that this could be paid in cash, in credits to be accepted at face value, or in tolls. In the unlikely event that the states might wish to pay in cash, they could make their contributions over a period of thirty-six months. Finally on October 10, 1835, the government ordered that one-half of departmental income be used to pay troops and the contingente was eliminated. However, the centralists went to some trouble to keep the departmental fiscal identity intact. They specifically retained state methods of collection and accounting used since 1824 and ordered that officials from the national treasury had no power over departmental offices (January 9, 1836).[16]

After the successful Texas revolt and other uprisings had undermined their ability to control national affairs, the centralists abruptly shifted gears. They closed department offices and demanded that all tax collections and disbursements be taken over by national offices and officials (April 17, 1837). As a result, state treasuries ceased to exist. National treasury reports beginning in 1839 did not list separate accounts for state/department collections, and they stopped issuing their own treasury reports.[17]

On February 26, 1840 the centralist fiscal system eventually decentralized completely.[18] Whereas, under federalism national taxes and state taxes were collected by two separate agencies and reported as such, under the new centralist accounting, *all* revenues were reported from the states/departments, including those which were unmistakably national like customs revenues. For example, according to the *Memoria de Hacienda 1844* the Department of Veracruz collected $ 5,933,105 of which $ 4,009,483 came from taxes on foreign trade. Under centralism after 1840, all funds went to the national government, but it paid collection costs, salaries, and expenses for the governor, his staff, and other state functionaries, the congressional delegation, and the jurists. And the departments paid no contingente.[19]

After independence, Mexican politicians had been very hesitant about granting the national government the power to decree new taxes. When they wrote the Constitution of 1824, lawmakers divided taxes already in existence between the nation and the states. They devised no new ones and differed on the issue of whether the national government could do so in the future. In fact, no new taxes were created during the federalist years from 1824 to 1834.

The centralists promised to fill the treasury by getting more revenue out of the states and by trimming bureaucratic expenses. The new leaders were equally wary of decreeing additional taxes and, in fact, the return to centralism throughout Latin America was in part a response to the threat of anticlericalism and new taxes. For example when Juan Manuel de Rosas, the dictator of Argentina and acknowledged representative of the cattle barons of Buenos Aires province, taxed rural property, he too was forced to accept extremely poor collections.[20] Indeed, much of the reasoning behind the adoption of centralism in the 1830s in so many countries was its tacit promise to avoid such taxation.

The Texas revolt ruined whatever plans centralists had of balanced budgets without new taxes. They had recognized problems even before the revolt in Texas but were too timid to test their new popularity by addressing them. On November 21, 1835, they tried to impose an "extraordinary war subsidy," a surcharge on the sale price of urban property. When resistance proved too strong, they capitulated and converted the tax into a loan paying 6 percent a year. By January 11, 1836, the government had to suspend payment on credits issued for back salaries and pensions.

On June 16, 1836, the government decreed a forced loan on religious corporations, landowners, and merchants to "cover the national deficit." When this strategy failed, the treasury devised a series of taxes on urban property (two pesos per mill), rural property (three pesos per mill), and income taxes on urban businesses proportional according to type and location.[21] These new taxes (listed officially as *"propiedades, rentas, y giros"*) yielded only $ 582,940 or 4.5 percent of total tax receipts for 1836–1837, their first year of operation. Treasury Minister Manuel Gorostiza blamed the poor collections on "the custom established by our predecessors of not having citizens contribute directly to the public treasury" and presented it as a way out of Mexico's "dependence until now on the vicissitudes of maritime trade."[22] Gorostiza's levy of direct taxes undoubtedly hurried Mexico's adoption of its new

Table 6. Property and Urban Business Taxes 1836–1844[23]

Year	Total Tax Collections	Property and Business Taxes
1836–1837	12,950,545	582,940 (4.5%)
1837–1838 (18 mos.)	13,262,921	1,373,345 (10.4%)
1839	17,545,190	622,718 (3.6%)
1840	15,452,919	503,094 (3.3%)
1841	14,724,788	1,054,598 (7.2%)
1842	15,968,774	2,377,745 (14.9%)
1843	19,602,180	3,393,543 (17.3%)
1844	20,592,058	3,050,145 (14.8%)

Sources: *Memoria de Hacienda 1838*, p. 75; *Memoria de Hacienda 1840*, p. 21; *Memoria de Hacienda 1841*, p. 20; 2nd part 1841, p. 19; *Memoria de Hacienda 1844*, p. 5.

centralist constitution *The Seven Laws* on December 22, 1836. Yet direct taxes never produced more than $ 3,393,543 (17.3 percent of collections). (Table 6)

Direct taxes failed to produce large amounts of revenue because wealthy Mexicans and landowners in particular refused to pay them. Countless reports written by contemporary Treasury Ministers testify to a general unwillingness of the articulate Mexican public to pay the costs of government except for sales taxes (alcabala) which fell hardest on the poor, and trade taxes which seemed to hurt foreigners and merchants. Sometimes treasury ministers like Joaquín Lebrija were sympathetic to the elites' viewpoint. According to his biased analysis written in 1837, the wealthy would contribute to a fiscal system "consistent with freedom of industry and trade and established in proportion to the wealth of the contributor." However, "the people would be repelled by any addition to the burdens they now suffer" since "the greatest evil that can be inflicted on a people is an inequality in taxes" and because the Mexican fiscal structure had done nothing but absorb their fortunes during the past "twenty-six years of revolution." Therefore they were content to watch the gap grow between income and expenses and the "ruinous borrowing" it necessitated.[24]

On March 11, 1837 the government tried to increase revenue by lowering customs duties to their 1821 levels—a 10 percent drop. The treasury ministry believed that by reducing rates, it could decrease contraband and thus improve revenue collections at the ports. Some historians have also seen this new approach as an attempt to placate the disgruntled French on the eve of the Pastry War and/or to win British support in the upcoming renegotiations of the British debt.[25]

The new rates were repealed before they had much of a chance to affect illegal trade because Santa Anna had to please Veracruz cotton growers and empresario constituents, but its results from 1837 to 1842 were hardly spectacular (Table 7). The figures for their first eighteen months in operation (July 1, 1837 to December 31, 1838) show a disproportionate reduction in receipts, due to the French blockade of Veracruz during the Pastry War. The new tariffs produced their maximum amount in 1840 with $ 7,474,192 (48.4 percent of total tax collections), but the rest of the fiscal system did so poorly that total revenue actually declined.

Because of the decline in revenue due to the French blockade, the Bustamante government on June 8, 1838, declared an "extraordinary tax levy" on trade, professions, capital (invested or in bonds), and on luxuries (defined as carriages, horses and other carrying animals, housemaids, boats, estates, and litters) divided among departments. The government assigned such collections to the office which gathered the 1836 direct taxes and gave it 8 percent of their proceeds. Yet these new taxes failed to yield impressive sums—only $ 514,906 (1839) and $ 650,735 (1840) respectively.[26] When the government established a monthly tax on heads of families, communities, and ecclesiastical corporations (capitación mensual) it met such resistance that only $ 10,717

Table 7. Customs collections due to changes in tariff rates, 1837

Year	Customs Receipts	Total Tax Collections
1836/37	$4,737,767 (36.6%)	$12,950,545
1837/38 (18 mos.)	4,258,411 (32.1%)	13,262,921
1839	5,574,887 (32.0%)	17,545,190
1840	7,474,192 (48.4%)	15,452,919
1841	5,892,661 (40.0%)	14,724,788

Sources: Memoria de Hacienda 1836/37, pp. 73–74; Memoria de Hacienda 1839, p. 10; Memoria de Hacienda 1840, p. 10; Memoria de Hacienda 1841, p. 19.

was collected. Treasury Minister Javier Echeverría, like many of his predecessors, attributed the low amounts to lack of cooperation from treasury officials.

Since neither tariff reductions nor direct taxes had increased revenue substantially, the centralist government raised the tax on imports sold in the interior (consumo) from 5 to 15 percent (November 1839) only to repeal it the next month. On March 11, 1841, the administration decreed a three mill tax on property, and on April 8 added a monthly head tax of between one-fifth real to two pesos on each Mexican over 18. The combination of the 10 percent increase in the consumo and the direct taxes on property and individuals finally destroyed the centralist coalition. On September 28, 1841 Santa Anna, Paredes, and others issued the *Bases of Tacubaya*, which called for Congress to draw up a new Constitution. The original centralist experiment was over.

At first, Santa Anna sought popularity by eliminating the 15 percent consumo (October 19, 1841) and modifying the three mill tax on urban and rural property (January 13, 1842). He also suspended payments on the foreign and internal debts.[28] But it was not to last. Treasury Minister Trigueros levied new taxes on "industrial establishments" (April 5, 1842), wages and salaries, professions and occupations, luxuries, and a head tax of one-half real per month (April 7, 1842). This system in effect taxed every person living in Mexico.[29] The tax package closely resembled a modern tax system and as such required a well-organized and efficient administration or its equivalent to assess and collect the new levies, which Mexico did not have.

The new levies produced more revenue—in 1842 alone collections increased from $ 2,684,630 to $ 6,726,673 and the proceeds amounted to 42.1 percent of total revenue for the year. Unfortunately, however, total collections hardly rose since the new taxes cost $ 2,731,006 to collect or 69 percent of the operating costs for the entire treasury! The next year collections dropped to $ 6,202,044, but costs rose to $ 3,473,004 or 56.0 percent of the amount gathered and 72.8 percent of total costs. In 1844, collections reached $ 6,818,979, but overall costs rose to a phenomenal $ 5,967,670 and deficits continued (Table 8).

In September 1843, the government increased import duties to their highest level at 30 percent with a 1 percent surcharge and an extra 5 percent sales tax at the ports and in the interior. The

Chapter 2

Table 8. Tax collections, expenses, deficits
1826/27–1844

Year	Tax Collections	Expenses	Deficits
1826/27	15,137,981	16,364,218	1,216,237
1827/28	12,446,893	12,982,092	535,199
1828/29	12,787,994	14,016,978	1,226,984
1829/30	11,656,479	13,828,491	2,172,012
1830/31	14,521,690	17,601,289	3,079,599
1831/32	13,033,698	16,937,384	3,903,686
1832/33	11,891,909	Not available	Not available
1833/34	12,838,721	19,934,390	7,095,769
1834/35	Not available	Not available	Not available
1835/36	17,036,042	28,876,024	11,839,982
1836/37	12,950,545	19,802,628	6,852,083
1837/38			
(18 mos.)	13,262,921	26,588,304	13,303,381
1839	17,545,190	27,318,729	9,773,537
1840	15,452,919	21,255,097	5,802,173
1841	14,724,788	22,997,219	8,272,431
1842	15,968,774	30,639,711	14,670,937
1843	19,602,180	34,035,277	14,433,097
1844	20,592,058	31,304,102	10,712,044

Sources: Memoria de Hacienda 1828, pp. 15–17; Memoria de Hacienda 1829, pp. 17–19; Memoria de Hacienda 1830, pp. 21–23; Memoria de Hacienda 1831, pp. 41–43; Memoria de Hacienda 1832, pp. 79–83; Memoria de Hacienda 1833, pp. 51–52; and Memoria de Hacienda 1870, pp. 118–19; Memoria de Hacienda 1835, pp. 55–61; Memoria de Hacienda 1837, pp. 33–34; Memoria de Hacienda 1839, pp. 73–75; Memoria de Hacienda 1840, pp. 3–7; Memoria de Hacienda 1840, 2nd part, pp. 5–7; Memoria de Hacienda 1841, pp. 19–21; Memoria de Hacienda 1845, p. 5.

treasury then added on a 2 percent surcharge to pay for the construction of a railroad from Perote to San Juan. The merchants immediately protested, calling the new taxes "the daughter of tyranny and reaction."[30] Finally, on August 21, 1844 Treasury Minister Trigueros proclaimed a two mill addition to the rural property assessment, a new levy of three mill tax on the appraised value of cloth and thread factories, the equivalent of a year's tax on bonds, and one and two mills on money invested either in the mining fund or in the merchant guild.[31]

These new taxes contradicted centralism's fiscal promises and indicated its political as well as financial bankruptcy. Subsequently, leaders in Jalisco and Querétaro convinced General Mariano Paredes y Arrillaga to "pronounce" against the dictatorship on November 2, 1844. By the end of the month, the country was under martial law, Congress had been suspended, and the Executive, i.e., Santa Anna, empowered to administer the treasury and the army. His government fell on December 6, 1844.

The fall of the elite-militarist dictatorship of the Organic Bases quietly ended an era in Mexican history. During the previous twenty years beginning with the adoption of the 1824 Constitution, Mexican leaders had tried to govern the republic using first a federalist, then a centralist structure. After 1844, even its proponents tacitly admitted that centralism had failed to fulfill its promises when they backed Paredes's presumably pro-monarchist coup. Subsequently, centralists presented themselves as protectors of the Mexican way of life from the federalists, and not as proponents of a superior method of revenue production.[32]

Why Centralism Failed

When historians have looked beyond the chaotic politics of the years from 1834 to 1847, they have advanced many explanations for the centralists' failure to create a viable fiscal system. Justo Sierra, the apologist for Porfirian order, asserted in 1901 that "when salaries are paid, revolutions fade."[33] In his terse explanation, fiscal insufficiency fueled political instability.

More recently, as historians have begun to examine official reports more closely, different explanations have emerged. Marcelo Carmagnani argued in 1984 that "in the tension between the central government and regional powers, the latter were the winners. The states impoverished the central state precisely to impede its operation."[34] He assumes that during the centralist period (1834–1846) the states possessed considerable resources which they deliberately refused to give to the national treasury.

Yet the picture painted of Sonora and Sinaloa in those years by Voss shows no sign of such hidden wealth. In fact, in 1837 the federalist revolt led by General Urrea was motivated by a desire to take control of departmental finance out of the hands of Mexico City officials and to use the funds in the war against the Apaches. The Sonorans felt that Mexico City was bleeding them dry and leaving them defenseless in a time of life-and-death emergency.[35]

Furthermore, the fiscal situation of the Mexican government under centralism was hardly that of "a state not only without territory, but also [that of] a state without financial sovereignty."[36] Representatives of the national treasury operated more effectively in some states (Mexico State, Guanajuato, Jalisco, Puebla, San Luis Potosí, Sinaloa, Tamaulipas, Veracruz, and Zacatecas) than in others (Yucatán, the Californias, and Nuevo Mexico), but they operated everywhere.[37]

The Bourbons ran a centralized treasury in New Spain and did so successfully, but the leaders of independent Mexico failed to reestablish the system which had worked so effectively before 1808. Governmental administrators in 1835 faced some of the same problems as had their Bourbon predecessors, but they were exacerbated by the breakdown of the imperial system during the insurgency, the deterioration of roads and other parts of the transportation system, and the drying up of internal credit resources except for ventures which promised large rewards. The advocates of centralism faced three problems vastly different from those which had confronted their colonial predecessors: regionalism, territorial expanse, and the novelty of the regime.

Regionalism had grown from a rebellion against Spanish authority and central control from Mexico City into an ideology sanctioned in the 1824 Constitution and championed by recognizable and militant supporters. Many countries in Latin America had faced similar entrenched federalist interests when they too switched to centralism in the 1830s. But in Mexico, the situation was complicated by a second difficulty—its sheer expanse of territory particularly in the years before 1848. In Chile, much smaller in the times before the War of the Pacific, narrowness facilitated easy centralization and communication between Santiago and the major port of Valparaiso,[38] while in Mexico the great distances between the capital and the major ports made centralization much more difficult. The Spanish Crown had handled the situation effectively because it had used an indirect tax structure and had not relied on customs receipts.

However, the third problem dwarfed the difficulties posed by regionalism and geography. The Mexican republic had yet to acquire the legitimacy and authority necessary to create new taxes, administer them efficiently, and stimulate investment. The centralists would have to persuade Mexicans to grant them the same powers and the same monies they had given so unquestioningly to the Spanish kings in order to preserve whatever remained of the traditional order.

The centralists failed to establish the national stability they promised. The government had rapidly crushed expected federalist uprisings in the nation's interior, but its inability to reconquer Texas inspired rebellion rather than greater confidence in the regime. Further uprisings resulted necessitating emergency fund raising which further eroded elite confidence. The centralization of a previously federal republic required frequent demonstrations of strength from the capital, as in Rosas's Argentina for example. The Mexican attempt to draw power from the departments in order to build up the capital was doomed almost from the beginning.

Centralism created a more reliable fiscal structure for the Mexican republic, but budget deficits for the years from 1836 to 1844 were greater in every year than they had been during the previous federalist period. These deficits were not caused by the increased military activity, for military expenses for the period of the first centralist constitution (1836–1841) never exceeded those under federalism and, in fact, were considerably lower. Meanwhile treasury expenses exclusive of collection costs without exception in every year outstripped those for the military.

This had not been true under federalism where Treasury expenses were consistently and considerably lower than those for the military. But beginning in 1835–1836, treasury expenditures overshadowed all others. For example, in 1839 the gap between the spending of the Ministerio de Hacienda and the Ministerio de Guerra y Marina exceeded ten million pesos, in 1842 it rose to almost twelve million, and in the following year it topped fourteen million. During the entire centralist period for which records are available, the 9.5 years between July 1835 and December 1844, Treasury expenses exceeded military spending by a total of $ 70,945,231 for an average of $ 7,428,820.

Fortunately Treasury Minister Manuel María Canseco revealed in his *Memoria de Hacienda* for 1841 why treasury costs had escalated so rapidly; the figures merely reflected governmental response to pressure to repay back loans. Canseco noted that although the expenditures for the Treasury Department in 1840 were listed as $ 12,484,048, they could be broken down into $ 2,375,314 for true treasury expenses and $ 10,108,733 for "loans, interest payments, and repayment of money on deposit in the Treasury."[39] It would probably be incorrect to assume that the ratio of 4.21 pesos for loans to every peso for genuine expenses held true throughout the period, nevertheless it indicated a pattern which the centralists could not alter. They, too, had to contend with deficits, and in turn were forced to borrow from the omnipresent moneylenders. Worse still, they needed their cash even more than the federalists had. First, centralism, after all, was supposed to suppress the states in the name of fiscal efficiency. Therefore its proponents could hardly acknowledge that they still could not find enough funds with which to run a government even with a centralist system in place. Second, unlike the federalists who planned to solve the fiscal problem by expropriating the Church, the centralists had already put all their schemes into practice. So they borrowed more in every year than their predecessors.

It is, of course, possible that the army took a substantial portion of the collection costs for those years and that the published budget figures were fraudulent. Nevertheless, the printed figures confirm the ominous trend of rising treasury costs which had begun in 1834. Scholars can see the immensity of the problem from the amount of revenue which Treasury Minister Ignacio Trigueros had subtracted ($ 4,780,506 or 31 percent) from his estimate of gross tax receipts ($ 15,460,000) because it had already been pledged to one debt or another (Table 9). These sums did not include repayment of more current debts.

Centralism's basic inability to end federalism and the revolts it engendered necessitated ruinous spending, but it was the legacy of past debts—foreign and domestic—which kept the treasury empty, and the national government weak.

Loans and Their Consequences

Centralism, like federalism, was not able to collect enough revenue to pay the expenses of the Mexican republic. Borrowing be-

Table 9.   Deductions to be made from 1845 revenue collections

1)	20% of Veracruz and Tampico customs for bondholders of foreign debt	$1,397,912
2)	5% of Veracruz and Tampico import duties to pay army contract with Lasquetty (and Escandón). When that completed, then to be used to pay interest on bonds emitted by Lizardi and Company	305,468
3)	25% of all the import duties (excluding those from Matamoros) to pay the interest and amortization of funds held by public offices	1,565,398
4)	5% of all import duties (excluding those from Matamoros) to pay credits of Montgomery, Nicod and Company	313,079
5)	2% of import duties at Veracruz and 1% of those at Tampico to pay recognized credits owed the British	84,647
6)	1% of import duties set aside for chambers of commerce	223,000
7)	Revenue from official paper set aside for amortization of copper money credits	212,000
8)	Forced loan intended to cover debt owed to United States	500,000
9)	1% of the tax on the transfer of metals to go to the mining fund	79,000
10)	1/2% to go to mercantile court	61,000
11)	Personal contribution for departments	11,000
12)	Discount of 1/2 centavo on invalid pensions	28,000
	Total assigned revenue	4,780,506

Source: *Memoria de Hacienda 1844*, pp. 16–18.

came an inevitable necessity, a way of life, but under centralism the business of supplying funds to the governments changed. Centralist emergency finance was characterized, above all, by a reliance on short-term, high-interest loans from a favored group of speculators.

In 1827 when such activity had begun, any person who had cash to spare *(prestamista)* could lend it to the government and become an agiotista. Many of the agiotistas who became prominent in Mexico by 1834 started out as merchants in the import-export trade. Commercial transactions required credit operations—both for purchases abroad and for consignments within the country —as well as monetary exchanges involving *letras* (promissory notes for future payments), *libranzas* (letters of exchange written by one merchant on another's account), silver, and silver coin. All of these were frequently traded with premiums attached depending on the place and time of redemption. They also dealt in foreign currency exchanges as well.[40]

Involvement with foreign trade naturally led to relations with Mexican governments. By the late 1820s the treasury was accepting credits at face value in payment of customs duties, yielding increased profits since credits sold at considerable discount in the street. Drusina and Martínez in 1833 made 14.5 percent of its income from transactions involving customs duties and another 21 percent of its income from purchases of government credits. The pursuit of profit in the import-export trade quickly led to expanded operations involving government bonds and finally to lending money to the treasury *(agiotaje)*. This pattern holds true for Guillermo Drusina, Martínez del Río Hermanos, Jecker-Torre, Garruste and Company, C. A. Formachon, and Manning-Marshall later Manning-MacKintosh and probably for others as well.[41]

After the default on the British debt in 1827, lenders in Mexico supplied the government with funds. These loans were rarely completely in cash—they frequently included pre- or post-independence debt credits. National borrowing changed abruptly, however, on January 1, 1832, when the Bustamante administration stopped payment on all domestic debts and ordered them registered. Nevertheless, lending continued. In 1833, Drusina and Martínez, Antonio Garay, Antonio Zurutuza, and Francisco Gómes lent the government $ 300,000, of which $ 103,448 (34.5 percent) was in cash, $ 93,103 in pre-Independence credits and $ 103,449 in post-Independence credits. Drusina and Martínez made almost 25 percent of their profits in 1833 from such ventures.[42]

In November 1834, the government acknowledged its inability to repay its obligations to speculators and asserted its right to pay some in preference to others. Later it issued amortization credits in four separate classes paying up to 30 percent in cash from the customs and the remainder in credits *(vales de amortización)*.

Public functionaries, civil employees, military employees, and pensioners received another type of credit *(vales de alcance)* still redeemable at the ports. It also authorized the government to accept only loans which used the vales de amortización and vales de alcance and set amounts for each with a fixed percentage for cash.[43]

When the Bustamante government stopped repaying internal loans completely in cash in 1830, it changed the nature of agiotaje in Mexico; by 1834 with the decree which mandated payment in credits, the government created a new and potentially dangerous way of borrowing money. When the government began borrowing from lenders inside Mexico, merchants with cash supplied the Treasury with short-term, high-interest loans, from which they made good profits at rather low risk. They continued to lend, believing that the repayments in cash would permit future lending. When payments in cash ceased, the smaller lenders were forced out of business since they no longer had any spare cash. Consequently, governments fell increasingly into the hands of a small number of large-scale agiotistas.

After 1834 the government gave top priority to the demands of this powerful group. In exchange for a one million peso loan from the agiotistas, the government mortgaged one–half of the proceeds of the Fresnillo silver mines in 1835 and agreed to not raise taxes for twelve years. The Zacatecas mint was empowered to handle their output exclusively if speculators would finance and administer the mines. One of the thirty-five shareholders in the deal was the increasingly ubiquitous Manuel Escandón, who was then only twenty-three years old. The agiotistas slowly extended their influence into other areas of governmental business unrelated to their lending activities. In 1830 they were empowered as bondholder agents to collect the portion of the customs set aside for payment of the foreign debt directly at the ports. Thereafter they and their staffs could get to know official procedures and personnel, which undoubtedly led to more smuggling. Then in 1834, the government contracted with Manuel Escandón's stagecoach company to maintain key roads and collect tolls on designated roads. The new arrangement suspended the liens on such tolls held by prominent members of the former merchant guild like Bassoco, Fagoaga, and Villaurrutia for fifteen years. In 1835 the company also signed a five-year contract to carry mail on their

routes for $ 100,000.[44] These contracts show that under central-
ism, Mexico had begun to return to the pre-Gálvez colonial policy of tax farming in which agiotistas assumed responsibility for
duties and/or tax collections which the government itself could
not manage.

Since Mexico under centralism soon faced unexpected drains
on already inadequate revenue, short-term loans, previously seen
as a temporary device, became indispensable. On April 10, 1835,
in response to the growing crisis in Texas, the government specified that future loans must contain at least 55 percent in cash.[45]
But few agiotistas were willing to lend large sums without guarantees or substantial collateral after the suspension of payments
in 1834. In response, the Treasury Ministry won moneylender
support and new loans by creating "the Fifteen Percent Fund."
(January 20, 1836) It pledged 15 percent of the customs to pay
"all the orders issued by the government on loans on contracts
and those of the vales of amortization." The creditors selected a
representative *(apoderado)* to collect the money and oversee its
distribution. At first the Treasury wanted to give the creditors
15 percent in cash and 85 percent in letters on the treasury; on
July 2 and then on September 15, 1836 the government pledged
15 percent in vales de alcance and 85 percent in cash. When it
finished paying off their "Fifteen Percent Fund," as it came to be
known, it promised to use the 15 percent to repay the vales de
alcance.[46]

The "Fifteen Percent Fund" gave priority to credits derived from
agiotista loans, guaranteed their repayment from the largest and
most secure source of revenue, and pledged that almost the full
amount would be paid in cash. By contrast, holders of other internal debt credits rarely received even 5 percent of customs. In
fact, the "Fifteen Percent Fund" creditors received almost as much
as the British bondholders who by then were receiving 16 2/3 percent of the receipts from Veracruz and Tampico.[47]

The "Fifteen Percent Fund" reassured agiotistas and borrowing greatly increased in the crisis years of 1836 and 1837. The
month following the creation of the Fund, Santa Anna received
authorization to borrow up to another $ 600,000 at 3 percent
monthly, and the government decreed the sale of all possessions
of the Philippine missionaries.[48] When a Spanish friar, Padre
Morán, protested a sale, the government pledged to repay the mis-

sionaries while, at the same time, it authorized the transfer of the property to General José María Cervantes who coincidentally had loaned it $ 50,000.[49]

In June 1836, the government imposed a two million peso loan on all commercial houses, native and foreign. The French assessments averaged between $ 1,300 and $ 1,500; Drusina and Martínez were told to pay $ 1,000 and both groups complained to their respective Ministers (Martínez del Río was a naturalized British citizen) for assistance.[50] Prestamistas abhorred forced loans; loans at interest, however, were a different matter altogether, because in another venture in 1836, a consortium of British merchants lent a large amount to the government in exchange for advance payments in Veracruz against duties on shipments to arrive in the future. When the government failed to honor the agreement and put the debt into one of the Funds, the merchants appealed to their ministers once again.[51] Nevertheless in a period of great need, the man with money to lend was king. For example, in 1835 Ewen C. MacKintosh, later British consul to Mexico City and a prominent moneylender, procured licenses to export unminted bullion in future without a license. By 1836, he was powerful enough to quash an attempt by the British-owned Real del Monte mining company (backed by his superior the British Minister, and its banking house, Holdsworth and Fletcher) and others, to export *its* unminted bullion without a license. Soon he was renting mints from the government.[52]

The second Presidency of Anastasio Bustamante (April 19, 1837 to January 23, 1839; July 19, 1839 to September 22, 1841) ushered in a period of good will, high profits, and euphoria for the moneylenders. When Anastasio Bustamante became President, he quickly formalized his administration's negotiations with these "financiers" by establishing a national bank on January 17, 1837, ostensibly to amortize the rapidly devaluating copper coins in circulation. On that day he also authorized it to solicit a foreign loan of up to four million pesos. On April 15, 1837, he gave the bank the power to auction off the remaining Inquisition and Jesuit properties and entrusted it with the management of the reestablished tobacco monopoly. The "bank" soon revealed its true nature by renting the monopoly to a consortium of moneylenders made up of Benito Maqua, Cayetano and Francisco Rubío, Felipe

Neri del Barrio, Miguel Bringas, and, of course, Manuel Escandón among others.[53]

Bustamante also reverted to the policy of his previous administration by trying, this time, to find foreign support against the threats of Texas and later of French invasions. He also wanted to try once again to secure a foreign loan by renegotiating outstanding Mexican obligations to British bondholders which had come due but had gone unpaid in 1836. Bustamante's concern for Mexico's international debt position gave the foreign ambassadorial community additional clout when appealing on behalf of their citizens' credits. The government authorized moneylender Manuel Lizardi to offer the bondholders the right to colonize lands "which were or should be national" and issue them titles to four acres for every pound sterling owed and 5 percent from title date to settlement. The government also pledged the standard one-sixth of customs collections at Veracruz and Tampico.[54]

In June 1838 the Mexican government approved the final arrangement stipulating that "deferred bonds" could be used to acquire territory at the rates offered above; otherwise the creditor would forfeit any interest until October 1, 1847. As a result Mexico saved $ 17,853,512. When the nation began to default on its obligations yet again, Lizardi issued certificates on the customs of Veracruz and Tampico with a 10 percent bonus to compensate the creditors.

Meanwhile, Lizardi felt that his commission of 2 percent of the total face value of the amount converted was inadequate. He therefore issued additional bonds worth over $ 1,000,000 (exclusive of yet another £876,000 in deferred bonds which never left the vault). Thus, he gave himself a commission in excess of 10 percent of which the Mexican government remained unaware until 1842.[55]

The "Fifteen Percent Fund" began a new type of speculation well suited to the chaotic Mexican financial scene. Since the holders of the Fund's credits were recipients of 15 percent of the customs revenues and within three years most of the debt had been repaid, possessing *that* paper meant large profits. Therefore prestamistas like Martínez del Río became involved in buying credits for a maximum price of 80 percent of face value and then redeeming them. On May 20, 1837 the government initiated another such Fund, this time for 17 percent with similar, excellent results.

The era beginning in 1836 must have been a heady experience for speculators with cash to invest, but it led many of the unwary into disaster. In effect, some agiotistas faced with the temptation of easy profit through the Funds and initial success, became compulsive gamblers. The quick payoffs from the "Fifteen Percent" and then the "Seventeen Percent" convinced them to plunge further and, contrary to common sense and good business practice, to borrow cash in order to buy fund paper.[56]

When Santa Anna returned to the presidency in January 1839, his prestige restored, he borrowed still more. In 1839, because of the French blockade, the government was particularly in need of funds. In the same month (March) it borrowed $ 140,000 in credits and $ 22,150 in cash from Francisco María Iturbé, Antonio Garay, Antonio Zurutuza, and Hube and Company for a period of six months in exchange for $ 120,150 in letters on import duties (worth 58 and 68 percent of duties levied and $ 42,000 in letters on duties on the export of silver). As Meyer pointed out, this deal contained 86 percent in credits (purchased at 15 percent of their face value) and only 14 percent in cash. Thus, the loan of $ 140,000 involved $ 43,150 in cash outlay in exchange for repayment of $ 162,150 (a 376 percent profit).[57]

Later in the month, another group (Martínez del Río, Geaves and almost all the English houses, and the Echeverrías) formed to lend $ 1,350,000 promising to deliver pre-Independence credits, and vales de alcance in exchange for 1 percent per month interest on the cash in libranzas from Veracruz. The deal continued until April 30, 1839 when Santa Anna needed $ 300,000 to pay part of the French indemnity mandated by the settlement of the Pastry War. The money came as $ 200,000 in cash and $ 100,000 in credits payable at the customs which threatened the first group's repayment and received double the interest. Using the British Minister Richard Pakenham's good offices, the Mexican government on June 8, 1839 abrogated the original contract, promising instead that the $ 300,000 already lent would get 2 percent a month until repaid, and the first group would be paid from a newly created "Ten Percent Fund."[58]

The situation abruptly changed in July when Bustamante returned to the Presidency and appointed Francisco Javier Echeverría, an agiotista himself, as Treasury Minister. During his term (July 27, 1839 to March 24, 1841) Echeverría was frequently attacked for using his office to enrich himself even though he was already extremely wealthy. One visitor to his estate in Toluca was the highly observant wife of the new Spanish ambassador, Fanny Calderón de la Barca, who wrote:

> This beautiful hacienda, La Gavía, which formerly belonged to the Count de Regla, . . . is thirty leagues in length and seventeen in width—containing in this great space the productions of every climate from the fir-clad mountains on a level with the volcano of Toluca, to the fertile plains which produce corn and maize; and lower down, to fields of sugar cane and other productions of the tropics.[59]

When British Minister Richard Pakenham again intervened on behalf of the "Ten Percent Fund" creditors in September 1839 to protest the government's order that they pay a premium *(refacción)* or lose payment, he found a much more responsive audience in Bustamante and Echeverría. The Treasury told the creditors that they could choose between a 35 percent premium in cash on 2.5 million to get credits recognized at 56 percent or a 10 percent premium to continue the "Ten Percent Fund." The matter was resolved when the merchants let new credits enter the Fund in exchange for all the consumo tax collected from British merchants in the capital. In September 1840, the government actually began to print and market *new* "Ten Percent Fund" credits.

Another loan made in 1839 accounted for the creation of the "Eight Percent Fund." Originally Santa Anna agreed to use 12 percent of the customs to handle credits worth $ 2,200,000 with a monthly interest rate of up to 2 percent. In September 1839 the Treasury tried to hit up these creditors for a $ 40,000 premium and reduced the percentage to 8 percent. By 1840, both the "Fifteen Percent" and the "Seventeen Percent" Funds had been completely paid off with interest. As one member of Martínez del Río Hermanos noted, "Montgomery and Nicod (a British merchant house operating in Oaxaca) must have made plenty (on the "Seventeen Percent Fund"), since besides what they had originally, the former made additional purchases . . . and calculating today just what can be made on the interest, it is a beautiful profit."[60] It was a time of "beautiful profit" for many. In 1830, Juan Antonio de Béistegui opened a store with a starting capital of $ 16,000.

By 1835 he was already lending money; by 1838, he could boast a capital of $ 250,000—a 1562.5 percent increase over an eight-year period.[61] In 1840 Martínez del Río Hermanos held 9.8 percent of the firm's assets in debt credits, but they earned 44.9 percent of the total gross profits for that year.[62]

In some measure, the Bustamante government's attention to loan repayment weakened it considerably. By cutting back on the army in order to pay back debts, Bustamante made powerful enemies. Furthermore, the fiscal situation of the Mexican government was changing. With it came new priorities requiring Santa Anna once again.

In the summer of 1841, the failing government of Anastasio Bustamante began a new "Twelve Percent Fund" supposedly to amortize copper currency. It received 6 percent interest per year and sold for 46 percent cash (75 percent in copper, 25 percent in silver) and 54 percent of any kind of paper. The cash was to be repaid in seven months. The prestamistas involved themselves in this venture not simply for profit, but to help Bustamante for old time's sake and in recognition of his assiduous payment of their loans. But it was too little and too late.[63]

In 1840 as Treasury Minister Manuel Canseco noted, the Treasury spent over four pesos for debt payment for every one for genuine administrative costs. Furthermore, that money had come from the only reliable source of revenue in the country—the customs duties. The republic could not afford to continue the relationship with agiotistas so nurtured by Bustamante and Echeverría. It would honor fewer loans and spend its cash on other items.

During the Bustamante regime, Manuel Escandón had been building up an important network of contacts, clients, and employees in the government and outside it. By 1841, Manuel Escandón and his cronies served as bonding agents for customs officials, some of whom were often simultaneously on their payroll. Escandón, in fulfillment of another of his government contracts, constructed the piers, warehouses, and offices for the Veracruz customs facilities. Furthermore, there is considerable evidence that Escandón, MacKintosh, and other speculators often handled other merchants' customs payments, in cash or in credits, for a small fee.[64]

Manuel's brother Joaquín married into the wealthy and aristocratic Fagoaga family (the Marquis of Apartado), and thus united

the social and newly wealthy native elites. The Escandóns were
also closely tied to British interests in Mexico. Manuel frequently
acted in concert with Manning and MacKintosh, and his sister
Luz was intermittently engaged to Richard Pakenham, British
Minister to Mexico during the 1830s and 1840s. Escandón owned
stagecoaches, cotton factories, an estate, and silver mines in addition to his lending business and would become the most important financier in the republic during the 1850s.[65]

Escandón was also heavily involved with the speculators who
controlled the tobacco monopoly *(Empresa de Tabaco)* and it is
they who determined that Santa Anna and not Paredes nor Canal-
izo, should occupy the Presidency. Already by June 1841, Treasury Minister Canseco gave Escandón and Company $ 514,000 and
was trying for $ 300,000 more. He even went to the apoderados of
the Funds to beg $ 25,000 from each. A few more of these maneu-
vers and the rest of the agiotistas hopped onto the Santa Anna
bandwagon.[66] The tobacco consortium run by the moneylenders
provided the general with one hundred troops as he made his bid.
Soon after, Manuel Escandón, the unofficial chairman of the board
of moneylenders, rode with Lorenzo Carrera, a Spanish speculator, to meet with Santa Anna and discuss financial arrangements.[67]
Once they had been concluded, the new political shift had officially begun.

Santa Anna tried to rule in 1842 by rewarding each of his groups
of supporters—the army, the bureaucracy, the Veracruz planters
and import merchants, and regional interests—but by helping *his*
financiers most of all, as the others were soon to discover.

The sad story begins with the inauguration of a second "Seventeen Percent Fund" in 1840 as repayment for a two million peso
loan (45 percent cash, 55 percent in paper). The list of lenders
includes some extremely important figures in the Mexican political and financial scene. Nevertheless, the change from Bustamante to Santa Anna doomed this Fund—on October 11, 1841
Santa Anna stopped payment on all existing funds. Three days
later, he resumed payments but at half rates. Next the apoderados
of each fund selected an apoderado general to collect all the
libranzas from the customs. Despite the protests of the apoderado
general and all the individual representatives, Santa Anna suspended payments again on February 19, 1842.[68] The suspension,
in effect, penalized some large-scale lenders in the same way as

the one in 1832 had driven small and medium-size ones out of business.

Some of the agiotistas called upon the Foreign Ministers to help them. Walker asserts that because of the 1842 payment suspension, the prestamista community divided according to nationality.[69] Although this was true of the Martínez del Río, the family he studied, some agiotistas had good connections with both the national and the foreign side, such as Ewen MacKintosh, the British consul in Mexico City, a close business associate of Manuel Escandón. Some Mexicans like the well-connected Cayetano Rubio used the Spanish Minister to get credits paid. The Martínez del Río's poor judgment was hardly universal in the agiotista community.

On July 12, 1842, Santa Anna offered to pay holders of fund credits a flat 15 percent for a $ 40,000 premium, but the lenders ignored the proposal. Three days later, perhaps as a spur to them, perhaps as a gesture for Ignacio Loperena and Antonio Garay who owned much of that paper, Santa Anna resumed payment *only* on the "Fifteen Percent Fund." On September 20, the creditors were offered 16 percent for the remaining funds in exchange for a 10 percent premium. The group proposed $ 100,000 in order that half of the eight, ten, and twelve funds be paid; Nicod, representing the "Seventeen Percent Fund" refused to bribe the government, hoping for Pakenham's successful intervention.

When in early October, Spanish-born Gregorio Mier y Terán, Joaquín de Rosas and Yturbé (Iturbé) made private deals for less with the government, Martínez del Río and other foreign firms went to the British Minister. At first Pakenham did not want to become involved but when the Mier y Terán deal was made public, he agreed to demand a settlement. The result was the Pakenham Convention and included claims of Manning and Marshall (assumed by Manning and MacKintosh), J. P. Penny and Company, and Martínez del Río; the amount totalled $ 250,000 and would receive 2 percent of the Veracruz aduana, 1 percent of Tampico. Pakenham also helped Montgomery, Nicod reach an accord with the government on January 21, 1843. The Treasury agreed to repay the 2.2 million loan which was previously covered by the "Seventeen Percent Fund" in exchange for a 6 percent premium. The government issued new bonds to be covered by 8 percent customs, later reduced to 5 percent (and known as the "Five Percent Fund").[70]

Santa Anna, however, had other interests to protect as well. In February 1842, his administration renegotiated the British debt because of failure to meet interest payments. During the talks, the London Stock Exchange informed the Mexican Minister Plenipotentiary Tomás Murphy that the total amount of bonds issued for the 1837 agreement was greater than it should have been—proof that Mexico's representative to the bondholders, Manuel Lizardi, had either blundered enormously or had deliberately cheated the government. Santa Anna, however, paid no attention to such evidence and as part of the February 11, 1842 agreement giving bondholders 20 percent of the Veracruz and Tampico customs receipts and 5 percent of those from Pacific ports, he awarded Lizardi a 5 percent commission for the 1837 renegotiation and 5 percent in import duties.[71]

While Santa Anna favored some creditors and penalized others, he also hit hard at the Church. At first he helped his clerical supporters and their allies by permitting the Jesuits to return to Mexico and by allowing the establishment of the Congregation of the Sisters of Mercy. However, requests for funds quickly followed as Santa Anna soon demanded a $ 500,000 contribution only to settle for $ 200,000 in cash, and the right to sell a former Jesuit estate. Throughout 1842 and 1843, the government issued many anticlerical decrees, including a 15 percent tax on all newly acquired property and capital, and prohibitions against sales of church ornaments under penalty of prosecution for theft. Its most significant blow against the Church came with the forced sale of the properties of the Pious Fund of the Californias at prices determined by capitalizing the annual rate of return at 6 percent.[72]

Yet Santa Anna progressively alienated his moneylenders as well by favoring Manuel Escandón and his clique over the rest. He even authorized him and his partner Manuel Lasquetty to purchase $ 500,000 in European war materiel.[73] On May 11, 1843, the government stopped payment on debts owed to many speculators, and created a special "Twenty-Five Percent Fund" to handle all of them in exchange for yet another 6 percent premium. If creditors declined to pay, they would be forced to wait until all those who had received their due. Included in the new fund were five million in tobacco bonds (held by Escandón and his people) for the tobacco monopoly. Payments on the "Seventeen Percent Fund" were suspended until the middle of 1844 when it was reorganized as the "Five Percent Fund." By then Montgomery, Nicod was bankrupt; Nicod reportedly insane. As José Pablo Martínez del Río put it, "Santa Anna knows how to squeeze blood from stones and he who knows how to manage Santa Anna will always be able to do business."[74] Eventually, his excessive spending and venality proved too much. Santa Anna's government finally fell on December 6, 1844.

Diversification

During the period from 1821 to 1834, those who became agiotistas were primarily involved in the import-export trade. Although usually based in Mexico City, these transactions could be far-flung. Drusina and Martínez sold German and English goods to firms in Morelia, Oaxaca, and Zacatecas as well as to Mexico City, and shipped cochineal from Oaxaca. Their business had accounts from Chihuahua to Oaxaca, from Tecpan to Tampico, and commercial relationships with firms in the United States, Great Britain, France, and what would come to be known as Germany.[75] Another merchant, José María Rico, the partner of Antonio Alonso Terán, sold laces from Flanders and fabrics from China.[76] The 1830s and 1840s witnessed the transformation of some agiotistas from merchant to empresario or entrepreneur. At this time, the trader/lender branched out into various forms of investment in other areas of the Mexican economy.

The prestamistas became active in landholding and mining as natural outgrowths of their lending activities. These men quickly became property holders (both houses and haciendas) almost in spite of themselves in much the same way that trading promoted lending through deals concerning customs duties. Property was the most common form of collateral for loans and, with annual interest rates as high as 40 percent, moneylenders quickly became property holders. Sometimes, of course, agiotistas invested in land as a speculation. In the 1830s Guillermo Drusina and his family bought land in Texas and founded a company to settle some four million acres in the area between present-day Austin and San Antonio.[77] This and subsequent ventures involving Texas fell through when the department declared its independence. In general the prestamistas did not view agriculture as the best way to generate profits, however.

Mining was a different proposition. It too was a natural outgrowth of the prestamistas' regular concerns because of the trader's perpetual need for cash, exacerbated by the demands of the lending business. In 1835 Manuel Escandón was part of a group of thirty-five shareholders in the Fresnillo mines which agreed to finance and direct operations and, as part of another deal, to split the profits with the government which actually owned the mines. The following year he also invested in the Guadalupe and Calvo mines in Chihuahua along with Ewen MacKintosh and other British capitalists. In 1838, Martínez del Río Hermanos also invested in Fresnillo. It quickly paid high dividends and by October 1841, the purchasers had recouped their original investment and began to collect profits. In the years 1844–1847, the Fresnillo mines paid annual dividends of 24 percent to 60 percent.

The Martínez del Río investment in the establishment of the Casa de Moneda de Guadalupe y Calvo in Chihuahua was not so successful. In 1843 the Martínez del Río group merged with another, headed by Ewen MacKintosh to administer the Guadalupe and Calvo mint and the Culiacán mint jointly. Although the original Guadalupe and Calvo company paid off its debts by 1842, all profits went into the new venture. After the Mexican-American war disrupted profit possibilities, Martínez del Río Hermanos sold its shares.[78]

In the 1840s some moneylenders diversified their interests by investing part of their profits in the textile factories which had originally been financed by the Banco de Avío in the 1830s. According to Jan Bazant, by the 1840s textile manufacturing could yield profits of almost 50 percent, a heady lure for the funds of speculators. As one partner of Martínez del Río Hermanos noted, "All those who have yarn factories are profiting greatly," oblivious to the fact that some owners had had to sell out because they were unable to get government permission to import the necessary supplies of raw cotton.[79] In 1840 Felipe Neri del Barrio and Martínez del Río Hermanos, both heavily involved in lending, formed a partnership with $ 250,000 to rehabilitate a cotton factory at Miraflores containing just 3,912 spindles (malacates). In 1840, it produced 3,631 pounds of coarse thread; in 1841, 159,159 pounds, and in 1842, 202,455—15 percent and 26 percent of total national production, respectively.[80]

Cayetano Rubio, active in the cultivation of tobacco and representative for Spanish debts, also became an important textile manufacturer in the 1840s with a wool factory in Celaya and a cotton factory in Querétaro, "Hércules," valued at $ 800,000. In 1846 Antonio Garay, Escandón's partner in the stagecoach business among others, and a former Treasury Minister, owned a cotton factory, "La Magdalena," worth $ 1,000,000.[81] Another important lender, William Forbes, the American consul for Tepic, in partnership with Eustaquio Barron, the British consul in San Blas, operated a cotton mill in Tepic with machinery smuggled into that port. They were accused along with Manuel Escandón of using their cotton factories, "Jauja" and "La Escoba" respectively, to import British textiles and pass them off as Mexican.[82]

The Mexican textile industry flourished under the management of speculators and with their capital. Robert Potash estimates that approximately ten to twelve million pesos were invested in cotton factories between 1830 and 1846. This capital came from the original Banco de Avío seed money ($ 650,000), foreigners who invested in industry, and agiotista wealth.[83] Profits generated from agiotaje financed the development of native industry almost as if they had been lent by the Banco de Avío in the first place.

Although the moneylenders did not require government financial aid, they did need the statistical information necessary for making crucial production and marketing decisions. Therefore, the government established the Bureau of Industry headed by Lucas Alamán. Alamán was a logical choice for the post because of his early advocacy of industry, his part in the establishment of the Banco de Avío, and his well-respected intellectual capacities.[84]

Textile manufacturing, however, required access to cotton. Cotton was grown in Veracruz predominantly, the state with the most political influence (through Santa Anna) and the most experience in protecting its own interests outside of the capital. The growers had successfully preserved their market by making sure that importation of cotton was illegal without special licenses, more difficult to acquire than those permitting the import of finished goods. Naturally a few favored speculators with access to Santa Anna received such licenses while their competitors did not. In 1843 the government, on the pretext of a bad harvest, permitted

Agüero, González, and Company to bring in 60,000 quintales of prohibited cotton at six pesos per quintal and allowed Cayetano Rubio's firm of Rubio, Hermanos y Compañía to bring in a thousand "pack-loads of raw cotton."[85] It took the unprecedented emergency of the war against the United States for manufacturers to be able to buy permits to import cotton at $ 10 per quintal.[86] The high costs and frequent unavailability of cotton created serious problems for factory owners, who almost by necessity found themselves in the business of speculating. Martínez del Río Hermanos speculated successfully in cotton in 1844 and as a result made a $ 50,000 profit for the year. But until 1847, it preferred to let Cayetano Rubio buy the import permits and then purchase the cotton from him.[87]

Once the goods had been manufactured, factory owners faced two additional problems—competition from cheaper foreign products and difficulties in marketing their goods throughout the country. Protectionism had been the policy of the Mexican government during the 1830s, particularly during the Bustamante presidencies, where the long-standing promoter of native industry, Lucas Alamán, held some influence. But as Bustamante needed money, even that commitment fell by the wayside. For example, when Drusina and Rubio pressured Mariano Arista, Commander of the Northern Army, trying to find the money to outfit troops to reconquer Texas, he permitted companies to import yarn through Tampico in 1841. The rail of protest against this behavior was so powerful that it helped in Santa Anna's eventual overthrow of the Bustamante regime later in the year. When Santa Anna became president, he quickly ordered that all cotton goods imported by way of Arista's permits be burned. But, of course, Santa Anna was amenable to reason and by June 1842, Drusina and friends were allowed to bring in up to 700,000 pounds of yarn for 2–4 reales per pound.[88]

Rumors abounded that British Minister Pakenham working in concert with Manuel Escandón bribed Santa Anna to allow, in effect, a most favored nation status for British manufacturers and to keep the lower rates in place for a rather extended period. Cayetano Rubio stopped this plan and by November, manufacturers threatened Santa Anna with overthrow unless he terminated these negotiations.[89]

Ultimately, the manufacturers had to sell their wares. During the 1840s the Martínez del Río Hermanos factory at Miraflores sold finished products to Zacatecas, Guadalajara, San Luis Potosí, and Guanajuato. Demand was unstable, both because of changes in government and changing government policy toward imports which could alter very rapidly. Factories did extremely well from 1844 until the occupation of Mexico City in September 1847 when textiles from the United States flooded the market. Profits could run as high as 19.4 percent a year (1845) or as low as –1 percent (1842, 1843, 1847).[90] Yet production costs remained constant, and outputs kept increasing. The need for protection and access to greater markets considerably influenced the course of the postwar period as the cotton entrepreneurs tried to maximize profits from their considerable investments.

The Agiotista Community 1834–1847

When decrees in 1830 and 1834 allowed governments to stop paying debts in cash, agiotaje became limited to a small group of lenders with enough cash to continue to put together loans. Cash, however, was frequently scarce, so even the wealthiest moneylender was often forced to borrow from fellow prestamistas. Agiotistas also often joined forces by marrying into each other's families or into those of the colonial elite. By 1844, the community was heterogeneous and complex, native and foreign, bound together by wealth but often divided by self-interest.

Some of the agiotistas could trace their connections back to the colonial consulados. For example, of the thirty-one names listed by Kicza as members of the Mexico City consulado from 1790–1824, at least seven (de Agreda, de Terán, Bassoco, Echave, García González de Noriega, Icaza, and de Iturbé e Iraeta) reappear among the group prominent in the 1830s and 1840s.[91] María Ignacia Agreda married Edward Wilson, a minor English agiotista in the late 1820s and a director of the tobacco monopoly. The de Terán line continued through the nephew Gregorio Mier y Terán, who arrived in Mexico from Spain in 1818.[92] As one observer wrote, his hacienda, San Nicolás Peralta was "one of the most profitable in the country."[93] María de la Cruz Noriega y Vicario married the German merchant and one time partner of Martínez del Río, Guillermo Drusina, and her sister Ana married British

Consul Charles O'Gorman.[94] Bassoco, Echave, Icaza, and Iturbé were all agiotistas in the 1840s. Other prominent members of the colonial nobility show up as well—the Noriegas were allied with the Morán, Vivanco, and Moreno families and Felipe Neri del Barrio, the Guatamalan consul and agiotista, married Rafaela Rengel, niece of Francisco Fagoaga, great friend of Lucas Alamán, and brother of the ex-marqués del Apartado. They formed the Barrio-Fagoaga, Flores, Campero, Echeverría (Javier, the Treasury Minister under Bustamante) alliance. Barrio was allied by friendship to the Martínez del Río's and later became a partner in the Miraflores textile factory.[95] Another member of the Fagoaga family married Joaquin Escandón, Manuel's brother, while his other brother Antonio was wed to the daughter of Eustaquio Barron, the agiotista partner of William Forbes. As these marriages demonstrate, the agiotistas of the 1830s and the 1840s were connected not only to the colonial consulados and nobility, but also to foreign merchants and diplomats as well. Through consignments, exchange transactions and loans, the Mexico City group became linked to other traders in the countryside and major cities like Veracruz and Guadalajara.

The agiotistas also socialized and relaxed together. They frequently met at the Sociedad de Comercío, located at number 8 Coliseo Street or at La Lonja de México at the Palacio de Ayuntamiento near the Zocalo. The Escandóns, the Garays, the Martínez del Ríos, Felipe Neri del Barrio, Manuel Nicod, and Juan B. Jecker were all members of the Sociedad as was former Treasury Minister Manuel Gorostiza. These were good places to hear important financial gossip, consummate crucial deals, and arrange loans among themselves. During the years from 1834 to 1844, Drusina and Martínez and later Martínez del Río Hermanos made loans to Fagoaga y Barrio, Manning and Marshall, Tomás Murphy, Antonio Zurutuza, Gregorio Mier y Terán, Benito Maqua, G. Hammeken (a German consul), Antonio Garay, Escandón, and Agüero González and Company. In this period of prosperity, the firm borrowed from Antonio Icaza and Mier y Terán.[96] The moneylenders also went together to weddings and funerals, attended the opera, carried on flirtations and love affairs, and paid social calls on each other at their homes.

To have a good time sometimes meant mingling with all classes in society, and this was epitomized by going to San Agustín de las Cuevas (now known as Tlalpan) south of Mexico City at Whitsunday.[97] For three entire days in June, Mexicans "from the president down to the beggar" went to San Agustín to dance, flirt, eat, drink, dress up, drive around, socialize, and of course, to gamble. The agiotistas could actually stake their favorite players; in 1838, Lubervielle (a friend of the Martínez del Ríos and the Escandóns) began with 250 *onzas* and won 30 more, Antonio Garay started with 200 and left 20 onzas richer. Domingo Noriega emerged the big winner making 120 onzas from a stake of 150 and Manuel Escandón lost 30 of his 200 onzas. On an investment of 800 onzas ($ 12,800 at 16 pesos per) advanced by Martínez del Río Hermanos, it made a profit of 140 (2,240 pesos or 17.5 percent).[98]

The last day at San Agustín was, according to Fanny Calderón de la Barca (who went in 1840 and 1841) the best. The cockfight arena charged one peso admission and required jackets for the gentlemen. Men and women both bet on their favorites, and even Fanny, who compared the spectacle unfavorably to bullfighting, admitted that everyone behaved with decency and decorum "that hides the real impropriety even from themselves." After dinner at the Escandóns' hacienda, everyone went to the outdoor dress ball at the Calvario hill and then to the home of General Morán where President Bustamante was among the guests. Soon, however, the French Minister and others returned to the tables. Fanny herself watched the Spanish agiotista Lorenzo Carrera winning and losing thousands of gold onzas. Then the ladies changed for the fourth time that day to go to the evening ball at the Plaza de Gallos where people of various classes mingled, and where it was considered impolite for ladies of the highest class to refuse to dance with members of the lowest. Fanny remarked that naturally enough her husband, the Spanish Minister, expressed some disapproval of the scene, whereby Minister Luis Gonzaga y Cuevas, a noted conservative, replied that gambling was an innocent pleasure and that the social mingling kept tensions down. Then Calderón suggested that if that were the case, the government should at least tax "the house!"

Fanny went to San Agustín again in June 1841, but even in that vacation spot, the tensions of financial turmoil and weakening government were ever-present:

It is even whispered that one cause of the more than usual crowd
at San Agustín this year is that many failures are expected in mer-
cantile houses, and that the heads of these houses or their agents
are here in the desperate hope of retrieving their falling fortunes.[99]

San Agustín changed tone in the years from 1842 to 1844 with
Santa Anna. The "new" President, unlike his predecessor Bustamante, who "looked more like the head of a convent," was an
avid gambler and even bred fighting cocks himself. As Guillermo
Prieto, never a fan of "the cripple" *(El cojo)* as Santa Anna was
known, described the scene:

Santa Anna is the soul of this emporium of disorder and licentious-
ness. There he was in the Gameroom, surrounded by the potentates
of *agio* playing the banker at monte, taking money lying around,
mixing with lowly bureaucrats and enlisted men, asking for money
without repaying.[100]

The Mexican-American War

From December 6, 1844 to June 20, 1848, ten different governments "ruled" Mexico—Herrera, Paredes y Arrillaga, Bravo, Salas,
Gómez Farías, Santa Anna, Anaya, Santa Anna, Peña y Peña,
Anaya, Peña y Peña, and finally Herrera. During this chaotic period, no administration managed to decree or collect new taxes
and even declarations of such an intent only multiplied instability because they provoked revolts.

The situation also hindered agiotista business. For example, just
as Martínez del Río Hermanos thought it had concluded a deal
with the Herrera administration concerning the tobacco bonds,
it was overthrown by Paredes and they had to begin all over
again.[101] The only consistency during this difficult period came
from the omnipresent need for funds and the agiotistas' willingness to supply them. For example, the government of President
Herrera, which followed the fall of Santa Anna's dictatorship, believed that it could settle Mexico's dispute with the United States
through negotiation, and thus greatly reduce the overblown and
costly Santanista army. Consequently, it cancelled the August
24 extraordinary levies, the forced loan, the tax on the circula-

tion of cash, and pledged that much of the collection of direct taxes would go to the departments. However, the government disappointed its creditors as the "Twenty-Five Percent Fund" became the "Twenty-Six Percent Fund," but was slated to receive only 6 percent of the customs duties (March 1 and June 18, 1845).[102]

Both the Church and the army disliked Herrera's plans and branded his diplomatic efforts to avoid a war "unpatriotic." Lucas Alamán and his newly formed newspaper *El Tiempo*, allegedly funded in part by money from the Spanish Minister to Mexico, Salvador Bermúdez de Castro, and the Archbishop of Mexico, Manuel Posada y Garduño, all self-proclaimed monarchists, convinced General Mariano Paredes y Arrillaga to overthrow Herrera.[103]

According to Guillermo Prieto's characteristically uncharitable reminiscences, Paredes was an ignorant elitist and partisan of the colonial order who had married the daughter of a wealthy, devout, and extremely conservative Guadalajara family.[104] After he became president on January 2, 1846, Paredes convoked an "extraordinary Congress" to draft a new constitution, composed of 160 representatives chosen corporatively (thirty-eight property owners, twenty each of merchants, clerics, and soldiers, fourteen each for miners, manufacturers, and literati (!), and ten apiece for lawyers, judges, and bureaucrats).[105] The Congress never met because on May 13, 1846, Mexico declared war on the United States. Ten days earlier Paredes suspended all contracts to repay previous loans (May 2), and had cut all nonmilitary salaries by 25 percent (May 6). Many agiotistas were furious and blamed the new Treasury Minister Francisco Yturbé (Iturbé), one of their number. Even the British Minister, Charles Bankhead tried to change the policy, but his efforts were constrained by the new accord reached on the British debt and British policy to help Mexico during its war with the United States.[106] On April 28, 1845 the Herrera government had authorized Manuel Escandón to renegotiate the British debt with bondholder representative Ewen C. MacKintosh. The war had already begun when the British bondholders reached an agreement with the Mexican Minister, Tomás Murphy, on June 4, 1846. The settlement provided for a new issue of bonds worth $ 51,208,250 at 5 percent interest and saved Mexico $ 4,805,625.[107]

Paredes' fiscal policies alienated many speculators and bureaucrats. His desultory conduct of the war infuriated the army, which eventually convinced Mexico's most charismatic leader, Antonio López de Santa Anna, to return and save the nation. When Santa Anna arrived in Mexico, he pledged to reestablish the federalist Constitution of 1824 and on September 17, 1846, Congress decreed that the nation would receive all port taxes; the 4 percent tax on coinage, the revenue from land sales, the tobacco monopoly, the post office, the lottery, the salt deposits, official paper, the mints; and all monies from the Federal District, national territories, and Church property in government hands in addition to a contingente of $ 1,011,000 from the states. The states would collect the rest once the system became effective at the conclusion of the war.[108] It also abolished the alcabala and reimposed taxes on property as well as a 50 percent surcharge on businesses, income, and luxury taxes collected by the states.

When this law was repealed with a change of treasury minister, the government had the difficult task of deciding whether to nationalize clerical wealth.[109] The Church had provided a large amount of property and revenue for centralist regimes since 1834. In addition to loans, both voluntary and forced, the Church had been required to part with the properties of the Philippine missionaries to help raise money for the fighting in Texas. During his Organic Bases period, Santa Anna once again pressed the Church for support, including the forced sale of the properties of the Pious Fund of the Californias. In exchange for what Bazant has characterized as a "disguised nationalization," the government pledged to mortgage the profits from the tobacco monopoly as security and pay 6 percent of the proceeds. These sales set a precedent for the future, particularly since they were made to moneylenders who paid 25 percent of the purchase price in government credits. Manuel Escandón later wrote a pamphlet defending the purchasers' interests when public opinion demanded that the properties be returned. The tobacco company also argued that it should keep its new holdings because of claims it held against the government. As Juan José del Corral later complained, "Where are the assets of the temporalities, of the Pious Fund of the Californias, of the hospitals? They have become properties of the speculators."[110]

In October 1846, Treasury Minister Antonio Haro y Tamariz proposed a new plan for clerical disentailment which, according to Bazant, was probably written by his friend José María Lafragua.

It allowed Church property to be sold and specified that its renters would have the first chance to purchase their homes with prices to be determined by setting yearly rent as 5 percent of the total. This project would ultimately become the model for the eventual law in 1856. Lafragua later noted that his plan would have yielded more than 12 million pesos from sales tax collections.

The Church responded with a typical bureaucratic ploy—it pledged to name a commission to study the measure. Since Santa Anna was desperate for funds to defend the country after the fall of Monterrey, Haro could not afford to wait. He would have to go to the moneylenders, and so he reverted to an earlier plan to convince the clergy to use its property as security for a loan. On October 2, he decreed that all corporations had to give the government one month's rent, calculated at 5 percent of the total value of the property. A few days before his resignation on November 13, Haro drafted one last decree ordering the Church to accept a mortgage on its property of two million pesos, which would be supplied by the agiotistas.[111]

The treasury's desperation then forced the government to woo funds from the agiotistas and furnish them even greater assistance in fulfilling their goals. Some of these "incentives" are rather easy to spot; others remain lost to the historian because of the probably deliberate lack of treasury records for those years. The 1845 budget figures are the only accounts available for the period; Matías Romero reproduced them in 1870 from a manuscript copy of the Treasury Report presented in March 1849. They indicate that the borrowing continued although loans are listed euphemistically as "unproductive sources."[112]

The new loan cycle began in December 1844 when opposition leaders borrowed $ 500,000 to overthrow Santa Anna. The next administration tried to cut back on loans by announcing in March 1845 that contracts made during the previous administration would receive only 6 percent interest, and in June, that owed interest payments would not be capitalized except for contracts involving "items necessary for public welfare such as uniforms, arms, etc." Thereafter the speculators hid behind the smokescreen category of "necessary items."[113] In addition, Treasury Minister Luis de la Rosa borrowed three million pesos from the firm of Garruste and Company, among others, signing what the opposition press termed "ruinous contracts." On November 19, 1846,

the government ordered the clergy to accept responsibility for repaying loans to individuals who contributed money to the war
effort. It assigned one million pesos to the Archdiocese of Mexico, $ 400,000 to the Bishop of Puebla, $ 250,000 to the Bishop of
Guadalajara, $ 170,000 to the Bishop of Michoacán, $ 100,000 to
the Bishop of Oaxaca, and $ 80,000 to the Bishop of Durango. The
Church then issued letters to individuals in denominations rang-
ing from $ 200 to $ 20,000. The Archdiocese of Mexico divided
its assigned one million pesos into $ 800,000 for the Federal Dis-
trict, $ 150,000 for its part of Mexico State, $ 40,000 for Querétaro,
$ 2,000 for its part of San Luis Potosí, and $ 8,000 for its section of
Veracruz. All of these loans were secured by clerical property. Of the
$ 688,000 assessed at $ 20,000, $ 9,000, and $ 5,000, known moneylenders contributed at least $ 204,000 (30 percent). (Table 10)

After it refused to acquiesce in any plan to sell its property outright, the Church reached a temporary compromise with the government on December 5. The politicians promised to abandon
plans for disentailment in exchange for a loan of $ 850,000. An-
other loan, this time for $ 1,000,000 shortly followed using all
unmortgaged revenue as collateral.[115] Ramírez relates that Francisco Iturbé, himself a speculator and former Treasury Minister,
told him that the clergy "were accepting the drafts (on their property) openly and frankly."[116] In the first days of 1847, Santa Anna's
troops were desperately battling the American invaders at Buena
Vista and other army units were trying to repel the U.S. seizure
of Veracruz. The defenders badly needed funds, but the government had nothing left to secure more loans. Finally on January
11, Vice President Valentín Gómez Farías decreed the nationalization and sale of fifteen million pesos worth of Church property. The Church retaliated by convincing the national guard in
Mexico City to stage the "revolt of the polkos" (so called for their
supposed allegiance to U.S. President James Polk). Although the
revolt failed to overthrow the government, it forced Santa Anna
to return to Mexico City, repeal the law, and fire Gómez Farías
in exchange for a $ 1,500,000 loan guarantee. Nevertheless the
damage had been done. In the preceding months, the government
authorized loans of up to $ 20,000,000 to be secured by specific
pieces of Church property.[117] Because the Church had little cash,
it authorized the government to sell libranzas and use Church
property as collateral. Treasury Minister Juan Rondero and his

Table 10. Distribution of a $ 800,000 loan among residents of the Federal District*

m = moneylender

$ 20,000 each (total $340,000)	
Sr. Ex-conde de Berrio	Viuda de Echeverría é hijos (m)
Don Juan de Dios Pérez Gálvez	Franciso Iturbé (m)
Duque de Monteleone	Gregorio de Mier y Terán (m)
Viuda de Agüero (m)	Nicolás Carrillo
Alejandro Arango (m)	Manuel Rull (m?)
(for Manuel Escandón)	Rosas hermanos (m)
Joaquín de Obregón	Rubio hermanos (m)
Eusebio García	Manuel de la Pedreguera
Representative of	J. Miguel Pacheco
D. Ignacio Loperena (m)	

$ 9,000 each (total $243,000)	
Doña Francisca Pérez Gálvez	Casas y Dacomba
José Gómez de la Cortina	Felipe Azcárate
Flores hermanos	Juan Goribar
Ignacio Cortina Chávez	Felipe N. del Barrio for his wife (m)
Executors of Francisco Fagoaga	Cirilo Gómez Anaya
José María Flores	José Fernández de Celis
Doña Francisca Villaneuva	Manuel Fernández de Córdova
de Sevilla	Juan Moncada
Doña Antonia Vaquero de Villar	Juan Rondero (m)
Executors of Gaspar Cevallos	Benito Macua (m)
Muriel hermanos (m)	Anselmo Zurutuza (m)
Doña Josefa Adalid	Pedro Anzoateguí (m)
J. Miguel Cortina Chávez	Villa hermanos
Carlos Sanchez Navarro	

$ 5,000 each (total $105,000)	
Fresnillo Mining Company (m)	Bernardo González Baz
José Adalid	Francisco de P. Mora
Fernando Collado	Donato Manerola
Manuel Soriano	Francisco de P. Sáyago
Crescencío de Boves	Juan Antonio Béistegui (m)
Mariano Cosío	José María Cuevas
General D. Manuel Gual	Santiago Moreno, for la
Mariano Pérez Tagle	Sra. Vivanco
Dr. D. Luis G. Gordoa	José Delmonte
Juan María Flores	Ignacio Velázquez de la Cadena
Ignacio Nájera, for the Count	José María Martínez
of Altamira	

*According to the published list, the Archdiocese collected a total of $ 775,600. The remainder came from eighty-eight individuals in contributions ranging from $2,000 to $200.

Source: Dublan and Lozano, *Legislación Mexicana,* volume 5, pp. 210–16.

cronies, Gregorio Mier y Terán, Rosas Hermanos, and Francisco
Iturbé and others were able to choose their libranzas and pay 50
percent in cash and 50 percent in bonds. Others, not so well favored, had to pay two-thirds in cash and one-third in bonds and
could not pick their libranzas.[118] To raise more cash, the clergy
also had to sell $ 1,200,000 of pre-Independence debt credits at 8
percent of face value and then turn over the $ 96,000 to the gov-
ernment. The purchasers, among whom was Ewen MacKintosh,
then used the credits to form other loans.[119]

The Church had considerable difficulty repaying those speculators who had purchased the treasury bills in cash and often had
to borrow from some moneylenders to pay off others. Eventually
the Church had to sell sixteen properties in downtown Mexico
City at two-thirds of their assessed value to Mier y Terán.[120] In
response to clerical pleas, the government repealed a law prohibiting the Church from demanding the immediate repayment of
its loans to urban and rural property holders. In exchange the government received money from the Bishop of Michoacán to purchase muskets.[121]

Centralist demands on clerical wealth beginning in 1834 considerably weakened the Church as a financial institution. The
Mexican American War and its extraordinary pressures on an impoverished treasury contributed even further to this decline as
governments in need permitted agiotistas to break the sacred tradition of mortmain.

Many Mexicans by 1847 agreed with the perception of Treasury official Juan José del Corral that,

> the best urban and rural properties of the religious corporations
> have passed into the hands of speculators because, lacking cash to
> give in response to government appeals for help, the Church has
> given its properties as security, so that the speculators would lend
> money.[122]

Indeed by the time of the American occupation of Mexico City,
speculators had infiltrated the highest ranks of the Church. Juan
Manuel Irisarri, *Vicario Capitular*, the head of Church funds in
Mexico City, frequently compelled his subordinates to make deals
with agiotistas which ran counter to Church interests. Indeed,
Santa Anna may have nominated Irisarri to be the next Arch-

bishop of Mexico as a reward (or a bribe) for his cooperation. When the clerical junta empowered to raise money to repay bills evaluated Irisarri's performance after his death, it noted that the Vicario Capitular had had close ties *("relaciones estrechas")* with speculators.[123]

Speculators profited in other ways as well since the government desperately needed their money to defend the nation. These "financiers" became so powerful that once the war had ended, they had only to mention an unrecorded loan to receive prompt payment. British consul Ewen MacKintosh benefited substantially as the government rented him the Guanajuato and the Mexico City mints in 1847. But MacKintosh was not the only speculator to profit from the war—Mier y Terán and Béistegui acquired property cheaply, and Loperena peddled guns.

On August 20, 1847, the Mexican government officially recognized that the speculators were the only group in Mexico stable enough and powerful enough to negotiate a settlement with the United States. It named Ewen MacKintosh one of its three representatives to the armistice talks. Two days later, the negotiators assembled at MacKintosh's home to discuss cease-fire terms. Later a man described as "MacKintosh's attorney," Miguel Atristain was appointed one of the Mexican Commissioners who helped draft the Treaty of Guadalupe Hidalgo.[124]

As MacKintosh's role in the armistice negotiations indicates, by 1847 the agiotistas had become inseparable from the official government. But the agiotista group, like the government it fed on, was by 1847 in the midst of transition. The faction surrounding Manuel Escandón was on the rise, due in part to his close association with Santa Anna, but also to shrewd business decisions and friendly relations with many important politicians of all views. As money became scarcer and the war with the United States erupted, the government had to stop payment on its credits. Some agiotistas had too many of their assets tied up in the now worthless paper and went bankrupt. High profits were the reward for taking great risks; in a country like Mexico in the 1840s, some were bound to be on the losing side.

And there were costs. David Walker in his study of the Martínez del Río family includes a revealing anecdote. On June 17, 1847 as American troops neared the capital, the government called for a new forced loan. Despite the frequency of such demands, the

crisis was evident. Yet when Martínez del Río Hermanos was assessed $ 2,250, it appealed to a British official Edward Thornton
to get it reduced. When a group of soldiers appeared on July 21,
1847 with orders to embargo Martínez del Río Hermanos and seize
its assets, Thornton again came to the rescue and the action was
called off. Eventually Lord Palmerston, the British Foreign Minister, won an exemption for the firm. As one partner wrote to the
other, "I am very happy as much for the savings of money as for
the blow dealt to Yturbé and his friends, who were very vainly
boasting of having won the principle that foreigners should not
escape."[125]

But the Martínez del Río family had been in business in Mexico for almost twenty years, and this was no ordinary exaction
demanded by a rapacious government. If the agiotista community split in these years on foreign/national lines, it was perhaps
a seeming unconcern for Mexico's survival that helped it along.
In the loan of November 1846, Pedro Ansoateguí (a partner in
Martínez del Río Hermanos) paid $ 9,000, but Manuel Escandón
paid $ 20,000 as did Agüero, Loperena, Echeverría, Iturbé, Mier y
Terán, Rosas hermanos and Cayetano Rubio (Table 10). In times
of crisis, the native agiotistas paid their share, while those with
foreign connections balked.

Another even more significant split appeared in the community when some agiotistas branched out into factory production,
while others continued in the more traditional activities of lending and property-holding. As time passed, their ties to the government increased as they won concessions and privileges to
protect their new interests. Governments desperate for funds willingly favored their moneylenders, who gained influence and prosperous projects as a result.

These ventures in turn altered the entire Mexican economy.
The moneylenders were associated with many different businesses
in various parts of the country. A speculator like Escandón could
operate mines in Chihuahua, cotton factories in Guadalajara and
Orizaba, and haciendas in San Luis Potosí among others. Such
far-flung enterprises initiated a shift away from the pattern of regional isolation which had characterized the Mexican economy
since independence. Agiotista investment silently encouraged the
development of a national economy, making the protections offered by the federalist notion of state autonomy complete with

individual local sales taxes less attractive. These new factories, aided by unique government privileges, tended to produce larger and larger outputs which required a national infrastructure built and supervised by a central government. They also demanded free access to property to build better transportation links and a strong nation-state to direct large-scale development projects. By 1848 entrepreneurial requirements brought the empresarios still closer to conflict with the Church for control of Mexico's future.

3

Funding Federalism
1848–1853

The more one looks at an agent of the public treasury, the more one can imagine him to be an agent of the speculators working to increase their profits.

El Heraldo, January 29, 1849.

"The Chamber of Deputies is not a mint!"
President of the Chamber of Deputies
Manuel García Aguirre's response to
Treasury Minister Guillermo Prieto's
appeal for funds in December 1852.

When the troops from the United States marched out of Mexico City, they left behind a ransacked and demoralized capital, a government in total disarray, and a disrupted economy. Unlike the Spanish and French forces which had invaded Mexico in the past and had stayed in and around the ports of the Gulf coast, the army from the United States had pushed its way into the Central Valley from Veracruz and Puebla. After failing to defend the capital, Santa Anna had resigned the presidency on September 16, 1847, whereupon the entire government had collapsed. General Winfield Scott, whose troops occupied the Federal District, abolished its sales tax, and levied exactions on the Mexico City municipal council which had to borrow extensively to meet his demands.[1] In other cities, the invaders had imposed forced contributions on the wealthy and had confiscated whatever shipments came out of the mines and the mints. Although no agency assembled an actual budget for 1847, Matías Romero estimated that the government had earned $ 8,820,649, but had spent $ 26,977,951.[2]

Ironically the war with the United States gave new hope and energy to a Mexico battered by invasion and filled with self doubt. In accordance with the Treaty of Guadalupe Hidalgo which ended the conflict, the United States agreed to grant Mexico a fifteen million peso indemnity for its loss of 55 percent of its territory (522,568 square miles including Texas) and to pay all outstanding claims held by U.S. citizens against the Mexican government.[3] The award of this indemnity in 1848 was much like the receipt of the British loans in 1824 and 1825. Indeed, at least superficially, Mexico in the process of reconstituting itself after its defeat by the U.S. seems to resemble the republic at its beginnings recovering from the independence wars nearly twenty-five years before.

With the fall of the empire and the establishment of a federal republic in 1824, Mexican politicians began to elaborate two basic ideological positions—federalism and centralism—concerning the relationship between the national government and the states. Over the years, federalism became linked with what Mexican thinkers called liberalism. The federalist-liberal position called for reform of colonial institutions, the abolition of special privileges for the Church and the army *(fueros)*, and the promotion of Mexican agriculture and mining. Federalist-liberal ideologues looked to France, England, and the United States for models on which to base programs for Mexico's future and blamed Spain for all the "horrors" of the colonial past.

Carlos María de Bustamante opened the debate in the 1820s with his anti-Spanish *Historical Picture of Mexico (Cuadro histórico de México)*. In the 1830s José María Luis Mora and Lorenzo Zavala each furthered the liberal cause with histories of Mexico intended to show how Mexico's institutional problems derived from its colonial past. But by 1836 Zavala was dead in Texas and Mora in permanent exile.[4] In 1842 Mariano Otero advanced the liberal analytical tradition in his *Essay on the true state of the social and political issues which affect the Mexican republic* which warned against free trade and British influence. Many of his fellow liberals disliked him for his novel views, his arrogance, and his earning his living by influence-peddling, but few could match his forceful and insightful analyses of Mexico's position.[5]

The centralists held sway officially in Mexico from 1834 to 1846, yet except for José María Gutiérrez de Estrada's monarchist pamphlet, they did not respond to Liberal ideology in tracts of their own. Their policies in office promoted central control, suppression of the press, the protection of the traditional army and the Church, and the support of native industry.

From 1845 to 1849, Lucas Alamán published his polemical *History of Mexico* which argued that Mexico needed a monarchy to preserve the colonial order and Spanish heritage essential to its social stability and to restore the consensus necessary to fight the factionalism and chaos which had culminated in the Mexican-American War and the U.S. invasion.[6]

Yet Alamán had been mistaken for in the twenty-five years since the establishment of the republic, a very real, although silent, consensus had indeed emerged. Most wealthy Mexicans agreed that their first duty lay in withholding their property from whatever government ruled in their name. These citizens created pressure groups to protect themselves. By 1848 the army, government workers, merchants, miners, landowners, the Church, moneylenders, and industrialists all learned how to use the three major newspapers published daily in Mexico City to express their opinions. Whenever the government proposed some plan that might affect the self-interest of any one particular group, it retaliated with a torrent of press criticism, often forcing the offending minister to resign. Press opposition alone could not bring down an entire administration but it could undermine it substantially.

The liberals controlled two daily newspapers—*El Siglo XIX* and *El Monitor Republicano.* Ignacio Cumplido founded *El Siglo XIX* in 1841 to represent the moderate wing *(los moderados)* of the liberal group; it specialized in economic and fiscal issues likely to be of interest to merchants. It favored government budget cuts, lower tariffs and direct taxes, and the gathering of statistical information to help economic growth. A few years later Vicente García Torres started *El Monitor Republicano* as an outlet for the radicals *(los puros)* among those liberals who thought the moderates too stuffy. It supported free trade and the expropriation of the Church and tended to represent merchants outside Mexico City and government employees.[7]

The conservatives operated the third Mexico City daily—*El Universal.* Lucas Alamán and Rafael Rafael, a Catalan printer, founded the newspaper in August 1848 to promote high tariffs, centralism, monarchism, and the maintenance of a strong Catholic Church. *El Universal* generally reflected the views of the Mexico City-Veracruz traditional elites, the Spanish government, the cotton entrepreneurs, and the Church.

Postwar Federalism

On September 17, 1846 Santa Anna resurrected the federalist Constitution of 1824. The national government was to receive all import and export duties, the consumo, the proceeds from sales of vacant land *(terrenos baldíos)*, 4 percent on coins, the tobacco monopoly, post office, the lottery, the salt monopoly, official paper, mints, the incomes of the Federal District (Mexico City) and the territories, and national properties including those of the Inquisition, the Jesuits, etc. The contingente was resumed, but set at the much more realistic figure of $ 1,011,000. The more populous states of Jalisco, Puebla, and Mexico each contributed $ 144,000, while Aguascalientes paid $ 3,000.[8] The states retained the right to all other taxes.

Although the division of tax categories in 1848 was almost identical to that in 1824, two major revenue sources—the tithe and the alcabala—had been abolished. Yet as with the British loans of 1824 and 1825, the leaders who returned to Mexico City in 1848 expected that the indemnity payments (three million pesos per year for five years) would help the Treasury pay expenses until the federalist fiscal system worked properly. Again, as before, such expectations fell short.

After the war, budget reports became much less reliable. In part this was due to the fact that treasury officials submitted no accounts during the period from 1845 until 1848. In the post-war federalist years, they probably doctored their figures to show that the indemnity had closed the gap between income and expenses and that the government had only borrowed small sums. In fact the discrepancies between the amounts listed for loans and the deficits even with the introduction of indemnity funds indicate otherwise. Treasury expenses continued to be higher than those for the military, but the figures for 1850–1851 and 1851–1852 look suspiciously low. Some examples of fraud can be spotted rather easily as when Treasury Minister Marcos Esparza listed $ 6,058,378 in the 1850–1851 expense figures separately as "spent in payments, refunds and for other purposes which although legal are not included in the budget." He then reported that the Treasury Department had spent a mere $ 1,273,776 instead of $ 7,332,154.[9] Despite the fact that the figures appear highly irregular, it is impossible to prove that they are completely fraudulent.

Tax revenues for the years 1848/49–1851/52 were also low, far below those for the years under centralism. If Mexico had not received additional funds from the indemnity, it would have been in even more serious financial trouble, but the indemnity alone could not compensate for inadequate income. Furthermore, income figures for the indemnity years are even more misleading than those for expenses. For example in the report on income for 1848–1849, Treasury Minister Francisco Elorriaga included $ 2,433,419 in internal debt certificates used to pay customs duties and a $ 2,230,970 drop in the foreign debt; in his report listing income sources, however, neither appeared.[10]

In addition, it is highly unlikely that the Treasury borrowed less than one million pesos after 1848–1849, particularly since a severe cholera epidemic devastated Mexico in the spring and summer of 1850. During the crisis, those with money fled the capital, leaving the city in chaos. Congress stopped meeting for several months, and few officials were present to maintain order. By 1851, Mexico had lost thousands of pesos and 2,000 citizens including the extraordinarily gifted Mariano Otero, who had refused to leave Mexico City.[11]

Even these probably doctored figures show that Mexico suffered deficits of $ 2,080,021 and $ 4,345,168 in 1848–1849 and 1849–1850, respectively, despite over ten million pesos in indemnity payments. The small deficits given of $ 177,339 for 1850–1851 and the surplus (!) of $ 532,922 for 1851–1852 once again confirm that budgets published by the treasury in those years were fraudulent.

Mexico needed to create a viable fiscal structure so that taxes would replace indemnity payments after 1852. Unfortunately neither the Herrera nor the Arista administration was able to devise and implement a single significant alteration in the manifestly inadequate fiscal system.

The fiscal system, federalist once more, produced even less revenue in the years 1848–1852 than it had previously. In part, this was attributable to the damage wrought by the American invasion, to political troubles in Europe, and to the cholera epidemic in Mexico, but the tax revenues gathered were very meager. The

highest amount collected in a single year ($ 10,212,755 in 1851/52)
was *lower* than that collected in every year for which records are
available since 1826–1827.[12] Furthermore, the percentage of revenue provided by customs receipts had increased phenomenally.
In the years from 1836 to 1841, tariffs had never provided more
than 48.4 percent of total tax revenues. Yet after the war, they
contributed a minimum of 62.8 percent (1848–1849) and a maximum of 68 percent (1849–1850).

Why Federalism Failed

Federalism, like centralism, was unable to fulfill its promises.
The centralists pledged to create a strong national government
and an efficient fiscal system, but their program produced ever
growing deficits despite increases in revenues, and the eventual
loss of over one-half of national territory. The federalists, by sup-
porting greater autonomy for the states, hoped to make revolt unnecessary and promote union through cooperation. They also
expected the indemnity from the United States to buy enough
time for national recovery. Yet they were unable to implement
tax increases, and despite the additional money from the United
States, promote economic growth, and cut expenses. The resulting deficits led to a loss of control, army disaffection, and revolt.

Federalism dictated that all centralist revenue machinery be
dismantled, causing the government to lose the ability to collect
direct taxes and to absorb other revenues produced by state treasuries. This revenue amounted to over six million pesos in each
year from 1842 to 1844. In exchange the federal government received a paltry state contribution which reached only $ 382,000
(3.7 percent) in its best year. While federalism was a poor genera-
tor of revenue, it was a sacred cow in Mexican politics. Neither
the Herrera nor Arista administration dared to suggest its abolition, although they tinkered with the fiscal structure.

On November 24, 1849, the government passed a spending ceil-
ing of $ 500,000 per month, two-thirds of which would automat-
ically pay the military. The law also specified that the money could
not be used for back debts or back salaries. Treasury Minister Francisco Elorriaga then produced a budget with 25 percent reductions for all government salaries, except for the army on active

duty. Politicians and the press hailed the law as a landmark, but no real budget ever conformed to its impossible regulations.[13]

New taxes were necessary for the establishment of a workable fiscal system, but after 1848 it became more difficult for the government to levy new taxes because of the indemnity windfall. The extra money provided just enough added revenue to maintain the government without major catastrophe from 1848 to June 1852. Therefore neither the Herrera nor the Arista administration felt pressured to propose, pass, and implement new and politically risky tax packages. In addition, the techniques of procuring extra funds through some manipulation of sources outside Mexico sparked unconscious expectations of the possibilities of other financial windfalls in the future. As the indemnity money began to run out, the inability of the Herrera and Arista administrations to implement reform stimulated these hopes more as government officials began to explore such possibilities.

During the Herrera administration, treasury ministers actually proposed various kinds of taxes, each aimed at specific economic groups in Mexican society. For example on October 6, 1848, the government decreed new municipal taxes like those of the 1830s and 1840s which applied to urban and rural property, businesses of all sorts, factories, professions and jobs, luxuries, and wages and salaries. Complaints soon surfaced from such "urban property holders" as moneylender Francisco Iturbé, Bernardo Couto, former President Manuel Peña y Peña, and Lucas Alamán claiming that such levies represented triple taxation which merchants did not have to pay. A few months later Treasury Minister Manuel Piña y Cuevas lowered the urban property tax to a mere two mills of assessed value, less than the wealthy themselves had advocated.[14]

In 1850 Treasury Minister Manuel Payno proposed that the wealthy of the Federal District pay a total of $ 30,000 per month, an 8 percent increase in the internación, a 15 percent surcharge on liquor purchased by foreigners, an added one mill on the assessed value of rural and urban property, an 8 percent sales tax on imports and a 5 percent annual income tax on earnings exceeding $ 100. The Chamber of Deputies actually passed Payno's proposal, but the conservative Senate defeated his version and substituted one of its own. Then the matter was promptly forgotten.[15]

The Herrera administration also tried to tax the poor. In August 1849 Treasury Minister Bonifacio Gutiérrez proposed the re-establishment of the general sales tax (alcabala) and new taxes on cooking oil, pulque, rice, coal, cornflour, and corn—all of which were necessities for the urban poor. But when Gutiérrez declined the offer of wealthy Mexico City businessmen to formulate their own tax structures, they stonewalled on these proposals as well.[16]

The wealthy indignantly refused to submit to new taxes until Congress reformed the fiscal system. Finally on July 25, 1850, Treasury Minister Manuel Payno presented a new formula for a treasury structure. According to his scheme, Congress would revise customs rates adding an 8 percent sales tax on imports, divided between states and nation. He also suggested a reformulation of the relationship between the Federal District and the national government whereby the former received the property tax and one-half of that on renters, and all of the indirect and direct taxes on sales of national products. In exchange the Federal District, by far the wealthiest area in Mexico, would pay the national government 10 percent of its income. He then produced a budget under these terms of $ 10,100,000 with $ 7,000,000 for general expenses, and $ 3,100,000 for the foreign and internal debts.

The protests began immediately. Every group in Mexico from *El Siglo XIX* (too much centralization of collection) to the customshouse employees in Manzanillo (shift of tax burden from trade to the citizenry as a whole) to the mining fund (income protected by tradition) objected to some aspect of the idea.[17]

During the Arista presidency the schemes for remedying the treasury imbalance became more and more extreme as the indemnity payments drew to a close. In addition Arista himself had many powerful enemies. Lucas Alamán and the textile entrepreneurs resented Arista's attempts to import cotton duty-free from the United States in the 1840s and his proposal in the 1850s to make the area near the new border with the United State a free trade zone. Alamán and the Conservatives also blamed Arista for instigating a December 1849 attack on the homes of the Conservative-controlled Mexico City municipal council.[18]

Because of these conflicts Arista's treasury ministers faced much more organized opposition from the Conservatives than had their predecessors. One treasury minister, José María Aguirre, proposed a new 3 percent tax on gold, silver, and textile exports. The new tax scheme collapsed and he resigned. His replacement, former

Minister of Foreign Relations Mariano Yañez wanted to tax cotton goods in addition to new indirect taxes in the Federal District and increased duties on imports. Yañez coupled these proposals with a request for an additional $ 1,680,000 of indemnity money in order to avoid the necessity of confiscating the funds of special interests, corporations like the Church, and states.[19] Congress discussed the measure, but it adjourned on May 24, 1851, without passing the proposal. Such inaction left the administration with no authorization to meet its financial crisis and no treasury minister, since Yañez resigned in disgust.[20] Neither the Herrera nor the Arista administration was able to tax itself out of deficit finance; in fact, they were quite unable to pass any new tax at all.

Federalism, by definition, depended on each state's willingness to accept membership in the Mexican nation and to demonstrate allegiance by paying its share of the contingente to the national government. During the post war federalist period, efforts to implement these ideals seemed increasingly futile. From 1848 to 1852 many of the areas on the borders of the republic were in turmoil and talking secession. Yucatán, which twice rebelled during the 1840s, was in the midst of a brutal caste war which threatened to annihilate the white society settled there. In 1850, revolts in Chiapas, aided by Guatemala and Tabasco were put down only to be replaced by others which reached to the frontiers with Guerrero and Puebla. Other uprisings occurred near the Sierra Gorda mountains which separate Guanajuato from San Luis Potosí. In 1849 the governor of San Luis requested 2,000 more troops and quashed the uprising by October, exiling the most intransigent to the northern frontier of Mexico to fight Indians.

The new northern frontier was beset by far greater problems. After the end of the Mexican-American War, those areas where the new territorial division was not marked by any geographical divider such as a river, settlers lacked any clear means to distinguish where the official border actually was located. In addition, the Apaches took advantage of the postwar uncertainty and stepped up their raids into Mexico. Although under the terms of the Treaty of Guadalupe Hidalgo, the United States was supposed to take care of the Indians on its side of the border, its forts and local citizenry made deals with the marauders which guaranteed peace for them and gave the Indians free rein in Mexico. As a

result, the attacks in Sonora markedly increased and public security became nonexistent.

The Herrera government decreed in July 19, 1848 a plan to establish military colonies to protect the new frontier. Those who
volunteered for a six year stint received a piece of land, tax exemptions, and other benefits. By 1849 a thousand soldiers complete with appropriate administrative apparatus settled in the three
endangered areas (Tamaulipas and Coahuila; Chihuahua; and Sonora and Baja California). By 1851, half of the planned colonies
were established and the others were forming, but large areas were
still exposed and defenseless.

The northern frontier faced an additional set of problems, unlike those in any other region. The loss (or "sale") of so much
nearby territory to the United States made those living in land
still Mexican nervous about what the future might bring for them.
Many people left Sonora, some seeking gold in California, some
just seeking safety elsewhere. Those who stayed, convinced that,
as their chronicler Stuart Voss laments, "Mexico City did not truly
seem to care," might have believed the article in the *New York
Herald* which they read reprinted in *La Voz del Pueblo*, the official state newspaper published in Ures. In it, they learned, that
"an agent of the Mexican government" had confided to a New
York reporter that the politicians in Mexico City were consider-
ing selling Sonora, Chihuahua, and Baja California in order to get
money for the treasury and because they could not protect these
areas from Indian raids.[21]

State payments of their *contingente* to the national treasury
reflected these problems. Although some states undoubtedly paid
less than they should, others inexplicably paid more. In 1849–1850
and 1850–1851 the state of Guanajuato earned $ 661,520 and
$ 641,700 respectively, but paid only $ 57,451 (8.7 percent) and
$ 60,333 (9.4 percent). Oaxaca, whose income for 1848 was $ 365,226
paid $ 56,318 (15 percent).[22] By November 1849 many states were
bankrupt and in debt; in the newly created state of Guerrero,
Governor Juan Álvarez could not pay his chief assistants.[23] Because of poor collections, the *contingente* was revised downward
on April 10, 1851. The new law set the total at $ 790,000 with
$ 100,000 each for Mexico State and Guanajuato and $ 3,000 for
Colima for the 1850/51 fiscal year and 15 percent of income in
those following.[24]

The difficulties of maintaining federalism in a period of growing deficits came to a head when Manuel Piña y Cuevas became Treasury Minister again on May 26, 1851. He first abolished special funds like the Mining Fund and ordered their surrender to the national treasury. He next proposed seven new taxes. Four of them—taxes on factories, 5 percent on tobacco sales, a surcharge on coinage taxes, and a new consumo—belonged to the national treasury; the other three—levies on urban and rural property, head taxes, and new assay taxes—were equally shared with the states.[25]

By mid-July, the states of Mexico, Guanajuato, San Luis Potosí, Jalisco, and Oaxaca had repudiated the proposal, the vast majority of the governors had refused to attend the Mexico City meeting the Treasury Minister had called for August, and *El Monitor Republicano* had urged that Piña y Cuevas be fired.[26] Joaquín Angulo, governor of Jalisco, the self-appointed spokesman, offered to aid the national treasury by giving it port taxes and expenses— taxes it already collected—and noted that the best way of producing revenue was still the old-fashioned sales tax.

Only three governors—Mariano Riva Palacio (Mexico State), Octaviano Muñoz Ledo (Guanajuato), and Pomposo Verdugo (Sinaloa)—showed up at the meeting to listen to Piña y Cuevas outline his proposals for new land, head, and coinage taxes. During the speech, he untactfully reminded the governors and representatives that only Guanajuato, Michoacán, Oaxaca, Querétaro, and the territory of Colima paid their full contingente for the year; the other eighteen states and territories still owed part or all of theirs.

Next he told them that he projected that in 1851–1852 Mexico would collect only $ 8,395,822 in taxes of which 73 percent would come from customs duties. That sum would hardly cover regular expenses of $ 15,144,947 and another $ 10,867,293 for the payment of debts for the same period. Therefore, he suggested that unless the states paid the national treasury proportionally according to population and Congress passed a new 2 percent property tax and a tax on native cotton goods, Mexico would have to defer payment of the internal debt.[27]

The governors and their representatives wanted the government to continue repaying the internal debt particularly since many of them were its creditors, and so they suggested that the tobacco monopoly be established in each state as well as on the national level, and that tariffs on manufactured cottons be lowered to 35 percent of the current rate to cut smuggling. They pledged that if the national government cut its costs, the states would contribute 20 percent of their income up to $ 1,000,000 to help compensate for the loss of the indemnity payments. Although the proposals appeared to have been made in good faith, the poor payment of the contingente in the past gave such pledges little meaning. Had these been legitimate suggestions and the states prepared to help the government, the plan would still have required the national treasury to handle collections without receiving any additional revenue.

Piña y Cuevas resigned in disgust, citing the demand that he reduce expenses to $ 550,000 per month as the final blow.[28] The state representatives succeeded in protecting their treasuries from revenue agents or army officers sent by the national government and in preserving their anarchic version of federalism.

Debts and the Indemnity

A Mexico without money was no novelty, but a Mexican treasury with three million pesos extra per year courtesy of the United States indemnity was another matter. Everyone who held Mexican debt paper, native or foreigner, inside or outside the country, wanted his or her share and fought strenuously to get it.

While everyone grabbed at a piece of the indemnity, most Mexicans agreed that one obligation took precedence—paying the British debt. In fact, the Mexican government could hardly have avoided the resumption of payments. When bondholder representative MacKintosh learned about the proposed indemnity at the armistice talks, he relayed the information to his employer, the Committee of Spanish-American Bondholders in London.

Nevertheless, the British in London and in Mexico City and their allies were determined to receive as much as possible of the indemnity money. Chief among the group was bondholder representative and British consul in Mexico City Ewen C. MacKintosh of Manning and MacKintosh. His dual identity as bondholder representative and leading moneylender represented a confirmation of interest since he stood to make a large profit from the new settlement. Furthermore the draining of the indemnity money meant more business for the moneylenders in the future. As Mariano Otero, whose family sued MacKintosh for control of some mines, wrote former Mexican Minister to Great Britain José María Luis Mora, Manuel Lizardi was actively lining up support to get his agency officially entrusted with handling the payments and that MacKintosh and Escandón wanted a large commission, a new conversion, and the return of Santa Anna.[29] Most Mexican politicians wanted to use part of the indemnity to pay the British debt. Both Conservative Lucas Alamán and Liberal Valentín Gómez Farías welcomed British influence in Mexico as a counterweight to that of the United States. Alamán, of course, encouraged any possible tie between Mexico and Europe, and Gómez Farías wrote his sons that Great Britain was "jealous of its interests and power (in Mexico)" and would help keep the North Americans out.[30]

Accordingly, the president of the Committee of British Bondholders, George B. Robinson, sent William Parish Robertson to Mexico as a special negotiating representative. On July 6, 1849, Robertson and Treasury Minister Francisco Arrangoiz announced a settlement whereby British bondholders received four million pesos from the indemnity to pay owed interest in exchange for reducing the interest rate from 5 percent to 3.5 percent. The Mexican Congress rejected the pact, not because it called for the expenditure of a full third of the indemnity and a large part of the yearly tariff receipts, but out of hostility toward Arrangoiz and his Conservative backers.[31]

Treasury Minister Manuel Payno proclaimed the eventual settlement on October 14, 1850, in which Mexico acknowledged a debt of $ 51,208,250 and promised to pay a total of $ 5,000,000 ($ 2,500,000 from the indemnity and 25 percent of all import duties; 75 percent of the export duties collected at the Pacific ports, and 5 percent from Gulf ports) to cover owed interest at a reduced rate of 3 percent.

Although the 1850 settlement spent less of the indemnity, it placed a heavy burden on the fiscal system. The bondholders approved the arrangement on December 29, 1850, and the Mexican government began to issue new bonds and certificates for interest owed from 1846 to 1851.[32] According to Joaquín Casasús, the 1850 settlement was "the best of the financial operations brought about with London debt."[33] It saved Mexico $ 5,776,572 in owed interest and reduced annual interest payments by $ 1,653,707.[34]

Although the settlement of the British debt provoked few protests, attempts to solve the problem of the rest of the creditors were full of controversy. The laws of the 1830s and 1840s which suspended payment on debts had turned creditors into competitors and the defeat in the war against the United States made Mexicans even more sensitive than usual to the native/foreign dichotomy. A political war broke out over the rest of the indemnity between those who wanted all credits treated equally, and those willing to use foreign ministerial muscle both in Mexico and in Europe to ensure preferential treatment.

Those without access to diplomatic intervention marshaled the press and prominent politicians on their side. In the heat of these battles, many Treasury ministers fell victim to constant press criticism, and little of importance was accomplished.

Mexico's first full-time postwar treasury minister, Mariano Riva Palacio, came to the position with powerful political allies because he had married the only child of martyred president Vicente Guerrero, the *compañero* of Juan Álvarez, caudillo of Mexico State. On June 14, 1848, Riva Palacio announced a reorganization of the Mexican treasury based on radical cuts in military and civilian spending coupled with planned retirement for military officers. However, he pledged $ 550,000 to protect citizens in Yucatán and in the areas now belonging to the United States and on the new border, and $ 791,685 to moneylenders ($ 600,000 to Manning and MacKintosh and $ 191,685 to redeem pension credits).[35] Shortly thereafter in August 1848, Riva Palacio announced that he had rented the tobacco monopoly to Manuel Escandón, Miguel Bringas, and British Consul Ewen MacKintosh in exchange for 20 percent of its receipts. The press exploded with accusations of all sorts including a charge that Riva Palacio, who resigned a few days later, had received a $ 200,000 bribe.[36] The most powerful treasury minister since 1821 had withstood the pressure for two and one-half months. Happily treasury ministers, unlike moneylenders, were expendable.

Before Riva Palacio left office, he issued an estimate of the size of the internal debt to aid work on its eventual settlement. By 1848 the government had no idea of the size of this accumulation of debts, both because of faulty record-keeping but also because the credits were used since 1834 and perhaps earlier as part of new loans and to pay portions of customs duties. According to Treasury Minister Mariano Riva Palacio, Mexico owed $ 44,524,879 from the colonial period of which $ 34,650,000 was derived from unpaid loans and unredeemed bonds and $ 47,907,791 stemming from the Republican period made up of $ 22,907,791 of loans and $ 25,000,000 in unpaid salaries. By this reckoning, speculators owned credits totaling at least $ 57,557,791 (62.3 percent) of the $ 92,431,670 internal debt.[37]

Riva Palacio's successor, Manuel Piña y Cuevas, was as well connected among Mexican Conservatives as Riva Palacio had been among the Liberals—his nephew Luis Gonzaga Cuevas was Foreign Minister and another nephew, José María Cuevas, was a deputy. In October 1848 *El Siglo XIX* revealed that in July 1847 Treasury Minister Juan Rondero had given Manning and MacKintosh credits, mostly on the tobacco debt, worth five million pesos as collateral for a $ 600,000 cash loan to be repaid April 1, 1848. When the merchant house reminded the government of the unrecorded debt, the treasury was quick to repay it, only to discover that the agents for the company could not supply the credits in return. The treasury officials involved did not inform the president of this "contract" violation and presumably the treasury minister remained ignorant as well. When Congress learned of the transaction it demanded a full account, which subsequently appeared on the front page of *El Siglo XIX* in October. By that time Manning and MacKintosh had returned almost one-half of the credits and asked for more time to produce the remaining $ 2,500,000 in bonds. A short time later Manuel Escandón gave the Treasury $ 500,000 as a pledge of the firm's goodwill.[38]

Piña y Cuevas tried to use the hostility to MacKintosh generated by this scandal to gain support for his most cherished project —a national bank. He believed a national bank would eliminate the need for moneylenders, discourage revolts, promote confidence among creditors, and lend money to promote business and industry. He proposed that the government set aside the remainder of the indemnity, about $ 10,000,000, and supplement it with one-third of its annual revenue to create reserves for the bank.

Yet despite the official government support expressed in newspapers and in President Herrera's yearly address to Congress, the legislature never voted on Piña y Cuevas's bank bill; indeed it never even discussed it. Such neglect was due as much to the Treasury Minister's desire to divert indemnity money from the hands of eager creditors as to opposition from agiotistas, politicians, and holders of debt paper.[39] Native speculators wanted to keep the lending business going. By stirring up hostility toward MacKintosh, they only wanted to hurt the competition, not increase it!

The next public scandal involving the agiotistas demonstrated Mexico's need for a national bank. In November 1848, Piña y Cuevas borrowed $ 768,000 from Manning and MacKintosh and agreed to repay it $ 800,000 in May 1849 (an effective interest rate of 4 percent). By the time the transaction was completed, the government received only $ 722,698, but still paid Manning and MacKintosh the full amount (an effective annual interest rate of 10 percent).[40]

The campaign against Piña y Cuevas heated up even more when he announced his settlement of the tobacco credits which called for 6 percent of the "Twenty-Six Percent Fund" to go to Martínez del Río Hermanos and other holders of the tobacco bonds and an additional $ 16,000 per month from the tobacco monopoly. Piña y Cuevas arranged this settlement in accord with a secret agreement concluded between President Herrera, Martínez del Río Hermanos, and British Minister Percy Doyle on January 26, 1849. The contract stipulated that the bonds would be paid in accordance with a ruling of the Mexican courts given before the war that these credits be honored separately. The decision helped a group of British (Martínez del Río Hermanos 33 percent; others with 9 percent), Spanish (Béistegui 27 percent, Maqua 11 percent, Muriel Hermanos 5 percent), and Mexican creditors (Escandón 5 percent, viuda de Echeverría e hijos 4 percent, Francisco Fagoaga 2 percent, and Agüero, González y Cia 1 percent), but it was perceived as a foreign enterprise.[41] The newspapers blasted Piña y Cuevas and the bureaucracy in general for taking bribes and making disadvantageous deals with the moneylenders, but they could not yet dislodge him.[42]

The "Twenty-Six Percent Fund" creditors were outraged. The new "Six Percent Fund" contained recognized credits of $ 3,500,000; the "Twenty Percent Fund" total was $ 68,000,000 and each received 6 percent of the customs revenues. Worse still, the British Minister kept close tabs on payments to creditors of the "Six Percent Fund" while payments into the "Twenty Percent

Fund" were often diverted to other uses. Finally, native creditors were concerned that all monies would eventually go to the foreigners—33 percent were assigned to "British creditors" even though Manuel Escandón was no more British than they. The next round of battles was about to begin.

In March 1849 Piña y Cuevas asked Congress for early payments of half the indemnity in order to balance the budget. When debate opened on March 12, 1849, Cuevas's opponents noted that the treasury minister had listed amounts owed and governmental expenses in full, despite the fact that government workers never received more than part of their salary. Mariano Otero accused Piña y Cuevas of hiring favorites and characterized the deal with Manning and MacKintosh as a "contract half on paper and half in cash . . . obtained (with) a bonus of a hundred percent." He observed that 32 percent of the next indemnity payment was slated to go to four speculator firms (Hargous, Rubio, Pasalagua, and Drusina) and that all but $ 510,000 of the funds would go to speculators and the military.

Subsequently, Congress approved the advance payment in exchange for Piña y Cuevas's resignation, and then restricted its allocation so that his successor could only spend the exact amount specified as the monthly deficit under the scrutiny of government employees.[43] Naturally Piña y Cuevas's replacement, Francisco Arrangoiz, blithely ignored such strictures and in less than one month asked Congress for another $ 800,000 from the indemnity and that it borrow an additional $ 800,000 at 1.5 percent monthly interest to repay loans made during the war.[44]

In the meantime, native creditors saw their chances for repayment slipping away. On April 28, 1849, *El Siglo XIX* published the official notice of treasury receipts and payments for April 9–14; it showed that of a total of $ 261,713 distributed, moneylenders received $ 220,960 (84.3 percent) exclusive of an additional $ 7,823 paid to creditors of the internal debt.[45] In retaliation, representatives of the former "Twenty-Six Percent Fund" first went to the Supreme Court, where they received a favorable but unenforceable ruling. Next, they pressured Congress where many of their number were members.[46]

Congress had been working on settling the internal debt since the beginning of the Herrera administration in June 1848. During the first year of discussions, senators, deputies, treasury ministers, and editorial writers proposed two types of unworkable solutions. They either envisioned spending part of the indemnity for debt payments or they wanted to use large portions of the customs revenue to repay creditors. By September 15, 1849, the Congressional Commission working on the debt had reduced its principal to $ 47,000,000, halved the total of outstanding interest and lowered the interest rate to 3 percent. In exchange, creditors received a 7 percent bonus for redeeming their credits. This plan meant that *all* credits would be included in the same pot, including those previously settled by private arrangement. For example, tobacco bondholders indemnified at 88 percent received a bond of $ 88 for every $ 100 of face value, plus an additional $ 8.80 as compensation for losing half of the accrued interest, and a bonus of $ 6.73 from the indemnity.[47] Thus holders of the tobacco debt would receive $ 103.5 per $ 100 of face value for credits worth much less on the street, but they lost the preferential repayment, protected by the British Minister's watchful eye. The law passed the Chamber of Deputies, but failed in the Senate. In 1850 Treasury Minister Melchor Ocampo issued his classification of the internal debt where speculators dominated at least ten of the seventeen groups. (Table 11) But within those categories, the credits included in groups 1, 2, and 8 had already been settled by special convention and previously had been held apart. In the battle for repayment, the sides were clearly drawn. Each group was supposed to name a representative to gather an accurate listing of creditors including names, owed principal and interest rate, but by September 1850, members of the "Six Percent Fund," the Mining Fund, and the merchant guild of Mexico City had refused to negotiate. Gregorio Mier y Terán and Antonio de Garay, acting on behalf of the tobacco harvesters and the Veracruz merchant guild respectively, could not manage to reach an acceptable agreement with the government.[48]

On November 30, 1850 Treasury Minister Manuel Payno y Flores completed the settlement package, known as the Law of Public Credit. Its terms included a common fund of 25.7 million pesos, 20 percent of customs receipts, $ 3,000,000 yearly amortization, and an interest rate of 3 percent sliding to 5 percent. The government also pledged to pay creditors an immediate $ 2,500,000 for amortization, the net profits from the reestablished tobacco monopoly, and an additional 10 percent from import duties. Payno then

Table 11.   Categories of internal debt, 1850

S = speculator   E = elite   F = foreign (speculator?)

1.	Indemnization of English subjects, which is at present 2%	(F)
2.	That owed to Montgomery, Nicod, and Company	(F/S)
3.	That stemming from the debt to the Philippine missions	(S)
4.	That from the confiscation of the silver bars in San Luis	(S)
5.	From the harvesters of tobacco	(S)
6.	Bondholders for the old copper money	(S)
7.	Owing from the 26% Fund	(S)
8.	From the tobacco bonds	(F/S)
9.	From the mining fund	(S)
10.	Tolls from the consulado of Veracruz and the *avería*	(E)
11.	From the tolls of the consulado of Mexico	(E)
12.	Owed to civil servants	(S?)
13.	Debt prior to independence	(S)
14.	The floating debt from the forced occupation of property	(S)
15.	From loans made only in cash	(S)
16.	Loans made with the admission of credits	(S)
17.	From contracts for the care of property	(S)

Source: Documentos relativos al arreglo de la deuda interior de la república mexicana, mandados imprimir de orden del supremo gobierno (Mexico, 1850), pp. 66–67.

issued $ 40,000,000 in new bonds, set up an office in the Treasury Ministry to supervise debt registration and liquidation, and established a Committee of Public Credit with speculator Gregorio Mier y Terán as president.[49] If creditors did not agree to incorporate their paper in the common fund, they would not be paid for ten years.

Treasury Minister Payno acknowledged that the Law of Public Credit aimed "particularly at the foreigners who acquired Mexican credits at ruinous prices to afterwards make them valuable with the support and force of their Ministers."[50] But the internal debt settlement unraveled quickly even by Mexican standards.

First, Treasury Minister Payno, credited with creating both debt settlements, resigned suddenly while working on the Internal Debt Settlement.[51] His successor, Veracruz senator José Ignacio Esteva y González, reluctantly revealed that the government simply could not fulfill its Law of Public Credit. As Esteva explained, Payno had based his settlement on the idea that $ 2,500,000 would cover the necessary first payments to creditors. However, the accounting division soon revised that figure to $ 5,994,869, $ 4,048,712 (67.5 percent) of which was owed to moneylenders, and $ 2,941,667 of that had been or would be included in ministerial settlements outside of the common fund.[52]

Esteva did not oppose the basic premises of the settlement; he simply recognized that if Mexico fulfilled its commitments to the creditors of the internal debt, it would spend all but $ 280,000 of the 1851 and 1852 indemnity payments (Table 12). Eventually Esteva resigned when Arista refused to suspend payment on the internal debt. Once out of office, Esteva proposed that the Church mortgage its property to permit the government to buy up internal debt paper at market value with bonds backed by clerical real estate.[53]

Esteva's successor, José María Aguirre, also supported a mortgage of church property, and proposed among other ideas that Mex-

Table 12. Demands on 1851, 1852 indemnity payments

Total 1851, 1852 indemnity payments	$6,540,000	$6,540,000
Internal debt payment		1,000,000
Internal debt (1852 indemnity)		680,000
External debt payment		2,500,000
Debt to Agüero, González & Co.		200,000
Debt to Jecker, Torre (loan 8/50)		500,000
Settlement from court to Forstall		900,000
Settlement to Casimiro Collado		480,000
Total owed	6,260,000	6,260,000
Amount free to the Mexican government from United States indemnity payments 1851, 1852	280,000	

Source: *El Siglo XIX*, February 27, 1851, p. 4.

ico suspend internal debt payments while negotiating a five and one half million peso loan.[54] Although the Law of Public Credit was demonstrably unworkable, Martínez del Río Hermanos and other creditors resisted it out of self-interest. Their protests escalated when the Junta of Public Credit began to receive money from the customs. On February 14, 1851 President Arista ordered all customshouse officials to suspend payment to the British convention in order to induce those creditors to make peace with the others. Martínez del Río Hermanos insisted on some guarantee of payment, which the government refused to give. Consequently the firm applied to British Minister Percy Doyle, claiming that native bondholders received better treatment and that "we have had to submit to the most grievous sacrifices, though the public coffers were then most amply provided."[55]

Throughout the spring of 1851, Doyle threatened Arista and his ministers. The interim Minister of Foreign Relations, José María Ortiz Monasterio, told Doyle that the law was needed to induce native creditors to lend money to a government near bankruptcy. But the threats continued as Doyle dropped hints of possible invasion, encouraged by instructions from the British Foreign Office. Arista weakened but pleaded to Doyle that "if all the quotas are returned, you will take from us the means of carrying on the government, for literally we have not a dollar in the Treasury."[56]

Since the Law of Public Credit could not work and because of strong pressure, Foreign Minister José Fernando Ramírez concluded a series of special arrangements called Diplomatic Conventions to settle claims owed to citizens of Spain, Britain, and France, and negotiated by their respective ministers. These agreements had the force of treaties and, if broken, could result in military action.

Ramírez and Spanish Minister Juan Antonine Zayas signed the Spanish Convention on November 14, 1851. Indeed the Mexican government had entered into the first of these "diplomatic conventions" on July 17, 1847, to settle debts owed to Spanish citizens since preindependence days. Spanish Minister Plenipotentiary Salvador Bermúdez de Castro and interim Minister of Relations José Ramón Pacheco had agreed to put all claims into a special fund to be redeemed by 3 percent of the customs receipts, lowered in 1848 to 2 percent. Under the terms of the new accord, the

Mexican government would issue bonds totaling $ 7,500,533 bearing 3 percent interest.[57]

Then, on December 4, 1851, Ramírez signed an agreement with British Minister Sir Percy Doyle in which the Mexican government agreed to reserve 12 percent of all import taxes to pay $ 1,269,892 owed the bankrupt British firm Montgomery, Nicod and Company and $ 3,876,434 in tobacco credits held by Martínez del Río Hermanos. The latter firm was appointed apoderado of the Fund, empowered to receive payments at the customs. Doyle too received his reward; his Queen made him Minister Plenipotentiary. Not everyone was so pleased. Manuel Payno grumbled that no British squadron would come to demand that Mexico pay the two or three dozen widows who daily petitioned for pensions, but it might appear in response to Martínez del Río's complaints.[58]

On January 21, 1851, Ramírez concluded the last of these agreements with French Minister André Levasseur, in which Mexico agreed to pay the banking house of Serment P. Fort one-half of the proceeds of the tax on internal circulation of money and all of the taxes on the export of silver from the Gulf ports. They also agreed to pay the banking house Drusina and Company $ 109,143 from the import taxes collected at the Pacific ports. In all Ramírez added $ 14,000,000 in new debts.[59]

Since the three Diplomatic Conventions shattered the concept of a single fund for internal debt, Congress revised the Law of Public Credit on May 19, 1852. It increased the percentage of state contributions to the federal government to 20 percent and assigned the increase and 3 percent of the new customs duties to the creditors of the internal debt. Once again the foreign bondholders backed by their ministers had beaten the Mexicans.[60]

Agiotistas at Mid-Century

Historians have sometimes assumed that the indemnity payments eliminated the need for internal borrowing, and indeed the budget reports for those years tend to confirm that belief by listing loans in rather small amounts. Nevertheless, the national treasury was by no means better off. According to Manuel Payno the Mexican government had assigned fully 66 percent of its tariff receipts to pay debt obligations. After totaling up all the money slated to pay debts, Payno concluded that the government could rely on 20 percent of tariff revenue and 50 percent of the money derived from internal taxation.[61]

Mexico, then, still needed its moneylenders, although since 1827 no politician had ever acknowledged this dependence publicly. After 1848, newspaper articles attacking agiotaje became commonplace. Even political enemies like Valentín Gómez Farías and Mariano Otero opposed the British firm of Manning and MacKintosh and accused it and its chief partner, Ewen C. MacKintosh, of fomenting revolutionary movements in Mexico.

Because of such open hostility, the Herrera government could no longer make deals with its "bankers" with impunity. Although its close relationship with the moneylenders continued, the increased visibility of their activity during wartime caught the educated public off guard as attention shifted from troop maneuvers to peace, indemnity payments, and financial wheeling and dealing. Politicians and the press criticized the mechanics of arrangements which once were concluded without a murmur.

Political leaders also simultaneously attacked the speculators in public, while transacting business with them in private. Governor Juan Álvarez, for example, wrote several highly respectful letters to MacKintosh urging him to buy mines in Guerrero, and Otero earned his living by helping agiotistas consummate favorable deals.[62] The new, more watchful, atmosphere forced the moneylenders to behave somewhat more cautiously, but some grew ever richer as the indemnity payments flowed from public coffers to private pockets while others, less prudent or lucky, went broke.

After the Herrera Administration took power in June 1848, a group of agiotistas including Manuel Escandón, José Antonio Béistegui and Miguel Bringas formed a company to rent the tobacco monopoly (August 18, 1848) and share resources for other projects. On June 1, 1849, the partners in the tobacco monopoly and the mint bought the British-owned Real del Monte mining company for $ 30,000 and payment of its debt of $ 102,359. The new mining company elected Béistegui, Escandón and Alejandro Bellangé its directors. By 1852, the mines hit a bonanza. The Escandóns' share was worth $ 987,500 in less than three years, creating a paper profit of $ 923,707 on an investment of $ 63,792.[63]

As Béistegui, Escandón, and Bringas earned fortunes and were freed from the curse of future liquidity crises, Guillermo Drusina and MacKintosh collapsed. In 1850 MacKintosh owned contracts for several mints, and was a partner in the tobacco monopoly and other ventures. He sent his sons to Harrow for their education and lived in a house two blocks away from the Presidential Palace complete with rosewood piano, Dresden china, and double bed ornamented with marble and mother of pearl. Unfortunately 1850 was a disastrous year for Mexican business, in part because of the devastating cholera epidemic, but also because lenders held too much of their assets in debt paper which the government was increasingly unable to redeem. British Minister Percy Doyle assessed the situation very astutely. In the past, the agiotistas lent money to governments which had assets to sell. The lenders came to depend on the profits they made in these transactions. When the government had sold everything of value and could not repay its loans, the houses which supplied funds collapsed along with the governments they had once supported. MacKintosh's sons returned from England, and his beautiful house and its contents were sold to Manuel Escandón.[64]

Other moneylenders benefited from MacKintosh's collapse. For example, in 1850 Manning and MacKintosh owed Juan Antonio Béistegui and his brothers Nicanor and Isidro $ 304,601. At the time of his bankruptcy, he agreed to give the Béistegui family his shares in the Mexico City mint, the tobacco monopoly in Sinaloa, and in the La Purísima silver mine in Guanajuato. Manuel Escandón also profited from MacKintosh's debacle and he bought up much of MacKintosh's property after his declaration of bankruptcy.[65]

From 1848–1853, speculators diversified their holdings still further and entered new areas such as mining and commercial agriculture, while maintaining their interests in textile factories, contracts with the government, trade, and of course, making loans. Some firms such as Jecker, Torre and Company and Barron, Forbes greatly increased the size and scope of their activities. The first firm emerged out of the ruins of the British Montgomery, Nicod, and Company and in 1847 its partners Juan B. Jecker, Isidoro de la Torre and Felipe Terán changed its name to Jecker, Torre. It had been serving the government since 1845 as a tax collector, supervising the gathering of import surcharges in return for 3 percent of all tariff receipts. The firm also helped French merchants by paying their customs duties and by handling their shipments. During the war it provisioned troops particularly in California; later it collected minting fees for a four percent commission. In 1850 the firm moved its center of operations to the northeast— Mazatlán, Nayarit, Sinaloa—where it imported and distributed cotton, iron, coal, and mercury.

In 1850 French Minister Plenipotentiary André Levasseur formed a joint-stock company to settle Frenchmen in Sonora to work the mines. Jecker, Torre was to finance the venture up to $ 30,000. Eustaquio Barron and William Forbes, Spanish and American consuls on the Mexican west coast for many years, and owners of Barron Forbes and Company in Tepic, fought back with a firm of their own, the Sociedad Esploradora de Metales de Sonora (Forbes-Oceguera Company). Their excellent local connections as well as contacts with high-ranking officials in the capital quickly defeated both the French Minister and Jecker, Torre, who abandoned the project.[66]

Although Béistegui, Bringas, and Escandón shared a brilliant success with the Real del Monte, only Escandón invested subsequently in other ventures in the Mexican economy. The Real del Monte mines was not Escandón's only postwar purchase—in 1848 he bought the Cocolapan textile factory which had been founded by Lucas Alamán, aided by the investment of French capital provided by Prospero and Augusto Legrand, and then sold to Juan de Dios Pérez de Gálvez. Escandón paid $ 456,000 for the factory, $ 101,500 in bonds of the 25 percent tobacco fund and $ 218,674 in tobacco credits. At the time of purchase, the Cocolapan mill in Orizaba had 11,500 spindles and was the largest manufacturer in the country.

The Real del Monte bonanza and the acquisition of the Cocolapan textile plant merely confirmed Escandón's preeminence among speculators and entrepreneurs. Historians can document that by 1852 he owned stock in the Fresnillo and Real del Monte mines and in the tobacco monopoly as well as cotton factories in Tepic (La Escoba) and Orizaba (Cocolapan); the haciendas of Chalco and Cienaga del Pastor and properties in Mexico City. He also held contracts to repair roads, run mines, mints, salt pits on the Jalisco coast, buy military equipment, fix facilities at the port of Veracruz, bond customs officials, and renegotiate the foreign debt. However, the growth and extent of Escandón's activities and investments created new problems and indicated the basic difficulty facing every moneylender who had diversified his holdings in the 1840s and 1850s.[67]

The investment of substantial amounts in industry, mining, and commercial agriculture soon resulted in sizeable increases in production. For example, in 1845 the Miraflores textile mill owned by the Martínez del Río family manufactured 16,331 pieces of cotton cloth, but by 1854 it could produce 67,200 pieces—an increase of 411 percent. The textile industry's overall output for the same period grew by 442 percent.[68] Greater production required expanded access to markets, but Mexican roads were in wretched condition, and mule travel costly, dangerous, and cumbersome.

The speculators had realized in the 1840s that more support for national industrial development was needed, and therefore, had entrusted Lucas Alamán with spreading the word while gathering important marketing statistics as Director of the Bureau of Industry. Alamán was only too glad to further one of his own major interests and within one year he had established fifty-six industrial boards throughout the country, with particular emphasis on stimulating textile production.[69] Once factories had substantially enlarged their outputs, speculators became increasingly interested in building railroad lines to enable them to distribute their products over a wider area.

The idea of a railroad in Mexico was not new. Anastasio Bustamante had awarded the first concession for a line from Veracruz to Mexico City with a spur line to Puebla to Francisco Arrillaga on August 22, 1837. The terms of the contract between the government and Arrillaga, former Treasury Minister and Veracruz merchant, indicate that some powerful group must have opposed the project. For example, Arrillaga was required to pay the government a million pesos for the concession, and any lands needed would have to be adjudicated and the owner indemnified. Furthermore the railroad was forbidden to use existing roads and mail would have to be carried free (which would thereby save the tolls and mail service profits for the speculator consortium which owned them). The idea failed for lack of investors.[70]

In 1842 Santa Anna granted two new concessions—one for a communications link across the Isthmus of Tehuantepec on

March 1, and one for a railroad from Veracruz to San Juan on May 31. The latter concession permitted the creditors of the pre-independence debt of the Consulado of Veracruz to build a railroad in exchange for the promise to pay the full amount of the debt when the railroad was completed. On July 26, the Consulado signed over its rights and duties over the railroad to the speculator Antonio Garay, whose brother José had received the Tehuantepec canal concession.[71]

The war with the United States temporarily halted this promising development, but with peace came a renewed interest in industry and a fresh look at the obstacles which blocked economic progress. For example, Ignacio Ramírez openly wondered where Mexico would get the necessary funds for development "since our capitalists are accustomed to easy and large profits from large estates, secure investments, and contraband trade."[72]

The following year, on May 18, 1849, Congress passed a law which authorized President Herrera to negotiate with bidders for the construction of a railroad from Veracruz to Mexico City then to the Pacific within fifteen years time. The government promised free land for stations and rights of way and a fifty-year period of exclusive private ownership. On September 15, 1850, the government inaugurated a line running the eleven and one-half kilometers from Veracruz to Molino.[73] Despite this extremely limited success, the entrepreneurs still needed to find a way to capitalize the rest of this railroad, and to build many more.

The End of the Road

After Manuel Piña y Cuevas's desperate attempts to remedy the fiscal situation failed, and he resigned on September 1, 1851, the Arista administration and congress proposed various schemes to provide more revenue without having to impose new taxes. For example, Arista himself reintroduced his plan for a tariff-free zone along the new border with the United States, only to be thwarted once again by a coalition of Veracruz-Mexico City merchants and moneylenders.[74] The Senate Commission of Treasury and Public Credit proposed to rearrange the internal debt by promising to give creditors the entire state contribution and 3 percent of customs receipts until such time as the government could arrange to sell them its vacant lands (terrenos baldíos), but Congress failed to pass the measure.[75] When Congress tried to reestablish the sales tax in the Federal District as a prelude to setting it up throughout the country, the legislature quickly withdrew its program in the face of vigorous protest from the Mexico City municipal council.[76]

By 1852 the Arista administration was driven to seek additional revenue by trying to sell the right to build an inter-oceanic canal across the Isthmus of Tehuantepec to the United States. Mexican officials were well aware of American interest in the property. U.S. negotiators had offered a minimum of five million dollars and a maximum of fifteen million for the rights to build a canal during the talks which ended the Mexican-American War. In 1850 the United States reopened discussions and signed a treaty with Mexico guaranteeing joint sovereignty of the area. The two governments then began to think about a possible sale of the territory for as much as fifteen million dollars, the precise amount of the exhausted indemnity.

Conservatives in Congress strongly protested the sale of any land to the United States and forced Congress to pass a general law on May 14, 1852, (five days before the internal debt renegotiation), stipulating that any sale of rights to Tehuantepec must contain a clause preventing access to armed expeditions but permitting free use to all nations. The guaranteed international character of the area ruined any possibility that the United States would buy it and thus give the Arista presidency some hope of completing its full term of office.[77] Foreign Minister Ramírez did try to get twelve million pesos for the release of Article XI of the Treaty of Guadalupe Hidalgo, but after Congress had stated its will about Tehuantepec, the United States suspended negotiations.[78]

When Congress recessed on May 22, 1852, the opposition, now composed of both conservatives and moderates, began to formulate a strategy aimed at the overthrow of Arista and the installation of a new government. *El Siglo XIX* signaled the formation of its pact with the Conservatives when it accused the government of waste and corruption, of leaving the border unprotected against hostile Indians, and of paying García Torres, the publisher of *El Monitor Republicano*, a daily seventy-peso subsidy.[79] The anger expressed by *El Siglo XIX* over such a standard practice marked the final split between the moderates and the Administration and the resulting alliance with the Conservatives.

By the beginning of September, President Arista had few political supporters from whom to select a new cabinet. As always, not many Mexicans wanted to be named treasury minister despite Francisco Zarco's facetious instructions on how to be named to that post:

> speak little of the treasury, but a great deal of friendship with the rich and moneylenders: write in the press what appears good to you, but write a lot, study the subject of political economy as in *Fistol del Diablo* and write another book if you can. When they think little of it, present a project on the arrangement of the federal treasury, which shows everything in a bad way: but use many algebraic calculations, with many signs like & y x + etc. all of which they will judge as excellent because no one will understand it and think you are the best financier in the world. Don't write any work on the treasury which is filled with pretensions because then they will know your desire and you will continue waiting. With such a background, it is undeniable that within a short time you will be the Minister of the Treasury.[80]

President Arista soon selected thirty-four year old Guillermo Prieto as Treasury Minister. Despite his youth, Prieto had more experience in government and more knowledge of economics than most of his predecessors. He had begun his political career as personal secretary to President Anastasio Bustamante and had studied economics at the dinner table of treasury official Manuel Payno y Bustamante, father of future Treasury Minister Manuel Payno y Flores. After the war, he represented Jalisco in the Chamber of Deputies, contributed frequently to *El Siglo XIX* and published a monumental analysis of the income sources of the republic and of customs collections in particular. Yet despite his interest in fiscal matters, Prieto acknowledged in his memoirs that he became treasury minister because of his love of fame, fanfare, and ostentation, only to discover that the post involved little of these. He also had great visions of himself as reformer, and decreed half pay for all treasury officials on his first day in office.[81]

Prieto had little opportunity to institute any further reforms because army units began to revolt throughout the country. The treasury lacked the funds needed to pay loyal troops, and soldiers stationed in Chihuahua were reduced to pawning their rifles for the cash to buy food. Revenue declined for, as Prieto described it, "a gang of robbers has invaded the tobacco administration in Michoacán, the revolutionaries of the South have rushed the customshouses, and contraband has taken over on the immense northern border." By the end of October, Prieto had to order all government employees to remain at their posts and defend them against the rebels.[82]

The opposition presented its policy on October 20 in the *Plan of the Poorhouse* (Plan del Hospicio) which tried to unite all factions, excluding the radical federalists, by calling for tariff reductions and the reimposition of centralism.[83] The strategy worked, for by the close of 1852 both Veracruz and Tampico had pronounced against Arista. When Arista gave his address at the opening of Congress in 1853, no one bothered to listen to his report on plans for a loan to be secured by a general tax.[84] Every politician was concentrating on the essential question of who would replace him. The matter was soon solved, for on January 5, Arista resigned and the President of the Supreme Court, Juan Bautista Ceballos, became the interim president of the nation.

The United States indemnity had given Mexico a chance to duplicate the conditions of Guadalupe Victoria's administration and like Victoria, President Herrera did manage to keep the peace and bring Yucatán back into the republic. However, the political and economic forces still inchoate in 1824–1828 emerged stronger and more articulate in 1848–1852 to disburse funds once again on their own behalf. Thus, by 1852, the indemnity had not brought new water systems for Tamaulipas, nor new roads, nor new schools. Worse still, it had not led to the creation of a new and viable fiscal structure.

Yet Mexico had changed during the intervening years between the British loans and the indemnity payments. Speculator profits had fueled new manufacturing plants whose outputs demanded greater access to ever more distant markets. Indeed, at the very time state governors were fighting to preserve their federalist enclaves, a national economy was emerging which would subvert any pretense to genuine regional autonomy. As the speculators accumulated more and more wealth, they began to need different services from the national government.

By 1853 the moneymongers required a government strong enough to collect taxes and supervise the construction of the modern transportation and communication networks necessary to handle the needs of a growing economy. After the administrations of Herrera and Arista both failed to reform the tax structure and subsidize infrastructural development, even with indemnity funds at their disposal, the speculators once again placed their support behind a military dictatorship. They perhaps believed that their coalition with those interested in national development would be strong enough to dominate the new administration and direct its attention toward building for the future. Unfortunately, once again, they had to rely on Santa Anna, who was by that time inescapably mired in the past.

4

Santa Anna and the "Vampires of the Treasury," 1853–1855

> Escandón and his buddies carry the most weight. The influence of the industrial-financial group has been such that notwithstanding the tirades of Alamán, the hatred of Haro and the constant preaching against the "vampires of the treasury" as the agiotistas are called, the deal makers insinuate themselves everywhere, being represented by such cunning and subtlety that when he entered Mexico City, Santa Anna came in Escandón's carriage.
>
> Guillermo Prieto, *Memorias de mis tiempos*

The agiotistas and the Conservatives led by Lucas Alamán overthrew Arista's government and ended federalism. The moneylenders and Alamán's Conservatives both wanted political stability and a strong central government. They disagreed sharply about other aspects of fiscal and political policy.

Lucas Alamán still believed, despite evidence to the contrary from the 1834–1846 period, that the reimposition of centralism would make Mexico solvent and thus able to proceed with economic development. In his view, centralist finance would provide a secure and stable base for Mexico's hierarchical social structure and for the Catholic Church. The moneylenders wanted a strong efficient central government to collect enough revenue to provide the political stability and money to oversee large-scale nationwide infrastructural projects. However, these new development programs ultimately required that the traditional Church give way to the needs of the future.

Neither the moneylenders nor the Conservatives could win power without military support so they had to choose a general to assume the presidency. While the army, the moneylenders, and Lucas Alamán's group of Conservatives debated the merits of various candidates, Juan Bautista Ceballos, Chief Justice of the Supreme Court, served as interim president.

Ceballos decided to enlist the support of foreign merchants in order to retain his position. He lowered duties on manufactured cottons and mining exports and the traders raised $ 200,000 in a few minutes supposedly for his treasury, which sum never appeared in any budget report.[1] Ceballos also granted a mixed company of Mexicans and Americans directed by A. G. Sloo permission to develop the Tehuantepec canal in exchange for $ 600,000—half as down payment, the rest in six monthly installments.[2]

By the beginning of February 1853, the backers of the coup against Arista agreed to make Antonio López de Santa Anna president and forced Ceballos to resign. General Manuel Lombardini became interim president until Santa Anna returned to Mexico. Lombardini spent most of his time in office increasing the army and looking for the money to pay for it. Lombardini granted widespread promotions, drafted many Indians into the ranks, and generally strengthened the army. In a gesture to the monarchists he granted land valued at over $ 200,000 to the heirs of former emperor Agustín de Iturbide. Lombardini spent money freely despite the fact that the customs collection system had yet to recover from the overthrow of the government. In February, for example, the customshouse at Veracruz produced only eighteen pesos and the one for Tabasco gathered $ 861. Since each port operated at will with its own set of tariffs, Lombardini's reduction of the consumo tax to 5 percent had little effect.[3]

Lombardini filled the treasury instead by borrowing from moneylenders or by selling monopolies. In February the government operated in part on the $ 300,000 from the Sloo contract. In March, Lombardini rented the mints at Guanajuato and Zacatecas, worth $ 5,000,000 to Manning and MacKintosh for $ 250,000 and helped other moneylenders by alienating Indian lands to private ownership. As the French Minister Plenipotentiary and Envoy Extraordinary André Levasseur commented, "for two months the moneylenders and court favorites were the absolute masters of the situation."[4]

As Lombardini scrambled to find the funds to pay the army, the agiotistas, and the Conservatives, fully aware of his personal strengths and weaknesses, were busily planning their approaches to Santa Anna. Lucas Alamán, as the self-styled "representative of all the propertied people, the clergy, and all those who want good for their country," wrote a letter to the future president outlining how the Conservatives thought he should behave once in office. After reminding Santa Anna that he needed Conservative support, Alamán advised him not to surround himself with syncophants and not to entrust the government to others and retire to one of his estates. He counselled Santa Anna to avoid asking the Church for funds and to procure them instead by selling territory to the United States. In this manner he could remain free from deals "advantageous to (the speculators) but dishonorable for you."[5]

While Alamán was composing his message, the very speculators to whom he referred were writing a letter of their own. When Santa Anna landed in Veracruz in April 1853, two men greeted him at dockside: Antonio Haro y Tamariz gave Alamán's letter to the new President as his old friend Manuel Escandón, by then known as the "king of the agiotistas" presented his idea that a company of moneylenders purchase the rights to collect and retain all taxes for $ 9,000,000, $ 6,000,000 of which would pay governmental expenses and $ 3,000,000 to pay debts.[6] Thus from the outset Santa Anna confronted two sets of demands which were mutually exclusive.

Yet the two opposing groups were hardly equal in strength and resources. Despite Alamán's claim that the Conservatives had made the revolt, the army held true power and Santa Anna would have to fulfill its expectations with ever-larger loans from the moneylenders. Furthermore, the power of the Conservative Party rested on the moral stature and authority of Lucas Alamán since no other strong leader had yet emerged from its ranks. Alamán died two months later.

During the last few months of Alamán's life, Santa Anna's government adopted policies which were consistent with Conservative ideology. He appointed Conservatives to all cabinet positions including the two new ministries of Development *(Fomento)* and

Internal Affairs *(Gobernación)*, but reserved the military and treasury slots for his longtime friends and allies José María Tornel y Mendivil and Antonio Haro y Tamariz. Lucas Alamán headed the cabinet as Minister of Relations.

Centralism's Last Hurrah

The war with the United States strengthened Alamán's conviction that monarchy was the ideal form of government for Mexico. According to the French Minister to Mexico, André Levasseur, Alamán confided to him his admiration for centralized France, particularly after the recent elevation of Louis Napoleon to his new position as Emperor Napoleon III in December 1852. Alamán told Levasseur that the Conservatives wanted to give Santa Anna the power and authority of a monarch.[7]

Santa Anna issued his first decree, "Bases for the administration of the republic until the promulgation of the Constitution" on April 22, just two days after he took office. This decree abolished federalism and declared Mexico a central republic subject to the absolute power of Mexico City. Three days later, the government issued the Lares Law, named after Minister of Justice, Teodosio Lares, which stipulated the rules and regulations under which the press could function under the new regime. The newspapers *El Instructor del Pueblo*, *El Telégrafo*, and two of Vicente García Torres's, *El Monitor Republicano* and *La Biblioteca Popular*, promptly closed. Many of the laws issued during the first month of Santa Anna's administration were based on copies of French legislation requested by Alamán. The similarities between the two, particularly the press law, were so striking that some accused Levasseur of suggesting and drafting them himself.[8]

Once these laws were in place on May 14, 1853, the Santanista government centralized revenue collection and disbursement throughout Mexico. It closed all state legislatures and made state governors accountable to Mexico City. Then, Treasury Minister Antonio Haro y Tamariz reimposed the direct taxes of 1842 and 1843 on rural and urban property, factories, professions, and profit-making activities, wages and salaries, luxury items, and trading licenses (May 30). He also brought back the alcabala which was repealed by Santa Anna in 1846 (June 2). On July 14, the Treasury

Ministry ordered the offices in charge of collecting direct taxes to also gather statistical information concerning the treasury, tax revenues collected by the Ministry of Foreign Relations, and those from national property. Haro y Tamariz reestablished the 6 percent tax on the export of silver coins which Ceballos had reduced to 4 percent and specified stiff penalties for treasury employees caught skimming from the collections.[9]

In effect, the fiscal system used in Santa Anna's last dictatorship combined the structure which had evolved during his previous presidency and that which had been functioning since the war. In one critical aspect the reimposition of centralism in 1853 prompted quite a different response from that which followed its previous establishment in 1836. Not a single state revolted in favor of federalism as had Zacatecas and Texas. The government sought to use the Conservative vision as a starting point to reform the nation. It appeared that Lucas Alamán's idealization of Bourbon New Spain had been realized.

Despite Alamán's admonitions, Santa Anna and War Minister Tornel created a huge army of 91,499, many of whom were the poor Indians Lombardini had impressed into service. Consequently, military costs skyrocketed to an unprecedented $ 33,397,135 which Santa Anna expected Treasury Minister Haro y Tamariz to find.[10] Haro y Tamariz had been born in Puebla in 1811 and belonged to one of its prominent families. He had studied law in Rome and had served as treasury minister in 1844 and 1846.[11] He had been in office only a few days when Manuel Escandón presented his proposal for handling the additional burdens of the treasury. The company formed by Eustaquio Barron, Juan B. Jecker, and other notorious speculators offered to fund a "bank" with $ 6,000,000—$ 4,000,000 in cash and $ 2,000,000 in notes raised by selling 6,000 shares at $ 1,000 apiece. If the income of the banks exceeded $ 9,000,000, the government and the shareholders would divide the surplus.[12]

The bank would then handle cash transactions and loans and emit paper currency. In addition its founders pledged to give the national government a credit account of $ 9,000,000 each year to include monthly outlays of $ 50,000 for general administrative expenses. Further it budgeted an extra $ 800,000 for interest on the foreign debt, $ 200,000 for interest on the internal debt, and $ 250,000 for payment of diplomatic conventions all in semiannual installments. In return the company wanted to administer and retain all tax collections.[13]

The bank proposal suggested that by 1853 the agiotistas were no longer content to remain the invisible backers of governments. They were ready and eager to emerge from the shadows and expose their carefully constructed financial networks to the glare of public scrutiny. Although they expected to be well rewarded for their efforts, the speculators were offering in fact to place their resources at the service of the Mexican republic. By any standard this was a considerable display of confidence in a nation which less than four months before had endured another successful coup d'état. Their plan to sponsor a national bank represented a significant marker in the development of the Mexican entrepreneurial class and in the growth of Mexican nationalism.

Unfortunately the speculators miscalculated. They assumed that Santa Anna, never noted for his observance of the niceties of fiscal probity, would force Haro y Tamariz to accept the plans if the price was right. Under ordinary circumstances their analysis would have proved correct, but in his few months in office, Santa Anna behaved atypically under the watchful gaze of Lucas Alamán. Alamán wanted centralism; Santa Anna wanted a large, well-equipped and powerful army; their wishes conveniently meshed and led to the Santanista and Conservative marriage. The alliance would have crumbled eventually under the pressure of agiotista demands, but Alamán's death on June 2 merely hastened its demise.[14] No other Conservative possessed the personal authority necessary to keep Santa Anna in line, but Haro y Tamariz, an honest Conservative, refused to bow to strong presidential pressure.

The Treasury Minister rejected the bank proposal correctly noting that the company was to receive $ 2,000,000 in additional cash for itself (6,000 shares/$ 1,000). In addition the amounts projected for regular expenses and interest payments were inadequate and would lead to greater indebtedness. Finally such a bank would have too much power over Mexican economic and political life.[15] French envoy André Levasseur agreed and wrote to his superiors that the new bank would have placed the republic at the mercy of a "company of insatiable moneylenders, who would exploit Mexico at their own pleasure and would dominate every branch of public administration by means of the corrupt influence of their money."[16]

Although Haro y Tamariz had pinpointed its liabilities correctly, his outright rejection of the bank proposal was short-sighted. It killed any possibility that the government and the moneylenders could have negotiated more advantageous modifications. Mexico needed a bank and only the speculators had the means to fund one in 1853. Mexico's first bank opened eleven years later in 1864, owned and operated by foreigners under the auspices of the French empire.[17]

Perhaps Haro y Tamariz recognized that rejection of the bank proposal would affect his personal future as well as that of the Mexican nation. For example, the moneylenders would hardly be anxious to supply funds to a treasury which their adversary controlled, and eventually the treasury would be empty once again. Therefore Haro y Tamariz presented an alternative scheme for fund-raising which relied on clerical rather than speculators' wealth. He proposed that the Mexican government ask the Church to lend it $ 17,000,000 and issue an equivalent sum in bonds paying 6 percent yearly secured by its possessions. In return, the Church received the revenue from rural and urban property taxes, which Haro y Tamariz calculated would yield $ 1,600,000.[18]

Unfortunately Haro y Tamariz failed to consider several key obstacles to the successful implementation of his scheme. First, he projected the yield of property taxes without reference to the difficulty of collecting them. Property owners rarely volunteered to pay their taxes and the government frequently had to resort to threats in order to garner a reasonable amount of revenue. Secondly, he would need the cooperation of the Church, which strongly opposed mortgaging its property for any reason. The Conservatives proposed instead that the government itself issue bonds using property tax receipts for security.[19] This suggestion was completely ludicrous. The treasury had failed to redeem the internal debt credits already issued and could not expect to find buyers for another bond issue backed by such unreliable collateral.

The Church's refusal to ally with even a Conservative government to find some effective remedies to the fiscal problem parallels the state governors' unwillingness to cooperate with Treasury Minister Piña y Cuevas to save federalism. Haro y Tamariz's plan, although unworkable in its original form, offered a means to pay off debts without burdening the government with more interest payments. In addition it would implement a cherished aspect of Conservative philosophy by establishing a common bond between the government, the Church, and the creditors. The idea resembled one which José Ignacio Esteva had prepared in 1851 for some of the same reasons. It also resembled the Bourbon Law of Consolidation of 1804. However, when the Church rejected Haro y Tamariz's plan, it lost what proved to be its last opportunity to avoid the forced sale of its property.

Although Haro y Tamariz failed to convince the Church to aid the Treasury, Santa Anna expected him to procure additional funds somehow. Haro y Tamariz realized that Santa Anna's demands would soon force him to borrow once more from the agiotistas; therefore rather than involve himself with them, he resigned from the cabinet on August 5. His firm stand gained him a great deal of respect from Mexican politicians and, according to Alfonse Dano, a member of the French legation, well-wishers filled his house congratulating him.[20]

"The Napoleon of the West"

The death of Alamán and the resignation of Haro y Tamariz ended Conservative influence and their centralist experiment. From August 1853 until August 1855, Santa Anna governed Mexico, unrestrained by reason, surrounded by syncophantic courtiers and eager agiotistas. Encouraged by the creation of the Second Empire in France, Santa Anna determined to elevate himself to a level equal that of Emperor Napoleon III or at least to heights of power unknown in Mexico since the death of Moctezuma II.

Santa Anna's dream of absolute power required large sums of money. When his Treasury Minister rejected the speculators' plans and the Church refused to cooperate with those of his Treasury Minister, he decided to sell more Mexican territory to the United States. Its representative James Gadsden arrived in Mexico City on August 4, 1853, just one day before Haro y Tamariz resigned from the Treasury Ministry.

Gadsden's instructions were to buy land south of the border established by the Treaty of Guadalupe Hidalgo. The United States needed the land to build a railroad to connect California with the

East Coast. If Gadsden managed to secure the land, he could include in the purchase price an additional sum to discharge claims of the United States against Mexico and those brought by Mexicans now living in U.S. territory for damage to property sustained in Indian raids.[21] Gadsden himself envisioned no difficulty in procuring the territory for, as he wrote to Secretary of State William Marcy, "the Mexican Government needs money—their necessities are great, and their pretensions very extravagant. The most serious difficulty in the way of extension of Territory will be: *The consideration* to be paid. . . ."[22]

Santa Anna feared that if the sale did not go through as planned, the United States might simply invade Mexico and take possession of whatever land it wanted. Therefore he instructed his ministers in London, Paris, and Madrid to obtain defensive alliances or promises of help in the event of an invasion by the United States. In order to convince these countries to rally to Mexico's defense, Santa Anna tried to clear up outstanding claims against the republic brought by the citizens of those nations which seemed likely to give him the support he requested. The Mexican government flattered and cajoled the French minister at every turn, hoping to get some promise of assistance. On June 30, 1853, Manuel Díez de Bonilla and French Minister Levasseur signed a third French Convention which recognized a $ 1,374,926 debt to French citizens. The Mexican government eventually paid all but $ 190,845 of the debts and pledged 25 percent of the import and tonnage duties levied on French ships to pay the remainder. Despite these demonstrations of Mexican good faith, the French government never officially agreed to aid Mexico in the event of a United States invasion.[23]

Santa Anna also tried to woo Spanish support. On November 12, 1853, Manuel Díez de Bonilla and the Marqués de la Rivera signed a treaty ratifying an 1851 agreement which recognized Spanish credits totaling $ 2,427,941 dating as far back as September 27, 1821. The terms specified that credits incurred subsequently or transferred by Spaniards to non-Spaniards would receive 3 percent interest and 5 percent amortization from a fund derived from 8 percent of customs collections. It was later revealed that the Mexican government had accepted as much as 50 percent of the total amount in fraudulent and illegal credits bought for 5–10 percent of their printed value which it redeemed for full face value plus interest.[24]

The Spanish government proved somewhat more cooperative than its French and English counterparts. The Spanish Minister of State, Angel Calderón de la Barca, had been his country's first minister to the Mexican republic and he too feared possible reinvasion of Mexico by the United States. On November 30, 1853, Foreign Minister Díez de Bonilla sent a draft treaty to Spain which called for mutual sharing of equipment, vessels, and troops. As he waited for Spanish reply, Santa Anna ordered his ministers abroad to inquire about securing the services of Swiss troops and an Irish legion.[25]

Despite success with Spanish officials, the Mexican government received no assurances from the British Minister. Most of the contact between Percy Doyle and Santa Anna's government at this time concerned its failure to live up to its obligations under the 1851 British Convention. In March 1854, Mexico owed British creditors $ 188,000.[26]

On December 30, 1853, Manuel Díez de Bonilla and James Gadsden signed a treaty stipulating that the United States would pay $ 15,000,000 for the territory known in Mexico as La Mesilla (approximately 30,000 square miles of present-day southern New Mexico and Arizona) and $ 5,000,000 for the claims from Indian raids. In addition the two nations pledged mutual assistance in suppressing such raids and other incursions.[27]

Gadsden felt the treaty to be a great accomplishment since it was "concluded without 'brokerage,' a Mexican [term] where the broker greazes [sic] the officials and retains all the tallow," and because he had thwarted attempts by Hargous, Escandón, and Santa Anna to insert extra provisions giving themselves $ 3,000,000.[28]

As negotiations for the sale of La Mesilla progressed, Santa Anna prepared to assault the last bastions of federalist resistance by enlarging the army. During the second half of 1853, the government created a lance squadron in Toluca, an active squadron in Morelia, two permanent battalions of naval artillery in Veracruz, a second brigade of artillery and of cavalry, an active lance squadron in Texcoco, an active lance regiment in Monterrey, and two battalions of naval artillery in the Southern department. While the army received munificent salaries, other government employees were paid in small change.[29]

He also designed his gradual elevation to a position of power and pretension previously unheard of in republican Mexico. In November he reestablished the Order of Guadalupe as a way of promoting a pseudoaristocracy. On December 16, he informed the nation that he would continue in power at a higher salary with the title of "Most Serene Highness."[30]

Once the Gadsden Treaty was signed, Santa Anna launched the final phase of his plan to make himself the Napoleon of the West. The money it would provide, $ 15,000,000, was more than was necessary to maintain political stability for three years after the Mexican-American War. It also kept the government from having to call upon the Church once more for forced loans or new mortgages on its property. Finally he minimized the risk by securing a semiofficial assurance of protection from Spain should the United States invade Mexican territory.

Thus fortified, protected, and prepared, Santa Anna began his attack on his long-time enemy, Juan Álvarez, leader of the federalists. Santa Anna launched his offensive by announcing his intention to improve the road connecting Acapulco, the financial center of Álvarez's stronghold, and Mexico City. This project posed a serious threat to Álvarez's continued rule over Guerrero because once the road was improved, Santa Anna could send an army into the area to crush his enemy. Therefore the announcement of the construction of a new highway without consulting Álvarez was tantamount to a declaration of war. Soon Santa Anna removed Álvarez's protegé Ignacio Comonfort from his position as head of the Acapulco customs, named his own man military commandant of the port, and granted rights to explore Guerrero for gold, all without informing Álvarez.[31]

Álvarez finally "pronounced" on February 24, 1854, condemning Santa Anna for illegally selling Mexican territory to the United States, and for establishing a dictatorship. The rebels withdrew their support from the Santa Anna government and promised if successful to maintain the army, reimpose the tariff rates established under Ceballos, to end the poll tax, and the draft of Indians.[32]

Álvarez showed considerable courage in this revolt against the government because Guerrero had few resources to sustain a serious and prolonged struggle against the national army. Most of its revenue came from Acapulco, which had been Mexico's major Pacific port in colonial times. However, after independence its importance and customs receipts had declined as Mazatlán increased in importance.[33] Even by 1900, Guerrero was an underpopulated state with only 420,339 inhabitants, a mere 3.3 percent of the national total of 12,629,825.[34]

When Juan Álvarez and the men of Guerrero revolted in February 1854, they launched a traditional style uprising. The rebellion was financed at first from supporters living in the United States. In June 1854 Ignacio Comonfort left Guerrero authorized to borrow up to $ 500,000 to purchase war materiel, and to concede trading privileges with the port of Acapulco to any navigation companies which wanted them.[35] He first went to San Francisco, but the Californians declined to help him. Next he went to New York, where a Spaniard, Gregorio Ajuria, gave him $ 57,680 in drafts and $ 9,000 in gold in exchange for half the profits of the port of Acapulco and a pledge to repay $ 60,000 at high interest.[36] By November Comonfort had bought over $ 12,000 of arms and ammunition, and had purchased a boat for $ 20,400.

This initial sum was large enough to sustain the type of guerrilla tactics Álvarez and his men used in 1854. In addition, rebel leaders did not hesitate to spend their own money to further their cause. Comonfort sold one of his ranches to provide money in the opening days of the movement and according to legend the governor of Acapulco, without funds, went from house to house, hat in hand, requesting money from the wives of his friends so that the soldiers could eat. Sometimes they were lucky, as in December 1854, when Generals Huerta and Santos Degollado raided Michoacán and found $ 40,000 in cash.[37]

The rebels' scanty and vague financial records indicate that the port of Acapulco furnished hardly any cash and that loans labelled "voluntary" or "forced" amounted to very little. The military expenses noted in the accounts seem routine, except for an occasional unusual payment such as $ 10 for marching music.[38]

Santanista Finance

From the time of Antonio Haro y Tamariz's resignation in August 1853 until August 1855, the Mexican fiscal structure could no longer be described as centralist. Indeed, because of the paucity and unreliability of available data, it is difficult to describe the financial system of the last two years of Santa Anna's rule in Mexico.

Ignacio Sierra y Rosso, whom Dano characterized as "a man of almost ridiculous mediocrity," replaced the stubborn Haro y Tamariz.[39] However, this appointment was merely cosmetic, for Santa Anna acted as his own treasury minister. He did so because the collections had not improved and the treasury was desperate for funds.[40] When revolt broke out in Guerrero, Santa Anna appointed Manuel Olasagarre, an associate of Manuel Escandón and the Martínez del Río, and fellow textile manufacturer, to be his new treasury minister.[41] Olasagarre utilized his position to change the fiscal structure to suit the needs of the moneylenders. He suggested simplifying the trade taxes by combining them all into a flat 40 percent of the import duty. In addition, he favored liberalization of the internal sales tax and the inclusion of the sales tax on imports in the 25 percent import tax. Such steps aimed to make international and national trade flow more smoothly and more profitably for the merchants.[42] The war against the revolutionaries of Guerrero dragged on from March 1854 to August 1855 as the national army could not manage to invade enemy territory and crush resistance, and the opposition could not transform its struggle into a national movement.

Although actual battles were fought in isolated areas, they disrupted regular tax collection. In addition Mexico suffered a cholera epidemic and a locust plague during that period. The epidemic was less severe than the one in 1850, but the locusts severely affected crops, particularly in Michoacán and Oaxaca.[43] These two natural catastrophes also hindered regular tax collections and decreased revenue.

Treasury Minister Olasagarre did submit a budget report for the year 1853–54, but his figures are extremely unreliable since no one in the Santanista government had the slightest interest in them. For example, the report stated that the government had "probably" collected $ 18,924,235 in 1853–1854, although simple addition yields $ 19,053,566 instead.[44] And, many of his totals are part fact and part estimate.

The Treasury report indicates that the Santanista fiscal system in 1853–1855 was not as decentralized as its predecessor in 1842–

1844. Although "internal taxes" (alcabala, 3 percent on silver, consumo, tax on coins, etc.) were reported by states, the customs collections were not. Overall income as reported by Olasagarre had almost doubled, thanks to substantial increases in customs collections and the reimposition of the alcabala and direct taxes, neither of which Herrera or Arista could have passed.

The increase in customs revenue offset below normal collections from the 1848–1852 tax categories and the poor performance of those from the previous Santanista regime of 1842–1844. Direct taxes, for example, came to a mere $ 1,298,299 in 1853–1854, a loss of more than four million. Santa Anna, however, consistently outspent his resources. Therefore the government levied a vast array of indirect taxes. It put a $ 3 per spindle impost on machines making wool, linen, and cotton thread, which infuriated the textile manufacturers.[45] To compensate, the government reestablished the tobacco monopoly in 1853 only to rent it the following year to Manuel de Lizardi, Cayetano Rubio, and Nicanor Béistegui.[46] Meanwhile taxes in Mexico City steadily increased to the point that its citizens were forced to pay one peso each month for each family dog, and an additional amount for windows and external doors.[47]

Santa Anna failed to fulfill his part of the bargain with the speculators. He could not preside over a new authoritarian regime capable of maintaining peace and collecting taxes. As Olasagarre's figures demonstrated, Santa Anna failed to repair the damage done to the tax structure during the war and as a result of the revolt which had overthrown Arista.[48] Perhaps with peace, the fiscal system might have regenerated itself, but the war against Álvarez ended all hope of its restoration. The breakdown of the fiscal structure as demonstrated by the 1853–1854 budget report certainly contributed to the eventual attack on clerical wealth.

Santa Anna spent millions recklessly because of the La Mesilla windfall and because he had solid ties to Escandón and the moneylenders. In response to empresarial demands for strong central control, Santa Anna had established ministries for Development (Fomento) and Internal Affairs (Gobernación). The new ministries, like the abortive bank proposal, indicated the speculators' increased visibility and assertiveness and their willingness to invest their funds in projects to promote national development. The Ministry of Development, under the leadership of the Conservative Joaquín Velázquez de León and with Miguel Lerdo de Tejada as its deputy (official mayor), had the authority to impose its own taxes, some of which duplicated those levied by the Treasury. Miguel Lerdo de Tejada was closely connected to the moneylenders of Veracruz and Mexico City, and was one of the foremost advocates of Mexican infrastructural development. His presence in the Development Ministry hints at the connections between the speculators' new outlook and their participation in the last government of Santa Anna.[49]

Santa Anna's rapprochement with these "financiers" was part of his preparations for the outright sale of territory to the United States. The president needed the agiotistas to convert dollars paid in New York into pesos in Mexico City and the speculators needed Santa Anna to represent Mexico in the negotiations with the U.S. representative.

By the time the Revolt of Ayutla (as Álvarez's revolt came to be known) had begun, the speculators already had taken control over the treasury as they had during the Mexican-American War. The agiotistas even tried to bribe Comonfort and Álvarez. Escandón's employee José Gener and General Manuel Céspedes offered Comonfort $ 100,000 to lay down his arms. Comonfort declined the offer despite the fact that he had spent close to $ 50,000 of his own money.[50]

In the meantime the sale of La Mesilla ran into difficulties in the United States. By the time the U.S. Congress had completed the Gadsden Purchase, its boundary line had been altered, the territory included had been reduced by 9,000 square miles, and the provisions to cooperate with the Mexicans in suppressing Indians and filibusters and to protect work on the Tehuantepec canal had all been rejected. But the most important alteration was monetary; Congress would pay only $ 10,000,000.

British Minister Percy Doyle urged Santa Anna to reject the treaty, and indeed Santa Anna wished to follow his advice.[51] However, he was already at war with Álvarez and had to accept whatever crumbs the United States was willing to provide. Therefore he reluctantly signed the treaty as amended. Unfortunately he did not receive the first installment until July 1, 1854, when the United States government gave Juan Almonte a draft for $ 7,000,000 in New York.

Since funds paid in United States dollars in New York did not satisfy creditors wanting pesos in Mexico, the Treasury asked businessmen in Mexico City to lend money to the government until the funds arrived. The moneylenders offered to give the government only 90 percent of the face value of the credits received. According to an article published in *El Siglo XIX*, Santa Anna indignantly rejected these proposals publicly, but later accepted an 8 percent discount.[52] Furthermore the government promised them an additional 10 percent profit since the money entering or leaving the country would not be taxed.

The government busily spent these advances during the spring and summer of 1854. According to the accounts of former Treasury Minister Francisco Arrangoiz, by the time Almonte surrendered the funds to him in August 1854, only $ 4,449,964 remained out of the $ 7,000,000 received only the previous month. Published accounts later revealed what happened to the money from the sale of La Mesilla. Eighty-six percent of the funds which Arrangoiz deposited in New York banks was eventually handed out to six speculators to repay short-term loans at interest rates exceeding 100 percent. Manuel Escandón received almost 43 percent of the total disbursement, more than twice as much as his nearest rival, but others made greater profits on smaller amounts. (Table 13)

The administration spent the remainder of the money paying ten other moneylenders, installments on the foreign debt, the expenses of foreign legations, and various military expenses. Ac-

Table 13. Disbursements of funds from sale of La Mesilla

Name	Amount advanced 6/54-1/55	Amount paid—NYC
Escandón	1,136,958	2,500,000
Martínez del Río Bros.	1,096,080	1,072,000
Lizardi	100,000	750,000
Rubio	262,160	608,000
Jecker, Torre	255,000	600,000
M. Mosso	110,100	330,000
TOTAL	2,960,298 (50%)	5,860,000

Source: M. Olasagarre, ed., *Cuenta de la percepción, distribución y inversión de los díez milliones de pesos que produjó el tratado de la Mesilla, celebrado por el gobierno supremo de la república con el de los Estados-Unidos de América, en 13 de diciembre de 1853* (Mexico, 1855).

cording to Arrangoiz's accounts, even Ignacio Cumplido, owner of the opposition newspaper, *El Siglo XIX*, received $ 20,000 from La Mesilla funds. Since Olasagarre did not include Cumplido in his list of lenders to the government, it is possible that the money was paid to get Cumplido to tone down *El Siglo XIX*'s opposition to the government.[53]

By the close of September 1854, His Serene Highness was in deep financial trouble. As Olasagarre subsequently revealed, from June 1854 to January 15, 1855, the government collected only $ 280,672 in taxes.[54] In June 1854 it had less than $ 1,000,000 left from La Mesilla. By October funds had dwindled to $ 60,000. The Treasury simply borrowed more money. The government's desperate search for cash turned Mexico into the same wide-open field for lending it had been before 1834. Indeed, Olasagarre's record reads like a who's who of moneylending. (Table 14). Seven familiar names supplied $ 401,550, or 48 percent of the $ 828,132 listed. Curiously both Mosso and Lizardi, two prominent lenders in the La Mesilla advances, do not appear in this group.

Olasagarre listed only two clerical loans, but they were substantial ones. The Monte de Piedad or clerical pawnshop lent the government $ 235,517 or 28 percent of the $ 828,132 total recorded during the period.[55] By the end of 1854, the Church still supported Santa Anna, but the agiotistas gave him 20 percent more.

Empresarios and the Reform

Throughout 1854 Santa Anna attempted to maintain the goodwill of his group of agiotistas. In addition to reestablishing and

Table 14. Lenders to the government, 1854

Gregorio Mier y Terán	109,000
Jecker, Torre and Company	85,650
Cayetano Rubio	62,900
Eustaquio Barron	70,000
Francisco Iturbé	30,000
Manuel Escandón	30,000
Martínez del Río	14,000
TOTAL	401,550

Source: M. Olasagarre, *Manifestación que M.J. Olasagarre hace del ingreso y egreso de la tesorería durante le época que desempeñó el ministerio,* pp. 4, 9 ff.

renting the tobacco monopoly to a moneylender consortium, Santa Anna permitted Mier y Terán to import 2,500 quintales of prohibited cotton.[56] Furthermore he authorized the Compañía Restaurador del Mineral de Tlalpujahua owned by such speculators as Manning and MacKintosh, Martínez del Río, Nicanor Béistegui, Agüero, González and Co., and Francisco Iturbé to import another 100,000 quintales in exchange for $ 300,000 payable in easy credit terms over a three-year period.[57] The moneylenders supported Santa Anna from 1832 until 1854, but in 1855 they finally abandoned him.

A number of factors led to the empresarios' decision to begin a rapproachment with the Ayutla rebels and to side with the movement which would ultimately institute "the Reform." Many agiotistas had favored Santa Anna in 1853 because they wanted a centralized order with firm direction emanating from Mexico City, determined to promote economic development in general and railroads in particular. On October 31, 1853, Santa Anna awarded a concession for such a railroad to an English merchant Juan Laurie Rickards. Mr. Rickards doubtless had contributed generously to the treasury in exchange for the promise of free national land, importation of materials duty-free, exemptions for military service for employees, and the providing of special protection for himself and his possessions. In return, Rickards had agreed to organize a company in England, permit government inspection of his plans, and allow free passage for government troops and supplies within eight months. In June 1854 the government extended the deadline for formation of a company.

According to Chapman, in April 1855 Santa Anna cancelled his agreement with Rickards, although the official announcement was delayed until August, when the entire government was fleeing the capital. Scholars have speculated that Santa Anna ended the contract because he wanted the railroad line to extend to his El Encerro estate and decided to make more money by reselling the rights. This time he awarded the privileges to the moneylending firm of Mosso Hermanos Company which had already been granted a concession for a railroad at Santa Anna de Tamaulipas on April 27, 1855.[58]

Despite these concessions and the new ministries of Development and Internal Affairs, Santa Anna disappointed the agiotistas. He failed to reinstitute order and authority. Worse still, he squandered money, and embroiled the nation in an unnecessary war. As a result of his activities, the republic was in even worse financial shape than it had been under Arista. In addition, the fighting he had instigated was destroying the roads they wanted to improve.

When the agiotistas became empresarios, their vision of Mexico's future altered. Textile production boomed in the 1850s. Miraflores, the Martínez del Río's factory, made a 9 percent profit in 1854, its best since 1846. Cocolapan, Escandón's factory, registered a 7 percent gain in 1853. Cayetano Rubio, Antonio Garay, and Barron and Forbes all owned important textile factories as well.[59] These factory owners shared a serious problem—as production increased substantially, marketing and distribution possibilities failed to keep pace. In the 1850s Manuel Escandón, always the empresario with the most foresight, devoted his attention to a project which had gripped his imagination during a trip to Europe—the construction of a railroad from Mexico City to Veracruz, designed to stop at his factory at Orizaba.

In previous decades the speculators had not yet felt strong enough to challenge the Church for control of national lending activities or national real estate, but by 1855 some of them recognized that Mexico's further development necessitated a new relationship with its Church. Empresarial needs shattered the long-standing alliance between Santa Anna and the moneylenders because His Serene Highness was irrevocably wedded to a proclerical policy. The moneylenders had already convinced Santa Anna to permit the sale of government owned land (terrenos baldíos), but they realized that he could never sanction the expropriation of Church lands even if vital to the construction of railroads. Therefore the moneylenders made their rapprochement with the leaders of the Ayutla movement, and large sums started to appear in their accounts as "loans from sources unknown."[60] This change in empresarial loan policy helped to transform a regional revolt into the national movement for change known as "the Reform."

The End of a Era

Santa Anna continued to borrow money from speculators, but this time they came from the United States. Gadsden, who supported Álvarez in his war against the government, referred to that group of compatriots as "plundering cliques" and claimed that they had "wrested from him every diplomatic lever" and had written to Secretary of State Marcy that he (Gadsden) was insane.

Meanwhile, Santa Anna badgered Gadsden for the final $ 3,000,000 due to the Mexican government for the sale of La Mesilla. The United States was not supposed to pay this additional money until the borderline between the two nations had been fixed, but Santa Anna disregarded this stipulation.[61] The Mexican government refused to wait for the official transfer of funds and solicited the cash not from the usual group of lenders, but from American bankers in Mexico—Howland and Aspinwall and Hargous Brothers—at an official discount rate of 5 percent. However, the traditional Mexican rate prevailed, and one observer stated that the government received only $ 256,000 in cash in exchange for a credit worth $ 650,000. Gadsden asserted that the two banking houses had made a profit of $ 1,000,000 on the deal.[62]

After all the money from the first sale of property had been spent, Santa Anna tried to interest the United States government in buying more territory. Gadsden, however, refused to consider the idea proclaiming that he did not want to be considered "a ministerial land jobber."[63] He must have received further orders from Marcy, for he met with Santa Anna and Díez de Bonilla on July 8, 1855, to discuss another possible sale. The meetings continued for the next few weeks, but Gadsden managed to stall the negotiations until Álvarez's victory was certain.

National authority began to crumble as Santa Anna's revenue sources dried up. Mexico State revolted against the regime, jeopardizing all revenue shipments to and from the capital. By May 1855, there was no money left to pay any of the civil employees. By June the government could not even manage to pay its troops. General Corona gave his men daily allotments for food, and Santa Anna told him to confiscate all necessary funds. In order to raise cash, Santa Anna ordered all property owners to give the government one month's rent and then suspended all debt payments. In addition His Serene Highness started to charge up to $ 2,000 for the privilege of an interview.[64]

As the money shortages became more severe, public indignation over unpopular financial policies increased. Governors complained that centralized revenues, too small to handle the needs of the national government, often failed to meet local expenses as well.[65] Gadsden reported that Mexicans, who had despised the La Mesilla treaty since it sold territory to the hated Yanquis, were outraged that the money from the United States had disappeared so rapidly. According to him, some believed that Santa Anna had taken $ 700,000 of the funds to reimburse himself for damage done to his property during the Mexican-American War.[66]

Popular outrage also focused on the mounting incidence of large-scale governmental corruption. The administration had acknowledged the fraudulent bonds issued by Manuel Lizardi; Rafael Rafael, the publisher of *El Universal*, left the country with $ 50,000 intended to promote colonization, and General Santiago Blanco, the War Minister, made little effort to hide his unlimited credit on the treasury.[67] Blanco also served as official influence peddler, since "there is no dirty business that could not be arranged through his intervention." He even permitted a German vessel loaded with contraband to land at Mazatlán for a promise of $ 20,000. Then Blanco became publicly furious with the Germans when the $ 20,000 was slow in arriving. As the French Minister told the Foreign Office, "simony is tolerated and natural in Mexico."[68]

Certainly Santa Anna was aware of the change for in June he declared war on his former moneylenders. He ordered twenty-two of the richest men in the capital to gather together a forced loan of $ 655,000. It was a poignant scene—Santa Anna compelling moneylenders to give him money when only the year before they had been anxious to do so. According to his list, Escandón, Rubio, Mier y Terán, Francisco Iturbé, and Pedro Echeverría were supposed to pay $ 50,000 each and Lizardi and Ignacio Loperena were tapped for $ 35,000 apiece. The other fifteen were ordered to pay $ 10,000 each.[69] Police Chief Juan Lagarde, who usually arrested the murderers and thieves of Mexico City, made his rounds in uniform on horseback with a saber in his waistband accompanied by an escort of dragoons from the garrison. Every potential lender refused to contribute to the government. Instead, Ignacio Loperena offered to lend the government $ 650,000 ($ 125,000 in cash and $ 525,000 in paper on the internal debt at par) against a promise of $ 750,000 cash payable in six months. Although Santa Anna rejected Loperena's offer, he proposed that the remainder of the La Mesilla funds be used as security for the forced loan. Merchants and speculators ignored the proposition, for by now most of the very wealthy men whom the government had sought to tap through the forced loan had started lending their funds to the rebels.[70]

Since he could not borrow abroad, or sell territory, or make his customary deals with the moneylenders, Santa Anna appealed to the Church for the funds to sustain his regime. Santa Anna had actively endeavored to please the clerical interests within the nation since 1834; he had permitted the Jesuits to return, and had appointed churchmen to high positions.[71] But none of these good works could outweigh the basic corruption of the regime and so, in March 1855, the Bishop of Michoacán and Papal Nuncio Clemente de Jesús Munguía ordered his subordinates not to conclude any transactions concerning clerical wealth without his written approval and to submit a complete inventory of all goods, their disposition since 1822, and the authorizations which had been given for either their passive or active use within the past three months. He also tried to make every property sale subject to papal approval in order to keep individual clerics from lending church money to the government without his knowledge or authorization.[72] In effect, his edict killed any possibility that the Church would provide Santa Anna with his much needed funds. It also virtually guaranteed the subsequent forced sale of Church property.

Antonio López de Santa Anna knew when he was beaten. He left Mexico City on August 8 and formally abdicated on August 12, 1855. The fiscal structure collapsed, a victim of localism brought on by a lack of national authority. After 1855, Mexico could no longer continue its postwar policy of selling land to the United States in order to stave off national bankruptcy. It needed to find a new solution to deficits and empty treasuries.

The moneylenders' frustration with Santa Anna led them to support a new generation of political leaders. Many agiotistas welcomed the chance to cure Mexico's inadequate fiscal structure and antiquated transportation and communication networks by forcing the Church to sell its property. Others were not anxious to risk drastic change in such an unstable environment. Their struggle marks the beginning of the Reform.

5

A Speculative Reform
1855–1856

From an economic point of view, the selling of
church lands should contribute greatly to the re-
generation of agriculture and to the increase of
national wealth . . . if it is distributed with the
purpose of making workers into property holders . . . But I do not believe that this is the concept motivating the present administration. The
friends of General Comonfort and some foreigners will be the sole administrators. They will talk
a great deal about the amortization of the national debt using these new resources. They will
discuss projects *ad infinitum*, but . . . everything
will be just words.

De Ambroy, French consul in Tampico,
April 30, 1856.

The triumph of the Revolution of Ayutla in 1855 inaugurates a
new period in Mexican history. By that time the standard remedies to the perpetual fiscal crisis had become exhausted. In 1848,
the indemnity from the United States had pumped new life and
funds into the old system. By 1855, the strategy of turning distant land into pesos had worn itself out, just as had foreign loans
in 1828. The liberals who joined the Ayutla movement such as
Benito Juárez (Oaxaca) and Melchor Ocampo (Michoacán) believed
that Mexican political development required a secular state in
which the Catholic Church could no longer dictate policy.

The empresarios were also eager for something new. They
wanted access to lands and property in order to build railroads,
highways, and telegraph lines and make their factories more profitable. But in order to realize such goals, property would have to

141

be available for new uses. Therefore, they wanted to empower a government which would abolish clerical mortmain, corporate ownership, and the special land tenure of Indian communities. Thus, as in 1853, two different groups shared a common goal for somewhat different reasons. The liberals wanted a secular state and the empresarios wanted to force the Church to sell its property. Out of this union the Reform was born.

The ending of clerical mortmain by decree posed at least as many risks and problems as selling territory. The Catholic Church had funded a successful revolt in 1834 after a liberal Congress had passed legislation which threatened its interests, and again in 1846 it protested attacks on its prerogatives and wealth by paying for the revolt of "the Polkos" during the Mexican-American War. The new government had to avoid a civil war and gain some clerical revenue at the same time. This dilemma would dictate much of the behavior of the Álvarez and Comonfort administrations.

The victors in 1855 were a generation younger than their predecessors at the Congress of 1833, yet they were equally committed to economic liberalism. They believed that no institution should keep property outside the free market, and that commercial and economic processes should be free from the contamination of governmental intervention. Furthermore, the political history of Mexico since 1834 guaranteed that they would have no ties to the Church as a political institution. It had not supported them as it had the Conservatives. Unencumbered by debts of cash or gratitude, they could consider much more thoroughgoing reforms of the national structure than the Liberals who had preceded them. Fiscal necessity forced them to go beyond daily political accommodations; once the Liberals accomplished their goal and wrested funds from clerical coffers, traditional patterns would be gone.

Their plans, unlike those of Liberals in the past, focused on an unknown future whose very structure and essence would likely differ fundamentally from anything they had previously known. The young men welcomed the challenge, the older ones feared it. Both generations suspected that their activities had become more serious. To register this new sense of Mexico's future, they convoked the first liberal Constitutional Convention since 1824.[1]

The younger men were intent on modernizing Mexico according to republican, liberal, and generally democratic lines. Scholes, among others, has characterized the goals of the movement as "Mexico's middle class revolution."[2] Indeed, these ideals were the products of genuine middle class movements in Europe, but, like the terms "liberal" and "conservative," the phrase "middle class revolution" lost much of its meaning when transported to the Mexican situation.

The Mexican middle class in the 1850s was hardly similar to the European industrial bourgeoisie. It was comprised of career soldiers, landowners, merchants, career government officials, some industrialists, and far too many lawyers. As Richard Sinkin demonstrates, in large measure unemployed and underemployed lawyers created the Reform.[3] And, although it produced many economic and social changes, its primary goal was to lay the foundation of the secular Mexican nation-state.

Winning Power

Once Santa Anna resigned from office, Juan Álvarez and his rebels faced four other generals who pronounced against the dictatorship in August 1855. The most dangerous of the new rebels, Antonio Haro y Tamariz, Santa Anna's treasury minister during his last term, was supported by the remainder of the Santanista army and the cream of its officer corps. He pledged to protect the class structure and the rights of private property, and had the approval of the Mexican upper clergy.

In addition to Haro y Tamariz's revolt based in the central valley, Santiago Vidaurri, the regional leader of Nuevo León and Tamaulipas,[4] had pronounced, as did Manuel Doblado, former governor of Guanajuato.[5] The final contender for power was General Martin Carrera, one of three men to whom Santa Anna had delegated his authority before fleeing the capital.

When citizens of Mexico City learned that Santa Anna had abdicated, they rioted and sacked the homes of Manuel Escandón and Manuel Lizardi as well as the homes of the Santanistas like Manuel Díez de Bonilla. General Romulo Díaz de la Vega mobilized the city garrison, quelled the riot, and proclaimed himself President under a revised *Plan of Ayutla* which omitted pledges for formation of rebel governments in localities, and for the restoration of the Ceballos tariff. Soon after, Díaz de la Vega assembled a committee which elected General Martin Carrera President of the Republic.

During Carrera's short-lived government (August 15 to September 12, 1855), he abolished the title of "Serene Highness," disbanded the secret police, forbade military control over the civilian portion of the treasury, lowered the tax on pulque by 25 percent, and restored all confiscated property. Every garrison still loyal to the government in Mexico City pronounced in favor of Carrera soon after.[6]

Carrera needed more than army support, he needed money. He could not even use tariff revenues because rebel chiefs either collected the money themselves directly, stole it enroute, or permitted enormous contraband trade in exchange for cash. Díaz de la Vega decreed an extraordinary contribution to keep the administration going and to pay the troops, which foreigners gave as a partial guarantee of public order. In addition, the Church reluctantly agreed to advance him $ 43,000 in cash. Carrera suspended all contracts made by Santa Anna still in effect and the government paid only the most pressing obligations, although it soon lacked the funds necessary to fulfill these.[7]

On September 11, 1855, the Mexico City garrison endorsed the *Plan of Ayutla.* Haro y Tamariz and Doblado made peace in exchange for Álvarez's promise to assume responsibility for the debts they incurred during the rebellion.[8] Álvarez became President.

Álvarez in Office

He selected a coalition cabinet which included radical liberals and moderate ones. Melchor Ocampo, the former anticlerical governor of Michoacán became Minister of Relations, and Ignacio Comonfort became Minister of War. Álvarez filled other positions with Benito Juárez, former governor of Oaxaca (Justice), Guillermo Prieto, resuming his old post as Treasury Minister, and Miguel Lerdo de Tejada as Minister of Development. The cabinet quickly fell apart when Ocampo resigned after only fifteen days in office citing differences with Comonfort. Meanwhile, Comonfort and his men did not want to continue working with Álvarez. The old federalist was too much of a *cacique* and too uncouth to win the support of the younger progressives. As Benito Gómez Farías confided to his brother Casimiro, "I do not think there will be anyone who expects something good from a man like Álvarez! Everything which originates from him will be dreadful." The French minister, Alexis de Gabriac, a prejudiced observer, reported, "one cannot find a single Mexican who does not say 'we are a lost people and without funds,' 'this is the beginning of the end,' 'there is no man who can save us,' 'the economic anarchy is even deeper and more incurable than the political anarchy,' 'within six months Mexico will no longer exist,' etc. Such expressions are heard even from the mouth of government officials."[9]

Meanwhile, the conservatives circulated stories about secret deals between Álvarez and the American Minister, James Gadsden. Gadsden was openly friendly to the new government, and repeatedly asked Secretary Marcy to permit him to deliver the remaining $ 3,000,000 to Álvarez, an act which would favorably affect U.S.-Mexican relations and diminish European influence. He wrote that "the Europeanizing of Mexico, of all South America in opposition to Anglo-American vandalism north of the Rio Grande has to be fought here," but he vigorously denied that any new agreement existed.[10]

Although the period known as "the Reform" began with Santa Anna's abdication, the battle to free Mexico from traditional institutions officially started on November 23, 1855, when Minister of Justice Benito Juárez announced his Juárez law. By 1855 the Mexican judicial system was ineffective and badly in need of reform. The Juárez law went beyond reform and tried to establish an egalitarian system in Mexico by stripping the army and the Church of their special right (fuero) to be tried in their own courts for all crimes. It attacked the traditional power structure, and the Church correctly perceived the new law as a blow to its position in Mexican society.

The Juárez law provoked a serious government crisis and, on December 8, Álvarez resigned in favor of Comonfort, now designated "interim President." Álvarez knew he was more suited to fighting than to peaceful governing, and realized that the Juárez law was apt to cause problems which he would be ill-equipped to solve.

Comonfort in Charge

Comonfort quickly rid himself of Álvarez' reform cabinet. The moderate Manuel Payno replaced the idealistic firebrand Prieto and Juárez was shipped back to Oaxaca as governor ostensibly to put down rebellions from the army garrison stationed there against the Juárez law. The Comonfort cabinet declared itself against "any dismemberment of national territory," an indication that its fiscal plans would likely involve gaining control of clerical funds. The new government hoped to accomplish this through moderation and conciliation in order to avoid civil war. Its policy quickly proved futile—Comonfort took office December 11; Puebla revolted on December 12.

The New Fiscal Structure

The revolutionaries of Ayutla differed from their predecessors. They refused to reinstitute federalism once in power. Since Álvarez was a long-standing federalist, and the regime he opposed was centralist, it is easy to suppose that he favored a return to the Constitution of 1824. Instead, the question of territorial organization was left unresolved until the proclamation of a new Constitution in 1857. As a result, the new administration did not reestablish or adopt a tax structure different from that used by Santa Anna. Rather, it retained that organization and lifted some of the more absurd taxes such as those on doors, windows, dogs, and the monopoly on ice.[12]

From the very beginning of the Ayutla revolt, its leaders were uncertain about which governing structure they preferred. Their confusion appears in the use of the word "states" in the original plan and "departments" in the reformulated *Plan of Acapulco*, written by Comonfort. This confusion emerged again in the *Organic Provisional Statute of the Mexican Republic* which Comonfort issued on May 15, 1856. In the clauses outlining the administration of the Treasury, the national government recognized that states and territories had taxes of their own, separate from those levied by the nation or by municipalities. But in the next clause describing the organization of states and territories, Comonfort declared that all governors would be named by the president in Mexico City and would have to submit budget reports to him for approval. The Statute was attacked during the opening sessions of the Constitutional Convention for establishing "centralism, more omnipotent even than that of the *Bases Orgánicas.*" As Antonio Escudero, a representative from Mexico State perceptively commented, "this is not what the *Plan of Ayutla* promised us."[13]

Treasury Minister Prieto believed that he could work within the Santanista framework by trimming the bureaucracy and the army. Indeed he once commented, "the organization of the treasury lies in the War Ministry," and estimated that with military reductions the budget could be brought to the manageable figure of $ 14,500,000. Unfortunately the government could not reduce expenses just as a new group of people entered office, and opposition forces had laid down their arms only a few days before. In addition the treasury was unable to increase revenue collections sufficiently to pay expenses.

Nevertheless in November Prieto wrote to the state governors about the condition of the treasury and his plans for the future. His report emphasized the blatant corruption of the previous regime and disavowed all pledges to pay creditors made by it, expressly including that of the bogus bonds owned by Manuel Lizardi. Prieto did not even trust his fellow ministers. He told the governors, "I have abolished the bureaus and brought them back under the Ministry. . . . I do not want General Álvarez to have omnipotent power to grab what does not belong to him and squander it on trifles."[14] Furthermore, he advocated reduction of the army against common sense given the political situation, and Comonfort's opposition.

Reductions in expenses do not, however, pay bills and Mexico needed funds immediately. Prieto asked the Archbishop of Mexico for $ 1,500,000 in loans. The prelate replied that he did not know if the diocese had that amount of money and that he himself did not own a single centavo. Next Prieto proposed to sell $ 12,000,000 in government bonds, require the Catholic Church to buy $ 1,500,000 and force government employees to subscribe in proportion to their salaries. Finally, he proposed that the Church mortgage its property and give the government $ 3,000,000 in installments. The Church would use its property as collateral for loans.[15] All these ideas were rejected.

Manuel Payno became Treasury Minister on December 14, 1855, two days after Puebla revolted against the government. He found only $ 72,830 in the Treasury at a time when the government was desperate for cash since tax collections suffered additional disruption, and officials had serious difficulties in transporting funds to Mexico City. In the midst of the chaos the Treasury received even less than its usual inadequate amount of revenue, and much of the customs revenue paid off short-term debts.[16]

Income from regular internal taxes continued to fall below normal levels because the revolts impeded tariff collections and internal taxation. The states continued to collect their own tariffs, and, until January at least, kept the revenues from the mail service, the official paper monopoly, the export of silver, the tobacco monopoly, and the lottery. The Mexico City customs, which generally produced $ 100,000 to $ 120,000 each month, yielded only $ 370,000 for the five month period. The silver taxes produced a mere $ 65,730 and the sale of cotton import privileges to speculators added another $ 38,000.[17]

The financial situation worsened as the Puebla revolt kept Veracruz customs revenues from reaching Mexico City. By January 1856, the insecurity of the roads threatened to disrupt national economic life. As Carlos J. Furber, a German merchant, wrote his friend Manuel Madrid, "a fly cannot go from Guanajuato to Silao without losing its little wings."[18] Since the national treasury was always short of funds with which to pay troops and employees, the new government inevitably turned to the agiotistas for the loans necessary to stay in power and defeat its enemies.

Even before Álvarez had entered Mexico City, Treasury Minister Prieto borrowed money from speculators with customs receipts as collateral. In return, Prieto supported free trade, the abolition of the internal sales tax that hindered shipping within the republic, and an end to the tobacco monopoly, which the moneylenders wanted to eliminate. At the same time he retained a 33 percent tax on property, industry, trades, and luxuries, and absorbed all special funds into the treasury.[19]

Mexico took in $ 3,682,930 in customs revenues, but the government received only $ 457,790 (12 percent) of that amount because Álvarez had accepted the obligation to pay bills of exchange which other rebel leaders had issued to moneylenders on the customs closest to their strongholds.[20] These amounts did not include the percentage of the customs collections assigned for the payment of Diplomatic Conventions and for the British bondholders.

The Comonfort Administration chose to pay its debts during a period of severe fiscal and political crisis, a time when the very existence of the government was in doubt. During Payno's six months in office (December 1855–May 1856) Mexico paid out a total of $ 600,382; which, except for the payment of the British debt ($ 175,000), went to speculators.[21] The government further curried favor with the agiotistas with the most advantageous tariff rates since 1841 (January 31). It divided them into two categories—the regular duty and a surcharge, up to 75 percent of the total duty, set aside for the payment of debts.[22] By setting revenues aside for debt payment, Payno protected them from political officials who had always used them when regular customs revenue was insufficient, and thrilled moneylender-bondholders.

Finally, Payno pleased the moneylenders when he abolished the tobacco monopoly, as Álvarez had pledged. He made no reference to the new administration's opposition to monopolies for restricting freedom of trade, and claimed instead that he ended it because of the widespread fraud which had occurred during the Santa Anna administration. Nevertheless, Payno made sure that the government paid the moneylender-owners not only all monies it collected but one-half of the value of goods which Álvarez' troops had stolen during the fight against the government as well. The former owners were happy to sell out because recent revolts had ruined their control over the production, distribution, and sales and they stood to be well recompensed. The government did not reorganize the monopoly and thus lost a substantial source of revenue. Payno complained that if he had had more time, he could have levied a small tax, but he ended the monopoly because he could not devise an imaginative solution to a difficult financial problem rapidly enough.[23]

On the eve of Comonfort's Puebla campaign, Payno borrowed heavily from the moneylenders acknowledging that for every $ 200,000 in cash he received, he had to issue $ 261,000 in letters payable at the customs—an interest rate of 30 percent. Although Payno did not record it, they also supplied an additional $ 100,000 against the sale of ships from England for which Santa Anna had already paid.

Payno borrowed from those moneylenders who had previously provided cash for Santa Anna. Lizardi, Jecker, Torre and Company, and Cayetano Rubio, who had benefited substantially from the sale of La Mesilla, contributed $ 702,353 (83 percent). But Barron, Iturbé, and Martínez del Río who lent $ 70,000, $ 30,000 and $ 14,000 respectively in 1854 do not appear on the 1856 list. (Table 15)

Lizardi gave the largest amount in hopes that former Treasury Minister Guillermo Prieto would uphold Santa Anna's validation of the fraudulent bonds, but he continued to lend even after Prieto ruled against him.[24] Comonfort also squeezed $ 200,000 out of Jecker, Torre and Company.[25]

Next Comonfort pressed Gadsden for the money owed from the La Mesilla sale. Gadsden had been willing to help Álvarez, but he considered Comonfort a reactionary and would have nothing to do with him.[26]

The Puebla Revolt and Its Consequences

On December 12, 1855, Antonio Haro y Tamariz, urged on by its rabidly anti-liberal priest Francisco Ortega y García, issued the *Plan of Zacapoaxtla*, a small town in the Sierra de Puebla.

Table 15.   Loans to the government, 1854 and 1856

	1854	1856
Clergy (last loan 12/27/55)	235,517	58,000 (7%)
Bishop of Michoacán		16,000 (2%)
Gregorio Mier y Terán	109,000	30,000 (4%)
Manuel Lizardi		154,000 (18%)
Jecker, Torre and Co.	86,650	349,897 (41%)
Antonio Escandón	30,000	39,700 (5%)
Cayetano Rubio	62,900	198,456 (23%)
TOTAL	523,067	846,053 (100%)

Sources: Olasagarre, *Manifestación*, p. 9ff; *Memoria de Hacienda 1855-56,* Chart No. 4. "Préstamos sin interés."

The rebels called for a restoration of full powers to the clergy and the army and a return to the Organic Bases Constitution of 1842.[27]

Anselmo de la Portilla characterized the fighting in Puebla as a true civil war since it was not unusual for a wife to have a rebel husband and a loyalist brother. The husband probably received better pay—by the end of January Comonfort could only give his troops a third of their monthly salary. President Comonfort was deeply pained by the uprising in Puebla because he still had ties to the region and many of his friends including Haro y Tamariz were fighting against him.

The revolt spread quickly through the country. In Oaxaca rebels attacked in favor of restoring the fueros to the military and the clergy. General Uraga pronounced in the Sierra Gorda for the Constitution of 1842. Other groups rebelled in Zacatecas and in Tepic.

The situation grew so dangerous that Comonfort had to move the forthcoming Constitutional Congress from Dolores Hidalgo to Mexico City, where he could guarantee protection by the national guard troops assembled there. Finally, he ordered Minister of Justice José María Lafragua to intercede with the clergy to offer prayers on behalf of a governmental victory. Pelagio Labastida y Dávalos, Bishop of Puebla, supported the government and advised the rebels to lay down their arms, but he went unheard.[28]

The Puebla revolt affected the course of the Reform movement in Mexico because it forced Comonfort to form even closer ties with the agiotistas. It accelerated the inevitable confrontation between the conservative Church bound by mortmain and the empresarios who wanted to open Mexico up to capitalist development. From 1828 to 1855 the moneylenders followed a policy of financing both sides during a political conflict unlike the Church which lent only to Conservatives. Yet the speculators refused to lend to Haro y Tamariz. Merchants were also loathe to help Haro y Tamariz because he had tried to halt contraband.

Alexis de Gabriac wrote to his superiors decrying such loans because they would wed French firms to Comonfort's cause in hopes of being repaid.[29] De Gabriac, however, had not perceived that some of the speculators supported Comonfort because they believed that his government would aid them significantly in their plans for infrastructural development. By denying funds to him, the agiotistas strengthened Haro y Tamariz's dependence on the financial backing of the Church, committing him even more to preserving mortmain and dooming country-wide rail development.

Lending to Comonfort was also good business. For example, the moneylenders supplied $ 20,000 in cash in return for a bill worth $ 100,000 on paper on the future customs receipts, or for pledges to allow their goods to enter at half tariff. They provided troops with clothing, ammunition, and arms worth $ 10,000 and charged the government $ 180,000. During his final days in Mexico City before marching to battle, Comonfort borrowed $ 45,000 from merchants. In exchange for the loan, merchants received a 5 percent discount on import duties. The French banking house in Mexico, Garruste Labadie and Company, lent $ 50,000 to Comonfort and promised to redeem paper for $ 100,000 on export duties. Thus the moneylenders stood to make small fortunes from the Puebla campaign.[30]

The historic battle of Ocotlán on March 8, 1856, determined the future of Mexican Reform. This single battle cost over 150 lives, left 200 wounded, and drained the treasury of an additional $ 1,000,000 it did not have. When Comonfort left Mexico City to meet Haro y Tamariz at the end of February 1856, he brought with him 48 cannons and 16,000 troops mostly green recruits who deserted at the first sign of difficulty. They threw their expensive equipment in the road—eight days later a rifle worth fourteen pesos would sell for six reales to a peso. In contrast to these troops, much of the remainder of the Santanista army supported Haro y Tamariz.[31] These rebels did not surrender Puebla easily, and the battle turned into a street by street struggle. Haro y Tamariz finally capitulated on March 22, and Comonfort took official possession of Puebla the following day.[32]

Comonfort sought to avoid civil war; he was convinced that other revolts would follow unless he moved carefully to mediate among all factions. To prevent future confrontations, the government had to keep money away from potential rebels. The Catholic Church was the obvious source of such funding and since it had not lent money to the government after Puebla revolted, it could not claim protection on the basis of past services. Radical liberals also suspected that Comonfort was a reactionary at heart and pressured him to strike directly at the Catholic Church. They wanted outright secularization of clerical wealth or the power to negotiate a $ 10,000,000 to $ 15,000,000 loan, using clerical property as security, which they thought Gadsden might help secure.[33]

Comonfort wanted to deprive the Catholic Church of its power to finance other revolts. On April 1, he declared that all clerical property in the diocese of Puebla must be sold to pay for the costs of the insurrection and to pay damages to families for loss of lives and property. He assured the Mexican public that the government could prove that the Church had used its funds to finance the revolt and therefore could no longer use its "anti-political nature as a defense against the confiscation of its property," and had to pay for the damages it caused. Church leaders in Puebla tried to compromise. The Bishop of Puebla, Pelagio Labastida y Dávalos, wrote to Mariano Riva Palacio, governor of Mexico State, and offered to loan the government $ 200,000 in exchange for delaying confiscation. Although the ploy failed, the offer provides insight into the Church's perception of the situation. Church officials reasoned that a bribe might convince the government to soften or abandon its anticlerical policy and since the Church had consistently contributed cash to the Conservative cause to protect its property, it was natural to try and stall its opponents with a similar contribution. That such bribes worked so effectively in the past confirmed the fact that lack of funds was a basic issue in Mexican politics.

Yet the government's refusal to accept this bribe does not point to a change in that fundamental condition. Nor does it indicate that ideological concerns had taken precedence over financial ones. Rather, the government's insistence on a hard line demonstrated its willingness to resort to drastic measures to solve Mexico's problems and fulfill its obligations to the moneylenders and their commitment to national development.

Once Riva Palacio had refused his bribe, Bishop Labastida y Dávalos reverted to a more ideological position and refused to supply the government with a list of diocesan properties. Eventually the government exiled him.[34]

The defeat of the Puebla revolt put the liberals into a difficult position. The victory had been costly and the new government had to find sufficient money to maintain tranquility during meetings of the Constitutional Congress. Unfortunately even with the addition of the extra funds to be collected from property sales in Puebla, Mexico was on the verge of bankruptcy. Payno kept this fact well hidden. In his accounts for his six months in office, Payno claimed to have spent only $ 3,029,595, of which $ 1,945,386 (64.2 percent) paid military expenses. Yet, he could not have recorded his disbursements accurately since during that time the army increased from 1,686 to 11,643 men.

Furthermore, the financial responsibilities of government mushroomed for soldiers had to be paid, some of the government's debt obligations had to be settled, and the bureaucracy needed its salaries. Yet the new administration cut customs rates and eliminated the tobacco monopoly and other taxes. The cost of the recent civil war when combined with the abolition of many of the most profitable national taxes and the added burdens on the customs of paying the debts of former rebels overwhelmed the already inadequate, inefficient, and customarily overburdened revenue system. In May, the treasury had collected a mere $ 178,002 which would not pay a month's costs in the yearly budget of $ 17,485,021. The treasury contained only $ 16,431 when Payno resigned on May 14.[35]

Crosses of Gold

Comonfort knew that his government had to have new sources of revenue, lest a conservative, or reactionary, regime replace him. However, the United States had withdrawn its support, and the Comonfort administration had pledged not to sell land. With the doors of Washington closed, the government had no prospect of an additional influx of revenue. Although Comonfort had defeated the conservative opposition in Puebla, the Church could still finance other challenges to his authority at any moment. The Comonfort administration would be in constant crisis and in fear of revolt until the government made peace with the Church or won its supporters away from it. The opportunity to tap clerical wealth to fund a bankrupt administration and deprive its enemies of a chance to finance new Pueblas seemed irresistible.

Of course Mexican leaders' general estimates of church wealth in 1856 bore no relation to the true worth of clerical holdings, and had even less to do with what they were worth at the time of sale. After three centuries of undisturbed accumulation, the Mexican Church was undoubtedly extremely wealthy at the time of independence. For example, when the properties of the expelled Jesuits were sold, the Spanish Crown received $ 10–12,000,000. Estimates of its holdings at independence varied from a low of $ 50 million to $ 300 million, representing ownership or mortgage on one-half of all the property in Mexico.[36] In 1837, José María Luis Mora published his calculations of clerical wealth which the liberal segment of the Mexican public generally accepted. Many scholars noted that Mora exaggerated because he capitalized at 5 percent all of the Church's annual income (i.e., tithes, parochial dues, first fruits, alms) in addition to its actual property. Also, he used Bishop Abad y Queipo's 1802 estimates for Church holdings despite their noticeable decline in value since then. Finally, he included in his totals his appraisals of such immovables as jewels, art works, and buildings, much of which was priceless and which would never be for sale.[37] Yet, Mora's estimates, in the context of the drive to expropriate the Church, could have added billions to his somewhat educated guesses and their impact and significance would still have remained the same.

Subsequent assessments did not differ greatly from Mora's presentations. In his famous analysis of the condition of the republic in 1842, Otero repeated Mora's figure of 179 million pesos. Brantz Mayer, Secretary of the United States Legation in Mexico in 1841–1842, thought that clerical holdings were worth between 90 and 100 million pesos during these years. In 1855, another student of fiscal matters, Y. O., subsequently identified as Isidoro Olvera claimed 100 million pesos to be a minimum evaluation of clerical wealth in 1855. The following year Treasury Minister Miguel Lerdo himself produced a figure of between 250 and 300 million pesos for Church property and his was not the highest guess to be printed at the time. Some went as high as 520 million pesos! Since the entire foreign and internal debt in 1850 (exclusive of diplomatic conventions) only equalled $ 100 million, the nationalization of Church wealth seemed the key to a solvent future for the Mexican republic.[38]

Although the use of clerical wealth to fill empty government coffers was motivation enough to attack the status quo, there were other reasons why a reforming government wished to alter the traditional place of the Catholic Church in Mexico. As Richard Sinkin shows in his biographical sketches of the most important leaders of the Reform, many had had painful experiences with the Church, particularly during their childhood. They had seen their way blocked by clerical intolerance and wished to lessen its power. Also, clerical mortmain frustrated many dreams of land ownership. In nineteenth century Mexican society, landowning still carried with it high social status and nouveau-riche merchants customarily desired to purchase estates. It was only after the passage of the Lerdo law that it was discovered that most of the Church's holdings were in cities. Even then, the opportunity to purchase rather than rent their homes thrilled many rising professionals and bound them to the Liberal cause.[39]

Comonfort selected a relative unknown, Miguel Lerdo de Tejada, as his new Treasury Minister. Despite his obscurity Lerdo had good credentials for the post. He had been president of the Mexico City Municipal Council in 1852, Minister of Development under Santa Anna, and was at the time of his selection an Undersecretary of Public Works.[40] Also, like his predecessors Prieto and Payno, Lerdo had written studies of history and finance: *Notes on the Heroic City of Veracruz* (1850), *Foreign Trade in Mexico since the Conquest* (1853), and *Statistical Picture of the Mexican Republic* (1856).[41]

Because so little data exists concerning Lerdo's private life and early days in Veracruz in particular, historians must speculate about his friends and associates. Some scholars have attributed Lerdo's post in the Development Ministry in 1853 to a long-standing friendship between his family and that of Santa Anna. Furthermore, as Bazant has noted, the state of Veracruz was an area especially concerned with financial and economic matters. It supplied fourteen Treasury Ministers from 1821–1856, including the two José Ignacio Estevas (father and son), the speculator Antonio Garay and, of course, Lerdo himself.[42]

When Lerdo left Veracruz for Mexico City, he met most of the leading merchants and moneylenders while serving on the 1847 liberal Mexico City Municipal Council. His fellow members included such influential figures as the partners of Manuel Escandón, Anselmo Zurutuza and Antonio Garay. In 1847, Lerdo was a decided partisan of free trade, not yet convinced about the merits of industry. In this period he also strongly believed that the United States should annex Mexico or ally with it. In 1851 he was reelected to the City Council and became a member of the Treasury and Public Credit Division dealing with all matters concerned with municipal property, city contracts, issues of mutual concern with the Cathedral Chapter, and the preparation of budget reports. In October 1851, Lerdo, Francisco Paula de Arrangoiz, and José Joaquín Pesado founded the Mexican Society for Material Improvements. Lerdo edited an issue of the Society's journal devoted especially to the need to construct railroads. He was reelected to the Mexico City Municipal Council in 1852.

By that time Lerdo was an advocate of industrial development. In 1853 he urged Santa Anna to implement economic reform, eliminating all obstacles to trade. He also proposed new road-building projects and "liberal concessions for railroads" in order to remedy the misery found in Mexico because of "the backwardness of crafts and industries."[43] Lerdo continued his advocacy of increased trade, railroads, and European immigration as Minister of Development. His strong support for railroads plus his control over repair work and toll assignments for major roads led to frequent contact with Manuel Escandón and other moneylenders. According to the French diplomatic corps, Lerdo had many friends among the community of liberal French emigrés resident in the capital.[44]

Lerdo's advocacy of industrial development reflected the beliefs of his empresario constituency. When many important moneylenders denied funds to Santa Anna in 1855 and to Haro y Tamariz in 1856, they demonstrated their belief that the Liberals were the best able to fulfill their needs. Lerdo knew that the agiotistas expected his government to satisfy their demands. That expectation was also new. While before 1848 much of the speculators' wealth depended on the fulfillment of creditor contracts with the government, privileges extended by the government, and arrangements to provide services for the government, there had always been the tacit understanding that all a government need do in return was not interfere with speculator activities in any manner that was not mutually beneficial. However, in 1856 moneylenders expected the government to eliminate all internal trade barriers, fix existing roads, build new and wider ones, and, above all, begin the planning, financing, and construction of railroads.[45]

But nineteenth-century Mexico presented two serious institutional obstacles to internal development. As the speculators well knew, Mexican governments until 1856 had shown themselves to be incapable of keeping the peace, let alone of directing substantial infrastructural projects. Indeed, they had been contracting them out to the speculators since 1834, which caused them to try to run the government themselves in 1854. However, the second and more serious institutional roadblock was the economic power of the Catholic Church. By 1856 Mexico had to reduce the Church to its purely religious functions in order to industrialize further.

If the Mexican government was ever going to create and maintain the peace and stability required for development, it would have to devise an adequate and consistent fiscal system. Since Mexican governments could no longer borrow from abroad nor sell territory to the United States, and since the moneylenders would use the greater part of their fortunes to invest in infrastructural projects, the new system would have to be based on the sale of Church property and its availability to be taxed in the future.

The agiotistas, for their part, wished to change Mexico's relationship with the Church for four reasons. First, it still had control over a significant portion of the unofficial banking business in the republic. Second, it held resources necessary for the creation and maintenance of a stable government capable of keeping the peace and supervising infrastructural projects. Third, it frustrated attempts to create a stable government by possessing both the finances and the willingness to resort to military action in defense of its possessions against governmental decree. Finally, it kept a substantial amount of rural and urban property permanently out of circulation, frustrating the development of efficient infrastructural planning and hampering the construction of any significant projects. Consequently, the moneylenders willingly put their money in the cause of the Reform in the hopes of destroying clerical opposition to their future.

The empresarios found a receptive audience in the treasury ministers of the Comonfort administration. Manuel Payno, seconding the thoughts of his good friend Manuel Escandón, verbally committed the government to speculator goals. When estimating costs for 1856, he allocated $ 1,099,464 (8 percent of the budget) for substantial improvements in the transportation and communication networks throughout the country. Furthermore, in his commentary on his expense calculations, Payno noted that $ 14,000,000 or $ 15,000,000 would be sufficient to maintain a 15,000 or 20,000 man army, make debt payments, and leave enough to "dedicate $ 1,400,000 to $ 2,000,000 annually to rail-roads or other material improvements of great importance to augment the wealth and movement of the nation."[46] This was the first time a treasury minister budgeted for development, and this during a serious revolt!

Miguel Lerdo understood this new alignment of forces and represented speculator interests quite well. In his report to President Comonfort in February 1857, Lerdo explained that he wanted new entrepreneurial projects and investments to provide jobs for those who formerly made a livelihood from rebellion and to give the treasury a permanent and solid base of support. He added that, in his opinion, the new group of entrepreneurs would in turn identify their interests with those of "an enlightened and progressive government," rather than with those forces "left over from the colonial system."[47]

Lerdo undoubtedly was aware of the previous projects for the expropriation of church wealth in Mexico and of other historical precedents. He had been in the Treasury Ministry during the time when José Ignacio Esteva had presented his plan for using clerical property, and he had worked in the government when Haro y Tamariz had proposed his expropriation scheme. Furthermore, he knew the details of the reforms presented by Mora and Zavala in the 1830s. In addition, he discussed the matter with his French friends who in turn described the expropriation of the French Church in detail.

The French National Assembly had been the first representative body to order the sale of Church property. France after the revolution, like Mexico, was faced with two huge internal debts—one owed to ordinary citizens *(dette constituée)* and one owed to moneylenders *(dette exigible)*. And as in Mexico, the Church was reputed to own as much as a third of the arable land in France. On November 2, 1789, the Assembly voted to nationalize Church property in order to pay debts and restore national credit and to sell the holdings in small groups to provide almost universal opportunities for the French people to buy an interest in the Revolution.[48]

But the French experience still frightened Mexicans. Even in 1856, apparently, the French Revolution and the subsequent execution of the royal family and mob violence had not lost their capacity to shock Mexicans. Indeed, Mexican political leaders,

liberal and conservative alike, had not forgotten the mass destruction wrought by the Hidalgo revolt, or, more recently, by the uprisings of the Maya against the whites in Yucatán. Furthermore,
most of them did not envision the glorious future they wanted
for Mexico in terms which included anything approaching social
equality.

Also France was a wealthy country with the second most powerful economy in Europe whose bureaucracy could handle the sales
in the name of the state. In Mexico, a poor, undeveloped country, the situation was reversed—sales of clerical property were in
part ordered to help moneylenders and entrepreneurs carry on their
work of national development. They were to create a nation-state
rather than assert the power of one already in place. Therefore,
the French model for the expropriation of the Church seemed in-
appropriate for Mexico.

The Spanish expropriation appeared more suited to the Mexican
case. Once again, as in France, the process had had a long history
under the Spanish monarchs. Begun in 1759 under Charles III,
by 1808 a sixth of the Church's property worth 1,600 million
reales had been sold. When Ferdinand VII returned to the throne
in 1814, he ended the sales of clerical property and tried to return everything which had been sold. From 1814 until 1835, the
ownership of some categories of clerical lands continued to see-
saw between private individuals (1820) and the Church (1823).

By 1835 when Prime Minister Juan Álvarez Mendizábal confiscated all clerical property, the Church controlled lands earning an estimated yearly rental income of one billion reales (seventy
million dollars in 1930 equivalents). When Narváez halted sales
in 1844, the government had earned over three billion reales, of
which 53 percent derived from the sale of the goods of the regular clergy. However, some 38 percent of the clerical lands still
remained unsold.

In May 1855, Treasury Minister Pascual Madoz decreed that
all lands belonging to the state, the clergy, to the military orders,
the sodalities, and the common village lands be eligible for sale.
He stipulated that the properties be divided up as much as possible and the purchasers pay a 10 percent down payment in cash,
and a 1/4 percent sales tax. Half of the sales receipts were to go
toward amortizing the debt, and the other half was earmarked for
public works.[49]

Of the two historical precedents for expropriation, the Spanish model undoubtedly seemed more appropriate, as Manuel Payno noted in his collection of disamortization documents, *Social Reform in Spain and Mexico*. Payno had written this carefully expurgated account to help his cause. He understood all too well that a true rendering of the French or Spanish case and its accompanying anticlericalism would bring up issues best left unraised. As Bazant perceptively notes, state expropriations of clerical property in Europe and in Mexico were responses to severe financial distress.[50] Thus, at bottom, they were really, as Payno suggests, not ideologically based. Furthermore, Lerdo did not plan to expropriate clerical property at all, he simply planned to abolish mortmain, and let the Church sell its property and keep the proceeds.

On June 25, 1856, Treasury Minister Miguel Lerdo de Tejada decreed that the Catholic Church must sell its property to its tenants, or after a stated period of time, to anyone who offered the money. The government was to receive a 5 percent sales tax, half of which could be paid in bonds of the internal debt. Lerdo explained that the government perceived the sales as a means to remedy two pressing fiscal problems. Tax revenues generated by the sales would help defray the immediate costs of government. The government would then use the property sales to establish a new revenue structure that would satisfy its needs and permit it once and for all "to abolish all those taxes that remain with us today as a baleful legacy of the colonial heritage, blocking trade, hurting agriculture, crafts, industry, and the nation as a whole."[51] Thus, Church wealth was to be the new panacea for all of Mexico's ills and the salvation from the dreaded evil of taxation.

The members of the Constituent Congress were under no illusions about the real intentions and serious deficiencies of the Lerdo law. During the debates on June 28, 1856, Francisco Zarco, floor manager for the measure, consistently emphasized that its provisions would give the government the revenue necessary to save itself from bankruptcy and overthrow by prudently uniting "the interests of the people, of the treasury, and of the clergy." He acknowledged that although the government would prefer that renters or subleasees buy the property, "it orders that sales be made to the highest bidder and it encourages buyers from every class of people, big and small capitalists, nationals and foreigners."

Zarco did not even pretend that the government hoped that the new law would begin a more socially equitable distribution of property; indeed it contained no provisions to help poor tenants acquire property and, even if there had been, a bankrupt government would have been unable to help them anyway. The government quite simply needed money and asked the Church once again to come to its rescue. The Church, for its part, would receive the proceeds of the sales and greatly increase its wealth. Zarco also reminded his colleagues of the substantial impetus to industrial and agricultural progress in a Mexico with easily purchased rights-of-way and new areas of cultivation to be opened up by railroads.

Two members from Jalisco, Ignacio Ramírez, an atheist and one of the most radical delegates, and Espiridion Moreno, spoke for the opposition. They complained that "the government is playing the role of the Conservatives," and focused on several issues. They pointed out that the law would make the Church even wealthier and give it final power over who could buy the property if the tenant could not. They explained that the new fiscal structure to be based in part on receipts from the new sales tax was designed to benefit merchants by shifting the heaviest burden away from tariffs and more onto internal duties, which Moreno claimed would hardly amount to much. Finally, Ramírez decried the fact that Congress had not studied the measure and that it contained no provisions to help poor people buy land. The deputies, a group of like-minded men, ignored all objections and the law passed seventy-eight to fifteen.[52]

The government had problems implementing the new law from the very beginning. On July 30, Lerdo decreed a statute to regulate sales. The law established which property was eligible, how renters could become owners and procedures for auctions and the like. Nevertheless the law was never consistently or efficiently implemented anywhere.

The purchasers of property, true to historical precedent, balked at paying the 5 percent sales tax which the government needed so desperately. By October, the government abolished all sales taxes on properties worth less than 200 pesos.[53] Most Mexicans were far too poor to acquire any property (although they were more likely to do so in the cities) and so were forced to renounce their rights. The Lerdo law and its successors sold moneylenders more land and, like the Spanish disamortization of 1855, permitted monied individuals to buy up communal lands as well.[54]

Ironically, the Lerdo law did not produce much revenue. By the end of 1856, only $ 23,019,280 worth of property had been sold, and the treasury had received a mere $ 1,083,611, of which sum $ 675,308 was in cash, $ 196,273 in debt credits, and $ 112,029 in moneylender credits known as "treasury certificates." In the meantime, the government cut the permanent army to less than ten thousand to reduce expenses.[55]

Although the Church would have benefited financially from the Lerdo law, it stood firmly against it and threatened buyers of its property with eternal damnation by denying them absolution. Nevertheless, as Knowlton documents, its attitude was inconsistent and contradictory. In some cases, clerical corporations sold to hand-picked buyers or sold property to a fictitious or safe buyer in order to retain it. Contradictions abounded as some clerics made fraudulent sales only to be reprimanded by supervisors for recognizing the law at all. Other clerics refused to give purchasers deeds to their new property so that buyers stopped paying interest on their mortgages. These problems were more severe in the rural areas where boundary lines were less fixed.

The Constitution of 1857 proclaimed on February 6 included the Lerdo law and other anticlerical legislation. It did not name Catholicism as the state religion, and specifically forbade burial in churches and the election of clerics to Congress and the presidency. Furthermore, on April 11, 1857, Minister of Justice José María Iglesias standardized ecclesiastical charges for services such as baptism and marriage. Finally, on September 14, the government closed the University of Mexico, then under clerical direction. These actions resulted in a number of consequences the liberals had not anticipated.

The Constitution and other anticlerical decrees increased nationwide chaos. Government insistence that all public officials swear allegiance to the Constitution or forfeit their positions caused further problems. The Church countered by threatening to deny sacraments to those who so swore, which provoked widespread resignations; forty employees of the Mexico City Customs alone lost their jobs.[56]

The speculators, however, found much they were seeking in the new Constitution. The legislators embraced centralism and national authority as well as the Lerdo law, a strong affirmation of the right of private property, and a dedication to law and order. Federalism, as embodied in the Constitution of 1824, was a dead letter. The empresarios found a home with the liberalism of the Reform and the Porfiriato its true roots.[57]

The government fulfilled its promises to the speculators because it desperately needed their money. Of course not every moneylender supported the Reform so the government felt justified in favoring its supporters in the distribution of contracts and concessions. On February 1, 1856, the government founded a Railroad Directorate, headed by Gregorio Mier y Terán, to assist foreign and domestic companies interested in building railways in Mexico. Simultaneously, the government stripped the Mosso brothers of the concession to build the Mexico City–Veracruz railroad and granted it to Antonio and Manuel Escandón. It tacked on a 15 percent surcharge to the Veracruz tariff collections to help pay for the construction. On July 4, 1857, the government inaugurated the five kilometer Guadalupe section of the railroad with great fanfare in order to spur greater interest in the project.

On August 31, 1857, Comonfort officially granted the Escandóns a new concession for building the Veracruz–Mexico City line. He pledged to issue eight million pesos in railroad bonds to be sold in Mexico and outside the country in exchange for eight million pesos in debt paper. The new bonds would pay 5 percent interest from the proceeds of a new 20 percent surcharge on imports. In exchange the company paid the government $ 750,000 for the existing Veracruz–San Juan line.

The Comonfort government was in no position to make such grandiose promises. In October 1858 General Félix Zuloaga seized power. Meanwhile Antonio Escandón went to the United States to hire surveyors. Upon his return to Mexico on July 9, 1858, he protested to the government, then in the midst of a civil war, that its failure to make the first interest payment made his bonds worthless.

According to Chapman, the Escandón family eventually made peace with the Conservative government. No doubt Manuel sided with the Liberals, Antonio with the Conservatives. After Manuel's death in 1862, Antonio continued his Conservative connections, but he took pains to guard himself against liberal vindictiveness. When the French established an empire in Mexico, Antonio went to Europe and formed the Imperial Railway Company on August 20, 1864, complete with a British board of directors. Thus when Juárez returned to the Presidency in 1867, Escandón managed to hold onto his share of the firm by hiding behind a facade of foreign ownership. The company, renamed the Mexican Railway, eventually finished the line in 1873.[58]

The Moneylenders' Miscalculation

By 1857, empresarios created the preconditions for the next phase of operations. They had a reasonably honest government dedicated to centralism and economic development, and they had access to all property necessary to their plans. They thought they had reshaped the social, political, and economic fabric of Mexico skillfully enough to avoid paying the costs of massive national change. They and the leaders of the Reform gambled that the moderation of the Lerdo law would prevent the clerical uprising feared by so many. They underestimated the Church just as Bishop Labastida misjudged the Liberals when he tried to bribe Riva Palacio. And without political stability, speculator dreams could never be fulfilled.

Some government supporters panicked as clerical opposition increased and convinced Comonfort that peace would bring greater benefits than the continuation of a controversial Reform. Comonfort concocted a scheme with General Félix Zuloaga to rule Mexico without the Constitution of 1857, but Zuloaga seized the presidency for himself on January 23, 1858, and suspended the Lerdo law almost immediately. Comonfort and Lerdo failed to avoid a civil war by gaining clerical revenue through compromise, and Mexico's entry into the railway age was delayed yet again.

Nevertheless, the Lerdo law ultimately accomplished its aim and ended an entire period of Mexican fiscal history. As in Spain, once the state had begun to direct the disposition of clerical property, it could not be stopped. Mexico and its various governments were too poor to permit Church wealth to remain inviolate any longer. Furthermore, the war which ensued between Zuloaga's Conservatives and Juárez's proponents of Reform provided the perfect rationale for the short step from the Lerdo law to the 1859 Law of Nationalization.

The government needed cash so badly that it abandoned its solicitude for tenants; anyone offering two-thirds of the appraised value of Church or other communal property, one-third in cash and the rest in bonds of the internal debt, could purchase it. The new owner had to supply the bonds immediately, but he or she could pay the cash over a five to nine year period at 6 percent.[59] Thus, Mexico entered its future by tying new landowners to the Liberal cause.

Some speculators also gave evidence of their loyalty to the Reform. In 1858 the Conservatives jailed Manuel Escandón, Santa Anna's favorite moneylender, and other agiotistas for refusing to lend money to their government. Only five years before, Escandón and others had hoped to create a national bank funded by government revenue. Indeed, in 1861, after the return of the liberals under Juárez, Escandón was described with Francisco Zarco as "the soul of the new cabinet."[60]

The Reform changed the relationship between speculators and the nation-state. As some historians have pointed out, the governmental battle for control over the Church was Mexico's real war of independence. The strengthening of the secular state allowed it to plan and supervise economic development projects and maintain national political control. But by the time national political control was achieved and civil wars ended, many speculators had lost whatever funds they had to foster national economic growth. Foreign capitalists rather than native would be the ones to profit most from the newly established law, order, and private property for which so many Mexicans had sacrificed their lives and fortunes.

6

Mexico in the Age of the Moneylenders, 1821–1856

I have limited myself to one overriding goal—to introduce [railroads] to my country. Twenty-eight years ago, . . . I started the first stagecoach line which ran from Mexico City to Puebla. Since then I have remained interested in that business even as I have involved myself in mining, agriculture, and in linen and cotton factories . . . Since I first saw railroads in Europe I have been obsessed by the idea of creating one in Mexico . . . and I have invested thus far more than two million pesos in the project without any hope of return.

Manuel Escandón

In 1800 New Spain was the richest colony in Spanish America, but the Mexican Republic during the decades from independence in 1821 to the Reform in 1856 sunk from greatness and strength to "chaos" and virtual dissolution. Many historical works use the term "caudillismo" to describe the years when the personality of charismatic leaders, especially that of Antonio López de Santa Anna, dominated national life as Mexico drifted into weakness, default, and semiobscurity.

Mexico's decline, in fact, did not begin with Independence. By the end of the eighteenth century, New Spain was in trouble. Budget reports beginning in 1795 testify to the Spanish Crown's increasing reliance on loans for revenue even in the midst of the silver age. The Bourbon Reforms themselves reinforced tendencies toward decentralization and regionalism. The movement for independence accentuated these problems as the Napoleonic takeover of the peninsula spawned mistrust of Spanish government in Mexico. Hidalgo and Morelos aroused Indian and mestizo masses to fight for freedom, and thereby fractured loyalties and patterns centuries old. Eleven years of pitched battles and guerrilla skirmishes destroyed property, scared capitalists into exile, and left many of the richest mines flooded, neglected, and useless, and the viceregal government heavily in debt to the elites. By 1820 the conservative creoles decided to accept Mexican independence to free themselves from the new liberal government in Spain. Such was the legacy of the glorious colony to its republican successor.

The Fiscal System

In 1824 Mexico adopted a federalist constitution and a fiscal system based on tariff collections. This first federalist period lasted until 1835. It abolished many profitable taxes from colonial days and simplified others. While waiting for the new fiscal system to bear fruit, it borrowed substantial sums from British banking houses to pay the costs of government.

But the federalist fiscal structure never worked as planned. The production of the export commodities which made New Spain wealthy—silver and to a lesser extent cochineal—declined considerably after independence. With exports reduced, the Mexican capacity to import fell off, markets were soon saturated, and overseas trade declined. Tariff revenues fluctuated so wildly that they could not fund a stable state over long periods. But Mexico had few other items to tax, particularly since the elites had no intention of giving the government a share of whatever wealth they still possessed. From 1824 to 1835, federalist governments also garnered funds from the tobacco monopoly, the state contingente, taxes on silver, etc., but these yielded little revenue, and the treasury always had to fall back on tariff collections. As a result, in 1827 Mexico defaulted on payments to British bondholders and could expect no more foreign loans in the future. Therefore when revenues were insufficient, and they usually were, governments after 1827 habitually resorted to internal loans.

Not many were anxious to lend. Wealthy colonists had often supplied funds to the Spanish Crown, but beginning with the Consolidation in 1804, the demands became more frequent and repayment rare. After independence, fewer Mexicans had funds to spare and even fewer wanted to lend them to the government. The elites' reluctance to supply funds and refusal to pay taxes made it impossible for the federalists to increase revenue through traditional fiscal means and forced them to consider the forced sale of clerical property as the only other alternative available. Most Mexicans, however, were not ready to take such a drastic step in 1833 and so Santa Anna revolted against his own government and deposed the federalists.

Their successors—the centralists—constructed a better fiscal system because they were more successful at wringing revenue out of recalcitrant taxpayers. The centralist years, 1835 to 1846, look less impressive than they should because of the Texas revolt, the Pastry War, Santa Anna's well-publicized antics, and the crushing defeat in the Mexican-American War. Nevertheless, in the midst of this turmoil, Presidents Bustamante and Santa Anna created a modern fiscal system in Mexico by decree, complete with income taxes, property taxes, and head taxes as well as tariffs. This structure too had problems at first—substantial commitments to pay previous debts and extraordinarily high collection costs—but before it had sufficient time to remedy them, the U.S. invasion discredited the entire centralist system.

Federalism was restored in 1846, but the new version bore little resemblance to its predecessor. The government which emerged out of the ruins left by the U.S. invasion was unable to replicate the original structure of the 1824 to 1835 period or use much of the fiscal system constructed over the past twenty years. From 1846 to 1856 the treasury relied overwhelmingly on tariff revenues because internal taxes produced virtually nothing at all. To compensate, the government spent U.S. indemnity revenues, the money derived from the sale of La Mesilla, and finally funds to come from the forced sale of Church and other communally owned property.

The Growth of the State

Fiscal records, particularly those from 1838 to 1845, reveal that the Mexican nation state after Independence was much stronger and had a tighter grip over more territory than has been generally supposed. Observers thought Mexico was weak because it suffered frequent invasions from foreign powers, countless military uprisings, and the loss of over one-half of its national territory. Given such evidence, it is difficult to present Mexico as other than an impotent nation which managed somehow to outlast its troubles.

Yet, once Mexico emerged as separate from its Central American neighbors, Texas was the only state to bolt successfully from the republic. Yucatán failed twice to gain independence, Sonoran revolts were defeated like those in Nuevo León and Tamaulipas, and Chiapas and Tabasco are still Mexican despite Guatemalan hopes. Voss's depiction of Sinaloa and Sonora and Berry's portrait of Oaxaca during those years show that the national government exerted considerable authority in both areas. Indeed, the last two reports of the Treasury Ministry issued before the war in 1844 and 1845 eloquently testify to the existence of an effective governing system at work throughout Mexico except Yucatán.

In fact, the considerable presence of the central state particularly in frontier areas led to unrealistic expectations. That Sonorans looked to the government in Mexico City for help against the Apaches says more about their faith in the nation than about its weaknesses when assistance was slow in arriving. Their basic trust in the republic explains why Sonorans became fervent nationalists so quickly with the emergence of the Reform in 1855. The frontier felt secure with a government in Mexico City which promised not to sell more territory.[1]

The composition of Reform leadership also reveals this same bedrock belief in Mexican nationality. As Sinkin has shown, the Reform was a regional movement, "an attack by the periphery on the center." Its participants were as likely to come from Jalisco or Oaxaca as from Mexico State, and some of the most distinguished were born in Nuevo León, Coahuila, Durango, and even Texas.[2] Its triumph in establishing the rule of law as the personification of Mexico, however, built on a solid legacy bequeathed by national administrations from 1824 to 1845 and on an equally strong sense of the nation already in power throughout its territory.

Moneylenders, the Nation-State, and Development

Most analysts view the agiotistas as vicious parasites who made fabulous sums by taking advantage of Mexican weakness and corruption.[3] This study, because of its emphasis on the fiscal history of the period, sees the moneylenders generally in a more positive light.

As shown here, Mexican governments after independence had to face three serious obstacles to their continued solvency and stability: the fiscal structure as elaborated in 1824 never generated enough revenue to handle expenses, the wealthy were unwilling to pay new taxes, and foreign capitalists refused to lend more money after the default in 1827. In response to these conditions, the Mexican government was forced to obtain additional funds by securing internal loans at the best interest rates possible. These were provided by merchants, some Mexican and some foreign, willing to invest their capital in a new republic which had just declared itself unable to repay its British creditors.

Moneylending in Mexico evolved through three distinct phases and was entering a fourth during the years from 1827 to 1856. In the first phase, 1827 to 1834, moneylending or agiotaje was a casual business in which merchants made short-term cash loans to the government at high rates of interest. Some lenders came to have greater influence than others, but there were enough of them so that governments had some flexibility in arranging terms. This phase ended when the government stopped repaying loans in cash and started issuing credits instead. Since merchants no longer received cash in return for loans, those with limited resources had nothing left to lend and dropped out of the business.

The second stage, 1834 to 1842 or the golden years of agiotaje, marks the consolidation of lending in the hands of fewer than thirty major agiotistas who dominated the business. They prospered during the Bustamante Presidency (1837 to 1841) because Treasury Minister and agiotista Javier Echeverría endeavored to repay as many debts as possible. His policy led to a growth in speculation in government credits which diverted moneylender cash, often for long periods, in hopes of high profits. It also forced the government to become an interest-paying machine until it fell in 1841. This phase ended when the new President, Santa

Anna, abruptly shifted gears and suspended payment on credits in order to pay the army.

During the second phase, the republic suffered a series of catastrophes which would seriously drain its revenues. Beginning with the federalist revolts in Zacatecas and Texas in 1835 and 1836, followed by the Pastry War in 1837–1838, and punctuated throughout by significant and costly rebellions and pronouncements, governments were constantly searching for funds. Although by this time stronger centralist regimes were able to decree some new taxes, these still fell far short of providing the revenues necessary to keep Mexico afloat and preserve national sovereignty. Once again, the agiotistas lent the additional funds.

In the third stage, 1842 to 1854, the community of moneylenders split into factions in the battle to redeem credits purchased during the Bustamante Presidency. Foreign agiotistas called upon their ministers to pressure the government to honor its commitments to them. These settlements called Diplomatic Conventions later provided an excuse for the 1862 Tripartite Invasion of Mexico by England, France, and Spain for nonpayment of debts. Mexican agiotistas castigated the foreigners for using tactics unavailable to them while marshaling their own networks of politicians and influence-peddlers to argue on their behalf.

Paradoxically, the battle over credit redemption forced the agiotistas to identify their own best interests with those of the Mexican republic at a crucial moment. Although Santa Anna's new hierarchical government was able to improve the fiscal structure considerably, it could hardly handle the demands placed upon it by the war with the United States. During Mexico's most serious crisis, the moneylenders virtually became the government and kept providing funds and services during its darkest hours, even though it had already become apparent that many loans would never be repaid. By the end of this stage, some well-known and established firms like Guillermo Drusina and Company, and Montgomery, Nicod, and Company and some notorious speculators like Ewen C. MacKintosh went bankrupt.

This delineation of the first three stages in the evolution of moneylending in Mexico deliberately omits the political controversies of the time. From 1827 until 1854, federalists, centralists, liberals, and conservatives all relied on the moneylenders to supply their governments with all-important funds. The agiotistas for their part were careful to maintain good business relations with all groups. In short, amidst the political factionalism which supposedly characterizes this period, the moneylenders served as the invisible stability which helped Mexico survive.

During the first three stages as agiotistas lent money to governments in need, they used their growing influence to win official contracts in other sectors of the economy. Beginning in 1833 when the government gave Escandón, Garay, and Zurutuza the right to maintain the roads in selected areas in exchange for payment of tolls, moneylenders took over many concessions, monopolies, and franchises for the nation. They built roads and port facilities, delivered mail, ran mints, and collected tolls when governments could not provide such services, and thereby maintained a vital national presence throughout the republic. They also established an informal banking network within Mexico and handled the international exchange of currency whenever the government received large sums from abroad.

During the 1840s, many prominent agiotistas invested their profits in the textile factories which had been founded with government support (Banco de Avío) during the previous decade. They also put their surplus capital into mines, ranches, and estate agriculture. They purchased most of the new ventures, but others were acquired when borrowers were unable to repay loans. Some speculators such as Isidoro de la Torre (the Northwest), the Béistegui family (the Bajío), and various merchants in Monterrey used their familial ties and political power to give their commercial houses control over regional economies.[4]

The continued growth of Mexican industry in the 1840s and 1850s required new kinds of commitments from national governments already aware of mining and agricultural needs. The factory owners or empresarios wanted better and safer roads and railroads to transport the increasing output of their plants. For the first time since 1827, these agiotistas expected more from a government than prompt repayment of loans and the awarding of lucrative concessions.

This alteration in priorities led to the emergence of the fourth stage in the evolution of moneylending in Mexico. In 1855, the agiotistas abandoned Santa Anna and pinned their hopes for the future on the liberals. They had made an apparently similar shift in 1841 when they deserted Bustamante for Santa Anna, but on that occasion, they were acting merely to insure payment of their credits and win a reorganization of the tobacco monopoly. During the fourth stage, however, they were looking for a new kind of administration for Mexico, which would end corporate property holding of all kinds and make land available for future infrastructural development. Their new political allegiance helped the Reform to succeed, but it pushed the nation into ten years of civil war, financed first by the Church in a vain attempt to protect its property and then mostly by foreign financiers under the auspices of the French empire.[5] By its end in 1867, Martínez del Rio Hermanos was bankrupt, Manuel Escandón was dead and his brother Antonio, an organizer of the Imperial Mexican Railway, was hiding his interests behind a British board of directors.

A few agiotistas maintained the positions of power they won for themselves and by century's end were even stronger. Yves Limantour was a minor moneylender and army supplier in 1850; his son, Finance Minister José Yves Limantour, was one of the most powerful men in Mexico in 1900. Conversely, as Womack tells us, by the turn of the century, the Escandóns dominated the social scene but little else.[6] In general, however, agiotista sacrifices made profits for others. The collapse of some entrepreneurs and the enrichment of others in the years since 1867 awaits the labor of some future chronicler, as does a detailed analysis of their interactions with the new foreign capitalists who arrived after 1880. By 1900 Americans, Englishmen, Frenchmen, and Germans owned the most important banks, factories, and transportation networks, which the agiotistas had hoped to build.

In the years from independence to the Reform, Mexico confronted many of the problems which all nations face in the difficult transition from colony to nation. Like many other republics in similar circumstances, it based its new fiscal system on taxes to be levied on international trade. Unfortunately, customs duties never produced enough revenue to pay for the ordinary expenses of government, leaving politicians in power unable to reward supporters and buy off opponents. Revolts inevitably ensued as ambitious officers struggled to control the few resources available, and other nations invaded hoping to capitalize on Mexican weakness. Governments tried one emergency strategy after another to raise additional funds—foreign loans, internal loans, sale of territory—finally culminating in the forced sale of Church property and its subsequent nationalization soon after.

Although Mexico did not fulfill the expectations of Von Humboldt and others and become a great nation after independence, it outlasted its troubles and emerged smaller but with its sovereignty intact. The moneylenders played a considerable part in sustaining the Mexican republic through its tumultuous beginnings. Most of them are forgotten now, but their close associations with Mexican governments formed the basis of the nation-state which exists today. As scholars and citizens alike anxiously watch how Mexico's foreign debt currently affects national life, they may wonder when the age of the moneylenders and the politics of penury will finally end.

Appendix

Mexican Finance 1821–1856 (Tables)

Table A: Breakdown of the Income of the Mexican Republic 1821–1856

Table B: Breakdown of the Expenses of the Mexican Republic 1821–1856

Table C: Income vs. Expenses 1821–1856

Table D: Comparison of the Proportion of Internal Loans and Military Costs to Total Expenses 1821–1856

Table A BREAKDOWN OF THE INCOME OF THE MEXICAN REPUBLIC 1821–1856

	Port Taxes[1]	Tobacco	Contributions	Loans (F)	Loans (D)	Total
1821	N.A.	N.A.	N.A.	N.A.	N.A.	N.A.*
1822/23 (9 mos.)						5,249,858
1825 (8 mos.)	4,593,545 (45%)	637,145 (6%)	1,114,615 (11%)	1,317,543 (12%)	131,113 (.1%)	10,303,232
1825/26 (10 mos.)	6,571,419 (44%)	1,356,127 (9%)	1,365,452 (9%)	2,458,559 (17%)	25,529 (.2%)	14,770,733
1826/27	8,049,399 (47%)	914,947 (5%)	979,145 (6%)	381,521 (2%)	46,280 (.3%)	17,017,016
1827/28	5,912,126 (43%)	1,212,462 (9%)	1,381,412 (10%)	11,061 (.08%)	802,216 (6%)	13,644,974
1828/29	6,684,157 (46%)	1,013,159 (7%)	1,435,970 (11%)	17,207 (.2%)	1,586,223 (11%)	14,593,307
1829/30	4,986,575 (35%)	841,375 (6%)	1,398,488 (12%)	0	2,379,957 (17%)	14,103,773
1830/31	8,483,006 (46%)	457,285 (2%)	1,356,564 (7%)		2,356,997 (13%)	18,392,134
1831/32	7,550,253 (43%)	7,116	849,240 (5%)		3,734,566 (21%)	17,582,929
1832/33	7,538,225 (37%)[2]	abolished in	624,969 (3%)		5,061,772 (25%)	20,563,360
1833/34	9,051,789 (43%)	Spring 1833	331,898 (2%)		4,239,731 (20%)	21,124,216
1834/35	9,241,054		710,503		6,041,190	N.A.
1835/36	6,199,871		3,142,223 (11%)		9,243,103 (31%)	29,524,527 [3]
1836/37	4,737,767 (22%)[2]		4,494,685 (21%)		5,530,447 (25%)	21,822,391
1837/38 (18 mos.)	4,258,411 (16%)[2]		3,964,914 (16%)[4]		7,497,344 (30%)	25,018,121

*Throughout Appendices NA means not available.

178

1839	5,574,887 (19%)[2]		3,684,548 (13%)		11,591,345 (40%)	29,136,536
1840	7,474,192 (35%)[2]		N.A.		5,802,178 (27%)	21,227,263
1841	5,892,661 (25%)[2]		4,299,445 (18%)		5,151,481 (21%)	23,995,766
1842	5,257,849 (17%)[2]		4,502,878 (15%)		8,031,849 (26%)	30,682,369
1843	7,653,260 (22%)[2]		4,810,686 (14%)		3,089,860 (9%)	34,138,581
1844	7,418,081 (23%)[2]		5,088,975 (16%)		6,240,747 (20%)	31,873,019
1845	5,814,048 (27%)		N.A.		8,502,564 (40%)	21,505,981
1848/49 (18 mos.)	6,954,390 (27%)	1,366,203 (1%)	618,674 (2%)	6,720,000 (26%)	1,109,949 (4%)	25,726,737
1849/50	6,574,091 (36%)	575,673 (3%)	357,874 (2%)	3,540,000 (19%)	209,696 (1%)	18,281,835
1850/51	5,554,502 (36%)	582,132 (4%)	241,687 (2%)	5,860,000 (38%)	440,541 (3%)	15,486,549
1851/52	6,926,641 (63%)	577,696 (5%)	382,800 (3%)	686,000 (6%)	115,852 (1%)	11,022,291
1852/53	N.A.	N.A.	N.A.		N.A.	N.A.
1853/54	9,011,010	735,000	6,304,532		N.A.	N.A.
1854/55 (8 mos.)	N.A.	N.A.	N.A.		N.A.	N.A.
1856[5]	7,283,489 (52%)	abolished	not collected		3,620,042 (26%)	14,131,699

1 "Port Taxes" include the *importación*, *esportación*, *tonelada*, 1 percent and 2 percent (*avería*) of *importación*, the *internación*, *circulation of money* and the *consumo* (after October 15, 1851).

2 All figures come from Lerdo de Tejada, *Comercio exterior*, chart 86, except those so indicated (by 2). Those come from *Memoria de Hacienda 1870*, pp. 119, 175, 206, 220, 232, and 251.

3 State income included.

4 "Internal commerce taxes" interpreted as state contributions.

5 *Memoria de Hacienda 1870*, p. 438.

Table B BREAKDOWN OF THE EXPENSES OF THE MEXICAN REPUBLIC 1821–1856

	War (incl. Navy)	Treasury	Collection Costs	Total
1821	N.A.	N.A.	N.A.	N.A.
1822/23 (9 mos.)	2,100,733 (40%)	1,443,707[1] (27.5%)	N.A.	5,241,337
1825 (8 mos.)	7,222,753 (72.5%)	1,740,811 (17.5%)	N.A.	9,965,789
1825/26 (10 mos.)	7,895,331 (60.2%)	3,673,042 (28%)	582,460 (5.8%)	13,112,200
1826/27	10,155,878 (62%)	2,536,810 (15.5%)	922,475 (7%)	16,364,218
1827/28	8,822,569 (68%)	1,028,977 (8%)	2,824,883 (17.3%)	12,982,092
1828/29	7,496,287 (53.5%)	3,719,632 (26.5%)	2,004,237 (15.4%)	14,016,987
1829/30	7,692,632 (55.6%)	3,461,165 (25%)	1,778,298 (12.7%)	13,828,491
1830/31	8,340,659 (47.4%)	6,729,988 (38.2%)	1,903,753 (13.8%)	17,601,289
1831/32	10,576,230 (62.4%)	3,350,025 (19.8%)	1,135,252 (6.4%)	16,937,384
1832/33	N.A.	3,507,575	1,206,968 (7.1%)	N.A.
1833/34	10,180,620 (51%)	7,066,368 (35.4%)	1,325,752 (6.7%)	19,934,490
1834/35	N.A.	N.A.	N.A.	N.A.
1835/36	7,686,926 (26.6%)	13,980,054 (48.4%)	2,397,515 (8.3%)	28,876,024
1836/37	6,618,142 (33.4%)	7,463,590 (37.7%)	2,191,899 (11%)	19,802,628

1837/38 (18 mos.)	8,790,662 (33.1%)	13,468,730 (50.7%)	2,462,600 (9.3%)	26,588,304
1839	7,088,140 (25.9%)	17,470,839 (64%)	1,617,959 (6%)	27,318,729
1840	5,998,908 (28.2%)	12,484,048 (58.7%)	1,368,791 (6.4%)	21,255,097
1841	6,720,383 (29.2%)	11,698,755 (50.9%)	2,722,288 (11.8%)	22,997,219
1842	6,777,073 (22.1%)	18,471,300 (60.3%)	3,998,672 (13.1%)	30,639,711
1843	6,366,327 (18.7%)	21,031,534 (61.8%)	4,815,158 (14.1%)	34,035,277
1844	6,677,663 (21.3%)	17,600,605 (56.2%)	5,967,670 (19.1%)	31,304,102
1845	7,924,147 (40.5%)	11,188,991 (57.1%)	N.A.	19,584,812
1848/49 (18 mos.)	6,239,520 (29.7%)	9,865,931 (47%)	2,239,253 (10.7%)	20,987,393
1849/50	5,046,719 (28.4%)	9,655,045 (54%)	1,516,073 (8.5%)	17,746,073
1850/51	3,452,129 (22.9%)	7,332,154 (48.6%)	1,773,570 (11.8%)	15,085,077
1851/52	3,621,519 (34.6%)	4,069,057 (38.9%)	1,860,360 (17.8%)	10,475,685
1852/53	N.A.	N.A.	N.A.	N.A.
1853/54	N.A.	N.A.	N.A.	N.A.
1854/55 (8 mos.)	4,214,531 (93.9%)	280,672 (6.3%)	N.A.	4,488,483
1856	7,738,778 (42.3%)	7,655,175 (41.9%)	1,922,639 (10.5%)	18,287,829

¹This does not include an additional $1,410,459 in paper money which was then retired. That sum was added to expense total.

Table C   INCOME vs. EXPENSES 1821–1856

	Total Tax Collections	Expenses	Deficit	Total Income
1821	N.A.	N.A.	N.A.	N.A.
1822/23				
(9 mos.)	6,418,814	5,241,337	+ 1,167,477	N.A.
1825				
(8 mos.)	8,384,863	9,965,789	1,580,926	10,303,232
1825/26				
(10 mos.)	11,921,128	13,112,200	1,171,072	14,770,733
1826/27	15,137,981	16,364,218	1,226,237	17,017,016
1827/28	12,446,893	12,982,092	535,199	13,644,974
1828/29	12,787,994	14,016,978	1,228,984	14,593,307
1829/30	11,656,479	13,828,491	2,172,012	14,103,773
1830/31	14,521,690	17,601,289	3,079,599	18,392,134
1831/32	13,033,698	16,937,384	3,903,686	17,582,929
1832/33	11,891,909	N.A.	N.A.	20,563,360
1833/34	12,838,721	19,934,490	7,095,769	21,124,216
1834/35	N.A.	N.A.	N.A.	N.A.
1835/36	17,036,042	28,876,024	11,839,982	29,524,527
1836/37	12,950,545	19,802,628	6,852,083	21,822,391
1837/38				
(18 mos.)	13,262,921	26,588,304	13,303,381	25,018,121
1839	17,545,190	27,318,729	9,773,537	29,136,536
1840	15,452,919	21,255,097	5,802,178	21,227,263
1841	14,724,788	22,997,219	8,272,431	23,995,766
1842	15,968,774	30,639,711	14,670,937	30,682,369
1843	19,602,180	34,035,277	14,433,097	34,138,581
1844	20,592,058	31,304,102	10,712,044	31,873,019
1845	11,723,664	19,584,812	7,861,148	21,505,981
1848/49				
(18 mos.)	11,078,423	20,987,393	9,908,970	25,726,737
1849/50	9,661,209	17,746,073	8,084,864	18,281,835
1850/51	8,607,097	15,085,077	6,477,980	15,486,549
1851/52	10,212,755	10,475,685	262,930	11,022,291
1852/53	N.A.	N.A.	N.A.	N.A.
1853/54	19,053,566	N.A.	N.A.	N.A.
1854/55				
(8 mos.)	280,672	4,488,483	4,207,811	N.A.
1856	10,806,128	18,287,829	7,481,701	14,131,699

Table D   COMPARISON OF THE PROPORTION OF
INTERNAL LOANS AND MILITARY COSTS TO
TOTAL EXPENSES 1821–1856

	Loans	Military Expenses
1821	N.A.	N.A.
1822/23 (9 mos.)	N.A.	2,100,733
1824	N.A.	N.A.
1825 (8 mos.)	131,113 (1.3%)	7,222,753 (72.5%)
1825/26 (10 mos.)	25,529 (.2%)	7,895,331 (60.2%)
1826/27	46,280 (.3%)	10,155,878 (62%)
1827/28	802,216 (6.2%)	8,822,569 (68%)
1828/29	1,586,223 (11.3%)	7,496,287 (53.5%)
1829/30	2,379,959 (17.2%)	7,692,632 (55.6%)
1830/31	2,356,997 (13.4%)	8,340,659 (47.4%)
1831/32	3,734,566 (22%)	10,576,230 (62.4%)
1832/33	5,061,772	N.A.
1833/34	4,239,731 (21.3%)	10,180,620 (51%)
1834/35	6,041,190	N.A.
1835/36	9,243,103 (32%)	7,686,926 (26.6%)
1836/37	5,530,447 (27.9%)	6,618,142 (33.4%)
1837/38 (18 mos.)	7,497,344 (28.2%)	8,790,662 (33.1%)
1839	11,591,345 (28.2%)	7,088,140 (25.9%)
1840	5,802,178 (27.3%)	5,998,908 (28.2%)
1841	5,151,481 (22.4%)	6,720,383 (29.2%)
1842	8,031,849 (26.2%)	6,777,073 (22.1%)
1843	3,089,860 (9.1%)	6,366,327 (18.7%)
1844	6,240,747 (19.9%)	6,677,663 (21.3%)
1845	8,502,564 (43.4%)	7,925,147 (40.5%)
1848/49 (18 mos.)	1,108,949 (5.3%)	6,239,520 (29.7%)
1849/50	209,696 (1.1%)	5,046,719 (28.4%)
1850/51	440,541	3,452,129 (22.9%)
1851/52	115,852	3,621,519 (34.6%)
1852/53	N.A.	N.A.
1853/54	N.A.	N.A.
1854/55 (8 mos.)	828,132 (18.5%)	4,214,531 (93.9%)
1856	3,620,042 (19.8%)	7,738,778 (42.3%)

Notes

Preface

1.   See Justo Sierra, *The Political Evolution of the Mexican People*, trans., C. Ramsdell (Austin: University of Texas Press, 1969); Bernard Moses, *The Railway Revolution in Mexico* (San Francisco: Berkeley Press, 1958); Wilfrid Callcott, *Santa Anna: The Story of an Enigma Who Once Was Mexico* (Norman: University of Oklahoma Press, 1936); Charles Cumberland, *Mexico: The Struggle for Modernity* (New York: Oxford University Press, 1968); Michael Meyer and William Sherman, *The Course of Mexican History*, 2nd ed. (New York: Oxford University Press, 1983).

2.   Charles Hale, *Mexican Liberalism in the Age of Mora* (New Haven: Yale University Press, 1968), chapter 8. For an exception to this, see Donathon Olliff, *Reforma Mexico and the United States: A Search for Alternatives to Annexation, 1854–1861* (University, Ala.: University of Alabama Press, 1981).

Introduction

1.   *Memoria de Hacienda 1870*, pp. 65–66.

2.   John J. TePaske with the collaboration of José and Mari Luz Hernández Palomo, *La Real Hacienda de Nueva España: La real caja de México (1576–1816)* (Mexico City: Departamento de investigaciones históricas, seminario de historia económica. Colección Científica, Fuentes [Historia Económica de México] 41, 1976), no page number, and a Xerox copy of "Sumario General de Carta Cuenta de Veracruz," supplied by Professor TePaske, Duke University. The author wishes to thank Professor TePaske for his generosity in supplying these materials and in sharing his hard-won knowledge of the royal treasury.

3.   TePaske, *La Real Hacienda*. The royal tenth was a 10 percent tax on all bullion brought to the mints.

4.   Herbert I. Priestley, *José de Gálvez, Visitor-General of New Spain*,

185

1765–1771 (Berkeley: University of California Press, 1916), p. 81. For a fascinating commentary on Gálvez and Priestley's interpretation of him, see Linda K. Salvucci, "Costumbres viejas, 'hombres nuevos': José de Gálvez y la burocracia fiscal novohispana (1754–1800)" in *Historia Mexicana*, vol. 33, 1983, pp. 224–264.

5.   Priestley, *Gálvez*, p. 43; Christon Archer, *The Army in Bourbon Mexico* (Albuquerque: University of New Mexico Press, 1977), chapter 6, pp. 136–167.

6.   Enrique Florescano and Isabel Gil Sánchez, "La época de las reformas borbónicas y el crecimiento económico, 1750–1808," Vol. 2 of *Historia General de México* (Mexico: El Colegio de México, 1976), p. 264.

7.   David A. Brading, *Miners and Merchants in Bourbon Mexico, 1763–1810* (Cambridge: Cambridge University Press, 1971), pp. 33–92. Florescano and Gil Sánchez, "La época de las reformas," p. 222 offer another description—"defensive modernization"—and add that other historians have decided that when such changes were made New Spain really became a colony.

8.   These figures are derived from the same sources listed in note 2. The work of TePaske and Klein in assembling the colonial *cartas cuentas* has piqued considerable interest in viceregal finance. For an extremely informative exchange on the problems of understanding the colonial fiscal system see Samuel Amaral, "Public Expenditure Financing in the Colonial Treasury: An Analysis of the Real Caja de Buenos Aires Accounts 1789–1791 with commentary by Javier Cuenca, John TePaske, Herbert Klein, J. R. Fisher and Tulio Halperin Donghi in *Hispanic American Historical Review* 64 (1984) pp. 287–322.

9.   Florescano and Gil Sánchez, "La época de las reformas," pp. 216–18; Robert Sidney Smith, "Sales Taxes in New Spain, 1575–1770," in *Hispanic American Historical Review* 28 (1948) pp. 2–37; Brading, p. 37.

10.   Revillagigedo, *Instrucción Reservada* art. 218–24, as quoted in Priestley, *Gálvez*, pp. 386–87.

11.   Priestley, *Gálvez*, pp. 135–50; Florescano and Gil Sánchez, "La época de las reformas," pp. 218–20.

12.   Fabián Fonseca and Carlos de Urrutia, *Historia General de Real Hacienda*, Vol. 1 (Mexico: Imprenta de Vicente García Torres, 1845), introduction, pp. i–xxxviii and chart 3; TePaske, *La Real Hacienda*, and "Sumario General."

13.   John E. Kicza, *Colonial Entrepreneurs: Families and Business in Bourbon Mexico City* (Albuquerque: University of New Mexico Press, 1983) pp. 13–42; Richard B. Lindley, *Haciendas and Economic Development: Guadalajara, Mexico at Independence* (Austin: University of

Texas Press, 1983), chapter 2. For another source of credit during the colonial period see Clara García, "Sociedad, crédito y cofradía en la Nueva España. El caso de Nuestra Senora de Aránzazu," in *Historias*, vol. 1, 1983, pp. 53–68.

14.   Enrique Florescano, *Precios de Maíz: crisis agrícolas en México, 1708–1810* (Mexico: El Colegio de México, 1969), p. 80; Doris M. Ladd, *The Mexican Nobility at Independence 1780–1826* (Austin: Institute of Latin American Studies, University of Texas, 1976), p. 97; TePaske, *La Real Hacienda*, and "Sumario General."

15.   Francisco Simón Segura, *La Desamortización Española del Siglo XIX* (Madrid: Instituto de Estudios Fiscales, Ministro de Hacienda, 1973), pp. 61–62.

16.   See Michael Costeloe, *Church Wealth in Mexico 1800–1856* (London: Cambridge University Press, 1967), pp. 1–29. For an exhaustive explanation of clerical wealth in Mexico see Arnold J. Bauer, "The Church in the Economy of Spanish America: *Censos* and *Depósitos* in the Eighteenth and Nineteenth Centuries," in *Hispanic American Historical Review* 63 (1983) pp. 707–33.

17.   Revillagigedo, *Instrucción* as quoted by Ladd, *Nobility*, p. 97.

18.   Ladd, *Nobility*, pp. 92–93.

19.   Ladd, *Nobility*, pp. 71–88.

20.   Ladd, *Nobility*, p. 99; table 20, pp. 100–101; pp. 102–103.

21.   Brading, *Miners and Merchants*, pp. 90–92. Federalist ideas were also spurred by the Provincial Deputation and by sending representatives to the Spanish Cortes. See Nettie Lee Benson, *La diputación provincial y el federalismo mexicano* (Mexico: El Colegio de México, 1955), and, edited by the same author, *Mexico and the Spanish Cortes, 1810–1822: Eight Essays* (Austin: University of Texas Press, 1966).

22.   Mention made here of Enlightenment economics should not be taken to obscure the impact of Spanish economic and political thought developed in the eighteenth century. See Richard Herr, *The 18th Century Revolution in Spain* (Princeton: Princeton University Press, 1958); Jean Sarrailh, *L'Espagne éclairée de la seconde moitié du XVIIIième siècle* (Paris: Klinckieck, 1954). Even Viceroy Revillagigedo called for greater freedom of trade. Revillagigedo, *Instrucción*, art., 318, 323, 338–41, as cited by Priestley, *Gálvez*, p. 298, n. 6, and p. 387.

23.   John Fisher has demonstrated that Spanish exports to the New World quadrupled during the years from 1778–1796 because of free trade. John Fisher, "Imperial 'Free Trade' and the Hispanic Economy, 1778–1796," in *Journal of Latin American Studies* 13 (1981) p. 36. In a subsequent article, "The Imperial Response to 'Free Trade': Spanish Imports from Spanish America, 1778–1796" in *Journal of Latin American Studies* 17 (1985) pp. 35–78 he shows that exports from Spanish America in-

creased 1000 percent after 1778 and that the increase particularly affected previously neglected natural resources. He further concludes that after 1796 the colonists realized that such expansion of trade could not continue "within the framework of Spanish imperialism," p. 63. As for belief in Mexico's glorious future see Alexander von Humboldt, *Ensayo político sobre el reino de la Nueva España* (Mexico: Editorial Porrúa, 1966), pp. 402–403 for example.

24. Lindley, *Haciendas,* pp. 89–122; Brian R. Hamnett, "Royalist Counterinsurgency and the Continuity of Rebellion: Guanajuato and Michoacán, 1813–1820," in *Hispanic American Historical Review* 62 (1982) pp. 19–48; Timothy E. Anna, *The Fall of the Royal Government in Mexico City* (Lincoln: University of Nebraska Press, 1978), pp. 151–58.

25. Hamnett, "Royalist Counterinsurgency," pp. 42–48; Fernando Díaz Díaz, *Caudillos y Caciques* (Mexico: El Colegio de México, 1972), chapter 1.

26. Lindley, *Haciendas,* pp. 95–111.

27. I have deliberately avoided the calculations made by Manuel Payno y Bustamante for 1818 and 1819 and published in the *Memoria de Hacienda 1845* because they are incomplete and less accurate than those for 1816 gathered by TePaske and Hernández Palomo.

28. Brian R. Hamnett, *Revolución y contrarevolución en México y el Perú (Liberalismo, realeza y separatismo 1800–1824)* (Mexico: Fondo de cultura económica, 1978), pp. 80–81.

29. Ladd, *Nobility,* pp. 148–49.

30. Hamnett, *Revolución,* pp. 87–88.

31. Hamnett, *Revolución,* pp. 93–94.

32. Anna, *Fall of Royal Government,* pp. 155–58.

33. Ladd, *Nobility,* pp. 134–48.

34. The amounts used in this chart are gross collection figures. They are meant to indicate a pattern and should not be read as exact since they do not take into account collection costs or the impact of inflation.

35. Ladd, *Nobility,* pp. 148–53.

36. Hamnett, *Revolución,* pp. 82–83. Hamnett has examined the impact of the independence wars and emphasizes that most damage came from theft, that loss should be evaluated in terms of "capacity to recover," and that mining did well in some areas. See Brian Hamnett, "The Economic and Social Dimension of the Revolution of Independence in Mexico, 1800–1824," in *Ibero-Amerikanisches Archiv,* 6 (1980) pp. 1–27.

37. Hamnett, *Revolución,* pp. 87–88.

38. Díaz Díaz, *Caudillos,* pp. 39–43.

Chapter 1

1. Ladd, *Nobility*, p. 127.

2. Manuel Dublán and José María Lozano, *Legislación mexicana o colección completa de las disposiciones legislativas expedidas desde la independencia de la república* (Mexico: Imprenta del comercio, 1876), 1: pp. 565–587; *Memoria de Hacienda 1870*, pp. 66–67, 72; Timothy E. Anna, "The Role of Augustín de Iturbide: A Reappraisal," *Journal of Latin American Studies* 17, pp. 86–95.

3. *Memoria de Hacienda 1870*, pp. 67–68. Charles W. Macune, Jr., *El estado de México y la federación mexicana 1823–1835* (Mexico: Fondo de cultura económica, 1978), p. 62. It should be noted that during the years under discussion, the Mexican peso and the U.S. dollar were equivalent and fixed at 5 per British pound sterling. The use of "$" in the text signifies Mexican pesos unless otherwise indicated.

4. Anna, "Iturbide," pp. 96–98. Even in this excellent article, Anna follows the contemporary evidence and does not look at the dual problem of fiscal insufficiency and elite unwillingness to help out in the short term.

5. William Spence Robertson, *Iturbide of Mexico* (Durham, North Carolina: Duke University Press, 1952), pp. 205–07; *Memoria de Hacienda 1870*, pp. 68–71.

6. Iimura, "The Financial Relationship between the Mexican Federal Government and the States: 1825–1828," M. A. thesis, University of Texas, p. 132, lent to the writer by Professor Nettie Lee Benson, University of Texas, Austin; *Memoria de Hacienda 1870*, p. 72.

7. Nettie Lee Benson, "The Plan of Casa Mata," *Hispanic American Historical Review* 25 (1954), pp. 45–56; Anna, "Iturbide," pp. 105–10.

8. See Ladd, *Nobility*, pp. 152–53 for hints of this attitude.

9. They were also busy in court actions designed to disentail their estates. *Ibid.*, pp. 154–61.

10. *Ibid.*, pp. 152–53; Robert W. Randall, *Real del Monte, A British Mining Venture in Mexico* (Austin: The University of Texas Press, 1972), pp. 27–45; Reinhard Liehr, "La deuda exterior de México y los 'merchant bankers' británicos, 1821–1860," in *Ibero-Amerikanisches Archiv*, 9 (1983) pp. 425–28; D. C. M. Platt, "Finanzas británicas en México (1821–1867)," in *Historia Mexicana* 32 (1982) pp. 226–61.

11. Jaime E. Rodríguez O., *The Emergence of Spanish America: Vicente Rocafuerte and Spanish Americanism 1808–1832* (Berkeley: University of California Press, 1975), pp. 108–12.

12. W. H. B. Court, *A Concise History of Britain from 1750 to Re-*

cent Times (Cambridge: Cambridge University Press, 1954), pp. 79–80; Celso Furtado, *The Economic Growth of Brazil* (Berkeley: University of California Press, 1965), pp. 85–92.

13. George Pendle, *History of Latin America* (London: Penguin Books, 1976), p. 89; Robert Randall, *Real del Monte*, pp. 32–35.

14. William W. Kaufmann, *British Policy and the Independence of Latin America 1804–1828* (Connecticut: Archon Books, 1967), p. 176, note 39; Judith Blow Williams, *British Commercial Policy and Trade Expansion* (Oxford: Clarendon Press, 1972), pp. 260–61; Pendle, *Latin America*, p. 112.

15. Rodríguez O., *Emergence*, pp. 111, 116–18.

16. For precise amounts see Edgar Turlington, *Mexico and her Foreign Creditors* (New York: Columbia University Press, 1930) and Joaquín D. Casasús, *Historia de la deuda contraida en Londres* (Mexico: Imprenta del Gobierno, 1885), pp. 110–111.

17. Macune, *México y la federación*, pp. 67, 72–79.

18. Josefina Zoraida Vázquez, "Los primeros tropiezos," Vol. 3 of *Historia General de México*, (Mexico: El Colegio de México, 1977), p. 16; *Memoria de Hacienda 1870*, p. 77.

19. Macune, *México y la federación*, pp. 75–76; *Memoria de Hacienda 1870*, pp. 77–78.

20. Macune, *México y la federación*, pp. 75–76.

21. British and Foreign State Papers (London, 1846), XIV, p. 865, as quoted by John E. Baur, "The Evolution of a Mexican Trade Policy, 1821–1828," in *The Americas* 19 (1963) pp. 234.

22. Stuart F. Voss, *On the Periphery of Nineteenth Century Mexico* (Tucson: University of Arizona Press, 1982), p. 80 on contraband in Mazatlán; Baur, "Foreign Trade Policy," pp. 237, 239, 242, 246–247, 251.

23. Romeo Flores Caballero, *Counterrevolution: The Role of the Spaniards in the Independence of Mexico, 1804–1838*, trans. Jaime Rodríguez O. (Lincoln: University of Nebraska Press, 1974) p. 88; Baur, "Foreign Trade Policy," pp. 229–32.

24. Vázquez, "Primeros tropiezos," pp. 58–60. For a fictional account of the difficulties of traveling see Manuel Payno y Flores, *Los bandidos de Río Frío*.

25. Iimura, "Financial Relationship," p. 31, n. 68 and table V, p. 38. Macune says that the Congressional Finance Committee predicted $ 1,500,000 for the tobacco monopoly; Iimura quotes $ 2,500,000 (p. 31, n. 68).

26. *Memoria de Hacienda 1828, 1829, 1830, 1831, 1832, 1833, 1835* and *1870*; Macune, *México y la federación*, pp. 108–13.

27. Rodríguez O., *Emergence*, pp. 120–24.

28. Tulio Halperin Donghi, *The Aftermath of Revolution in Latin*

America, trans. J. Bunsen (New York: Harper and Row, 1973), pp. 50–55; D. C. M. Platt, *Latin America and British Trade 1806–1914* (New York: Barnes and Noble, 1983), chapter 1.

29. The reader should be warned that Lerdo's figures on other aspects of trade—namely that of British exports—have been shown to be erroneous. See Robert A. Potash, " *El Comercio exterior de México* de Miguel Lerdo de Tejada: un error estadístico," *Trimestre Económico,* 20, (1953), pp. 474–79.

30. Rodríguez O., *Emergence,* p. 127.

31. Ladd, *Nobility,* pp. 154–61.

32. Lindley, *Haciendas,* pp. 101–11.

33. *Memoria de Hacienda 1870,* p. 87.

34. *El Sol,* November 28, 1827, pp. 3690–3691, and *El Sol,* November 29, 1827, p. 3693 as cited in Flores Caballero, *Counterrevolution,* pp. 102–104.

35. Shanti Oyarzábal Salcedo, "Gregorio Mier y Terán en el país de los especuladores, 1830–1869," in Ciro F. S. Cardoso, ed., *Formación y desarrollo de la burguesía en México. Siglo XIX* (Mexico: Siglo Vientiuno Editores, 1978), pp. 142–143; *Correo de la Federación,* January 23, 1829, p. 3 as quoted by Flores Caballero, *Counterrevolution,* p. 122.

36. *Correo de la Federación,* January 23, 1829, p. 3 as quoted by Flores Caballero, *Counterrevolution,* p. 129.

37. Flores Caballero, *Counterrevolution,* p. 129.

38. *Reflexiones sobre las leyes de españoles* (Mexico: Agustín Guiol, 1833), as quoted in Flores Caballero, *Counterrevolution,* pp. 129, 133, n. 74.

39. *Memoria de Hacienda 1870,* p. 96; Lorenzo Zavala, *Albores de la república* (Mexico: Empresas Editoriales, 1949), pp. 194–195.

40. *Memoria de Hacienda 1829,* pp. 13–14; *Memoria de Hacienda 1830,* pp. 19–20.

41. José María Bocanegra, *Exposición documentada que José María de Bocanegra, secretario de estado y del despacho de Hacienda, leyó en la camara de diputados el día 19 de noviembre de 1833, a consecuencia del acuerdo de la misma del día 16 del propio més, sobre dar cuenta con los contratos celebrados en los tres últimos meses.* (Mexico: Impreso por Juan Ojeda, 1833) pp. 6–8.

42. *Memoria de Hacienda 1870,* pp. 132–33.

43. Juan José del Corral, *Exposición acerca de los perjuicios que ha causado al erario de la República y a su administración el agiotaje sobre sus fondos y reflexiones sobre los medios de remediar aquellos males* (Mexico: no publisher listed, 1834), pp. 3–11.

44. Margarita Urías Hermosillo, "Manuel Escandón: de las diligencias

al ferrocarril, 1833–1862," in Cardoso, ed., *Formación de la burguesía*, pp. 37–38.

45. del Corral, *Agiotaje*, p. 15.
46. *Memoria de Hacienda 1870*, pp. 97–98, 100–102.
47. *Ibid.*, pp. 102–103.
48. *Memoria de Hacienda 1830*, p. 18.
49. Joaquín D. Casasús, *Historia Deuda*, pp. 132–40.
50. See especially Randall, *Real del Monte*, table 1, p. 73. He says that the British failed to make *any* profit in this venture until 1837, but it is doubtful that a firm would continue operations for so long on a losing proposition.
51. Irving Stone, "The Composition and Distribution of British Investment in Latin America," unpublished Ph. D. dissertation, Columbia University, 1962, table 30, p. 101A, and table 43, p. 153A, B, and F; Leland Jenks, *The Migration of British Capital to 1875* (New York: Knopf, 1927), pp. 356–357, n. 61. According to Stone's calculations, in 1865 British investment in Latin America was divided as follows: Brazil 25.1 percent, Colombia 9.1 percent, Mexico 31.6 percent, Venezuela 7.9 percent, and Argentina 3.4 percent, among others. But those percentages are extremely misleading for Mexico, since only 8 percent of the total amount (£25,575,000) was invested in anything other than loans to the government made originally in 1824 and 1825, and those made in 1864. Another 5 percent represents mining investments and stands for the probable depreciation of previous ventures, some made as early as the 1820s. Therefore, only 3 percent (£800,000) of the 31.6 percent (or 0.948 percent of total British investment) went to Mexico for infrastructural development or for much else between the years 1830–1864. The Brazilian case is quite different—27 percent (£5,375,000) of British investment went into railroads by 1865 as opposed to 2 percent (£200,000) for Mexico.
52. See Robert A. Potash, *Mexican Government and Industrial Development in the Early Republic: The Banco de Avío* (Amherst: University of Massachusetts Press, 1983). For an interesting commentary on the Banco de Avío, see D. C. M. Platt, "Finanzas británicas," pp. 240–41.
53. Of course, the government claimed that its policy of firm control promoted a climate appreciated by foreign traders, Flores Caballero, *Counterrevolution*, pp. 143–144. It used this ploy to get greater loans from the business community. The great rise was due to an increase from $ 4,397,927 (1829/30) to $ 7,765,528 (1830/31) in imports. Exports fell. Miguel Lerdo de Tejada, *Comercio exterior de México desde la conquista hasta hoy* (Mexico: Banco Nacional de Comercio Exterior, 1967), chart 36.

54.   Michael P. Costeloe, *La Primera República Federal de México (1824–1835)* (Mexico: Fondo de cultura económica, 1975), pp. 295–306.

55.   *Memoria de Hacienda 1832*, pp. 10–11 and estado general, *Memoria de Hacienda 1833*, charts 12 and 13.

56.   Jaime E. Rodríguez O., "Oposición a Bustamante," in *Historia Mexicana*, vol. 20 (1970) p. 230.

57.   Costeloe, *Primera República*, chapter 12.

58.   Juan Antonio de Unzueta, *Informe presentado al Exmo. Señor Presidente de los Estados-Unidos Mexicanos por el contador mayor gefe de la oficina que le confirió S. E. para que le manifestase el manejo, y estado que guardó la Hacienda pública en los años de 1830, 1831, y 1832* (Mexico: Imprenta de Aguila, 1833), p. 10. Although Unzueta's report had definite political motivation, nevertheless that the new government issued an elaborate decree stipulating the order in which such debts were to be recognized indicates that they were valid. *Memoria de Hacienda 1870*, pp. 121–22.

59.   Francisco de Paula Arrangoiz, *México desde 1808 hasta 1867* (Mexico: Editorial Porrúa, 1968), p. 362.

60.   Jan Bazant, *Alienation of Church Wealth in Mexico: Social and Economic Aspects of the Liberal Revolution 1856–1875*, trans. M. Costeloe (Cambridge: Cambridge University Press, 1971), pp. 20–21.

61.   Costeloe, *Primera República*, pp. 290–91, 318, 396. For more detailed discussion on the development of theories concerning the relationship between church and state, see Jesús Reyes Heroles, *El Liberalismo mexicano*, vol. 2, *La Sociedad Fluctuante* (Mexico City: UNAM, 1958), chapters 3–5, pp. 89–211; Charles Hale, *Liberalism*, chapter 4.

62.   José María Luis Mora, "Proyecto sobre la deuda pública, publicado el 20 de noviembre de 1833," as printed in Manuel Payno y Flores, *La Reforma Social en España y México: Apuntes históricos y principales leyes sobre desamortización de bienes eclesiásticas* (Mexico: UNAM, 1958), pp. 69–78.

63.   Proyecto de D. Lorenzo Zavala (sesión de día 7 de noviembre de 1833) in Payno, *Reforma Social*, pp. 65–67.

64.   Hale, *Liberalism*, pp. 138–41.

65.   Costeloe, *Primera República*, pp. 419, 422–23, 425. Frank Sampanaro, "Santa Anna and the Abortive Anti-Federalist Revolt of 1833 in Mexico," in *The Americas*, vol. 40 (1983) pp. 95–107.

66.   Costeloe, *Primera República*, pp. 419, 422–23, 425.

67.   *Ibid.*, pp. 425–29.

68.   *Memoria de Hacienda 1870*, p. 141.

Chapter 2

1. David Wayne Walker, "Kinship, Business, and Politics: The Martínez del Río Family in Mexico, 1824–1864," unpublished Ph. D. dissertation, University of Chicago, August 1981, pp. 289–90.

2. Dublán and Lozano, *Legislación mexicana,* 3, pp. 43, 75–78, 111–112; *Memoria de Hacienda 1835,* pp. 19–25; *Memoria de Hacienda 1870,* pp. 151–152; Costeloe, *Primera República,* pp. 430–436.

3. Voss, *Periphery,* p. 84.

4. Voss, *Periphery,* p. 90.

5. Hubert Howe Bancroft, *Complete Works,* 13 Volumes *(History of Mexico,* Vol. 5) (San Francisco: A. L. Bancroft and Company, 1885), pp. 146–47.

6. Vázquez, "Primeros tropiezos," pp. 69–75.

7. Voss, *Periphery,* pp. 96–101.

8. Nancy Barker, *The French Experience in Mexico, 1821–1861* (Chapel Hill: University of North Carolina Press, 1979), chapter 3, pp. 57–88. See also Iwan Morgan, "French Policy in Spanish America: 1830–46," in *Journal of Latin American Studies,* 10 (1978): pp. 309–28.

9. Bancroft, *History of Mexico,* 5:189.

10. For a copy of this remarkable document, see Gastón García Cantú, *El Pensamiento de la Reacción Mexicana, Historia documental, 1810–1962* (Mexico: Empresas Editoriales, S. A., 1965), pp. 215–31.

11. Arrangoiz, *México desde 1808 hasta 1867,* pp. 378–384.

12. Dublán and Lozano, *Legislación mexicana,* 4: pp. 36, 43, 60–62, 66–67, 75–76, 106–107.

13. Bancroft, *History of Mexico,* 5: pp. 240–45.

14. Bancroft, *History of Mexico,* 5: pp. 266–81.

15. *Memoria de Hacienda 1870,* p. 117.

16. *Memoria de Hacienda 1870,* pp. 142, 151–54.

17. *Memoria de Hacienda 1870,* p. 169; *Memoria de Hacienda 1839,* pp. 4–5.

18. Dublán y Lozano, *Legislación mexicana,* 3:pp. 691–692.

19. *Memoria de Hacienda 1845,* resumen general no. 21.

20. Miron Burgin, *The Economic Aspects of Argentine Federalism 1820–1852* (New York: Russell and Russell, 1971), pp. 193–94.

21. *Memoria de Hacienda 1870,* pp. 152–154, 162–163.

22. *Memoria de Hacienda 1838,* pp. 24–25.

23. This volume presents all tax receipts without reference to the cost of their collection; it shows collection costs in the expense calculations.

24. *Memoria de Hacienda 1837*, pp. 27–28.

25. *Memoria de Hacienda 1870*, pp. 165–167; Barker, *French Experience*, p. 63. For comparisons of these rates with others, see Guillermo Prieto, *Indicaciones sobre el origen, vicisitudes, y estado que guardan actualmente las rentas generales de la federación mexicana* (Mexico: Cumplido, 1850), pp. 211–16.

26. Dublán y Lozano, *Legislación mexicana*, 3:pp. 512–33; *Memoria de Hacienda 1840*, p. 22; *Memoria de Hacienda 1841*, p. 19.

27. Dublán y Lozano, *Legislación mexicana*, 3:pp. 667–68, 673–74; 4:pp. 5–9, 11–21.

28. Dublán y Lozano, *Legislación mexicana*, 4:pp. 39–40, 94–97; *Memoria de Hacienda 1870*, pp. 215–16, 222.

29. Dublán y Lozano, *Legislación mexicana*, 4:pp. 134–50.

30. Prieto, *Rentas Generales*, p. 16; *Memoria de Hacienda 1870*, pp. 245–246.

31. *Memoria de Hacienda 1870*, pp. 255–56.

32. See for example the Conservative manifesto, Lucas Alamán's five volume *Historia de Méjico*.

33. Justo Sierra, *The Political Evolution of the Mexican People*, p. 191.

34. Marcello Carmagnani, "Regionalism and the Central Government of Mexico During the Nineteenth Century," p. 7, presented at the Woodrow Wilson International Center for Scholars, Smithsonian Institution, Washington, D.C., July 25, 1984. The author wishes to thank Professor Carmagnani for sending this paper to her.

35. Voss, *Periphery*, pp. 95–105.

36. Marcello Carmagnani, "Finanzas y Estado en México, 1820–1880," in *Ibero-Amerikanisches Archiv*, 9 (1983) p. 288.

37. See, for example, *Memoria de Hacienda 1845*, Resumen general and departmental cuentas.

38. Simon Collier, *Ideas and Politics of Chilean Independence 1808–1833* (London: Cambridge University Press, 1967), chapter 9, pp. 323–360.

39. *Memoria de Hacienda 1841*, p. 14.

40. Walker, "Martínez del Río," pp. 27–29, 35–37.

41. Walker, "Martínez del Río," pp. 38–39, 184; Barker, *French Experience*, pp. 57–59, 128; Ma. Teresa Huerta, "Isidoro de la Torre: El Caso de un empresario azucarero, 1844–1881," in Cardoso, ed., *Formación de la burguesía*, pp. 165–74; Barbara A. Tenenbaum, "Merchants, Money, and Mischief: The British in Mexico, 1821–1862," in *The Americas*, 35 (1979):pp. 319–22.

42. Walker, "Martínez del Río," p. 185.

43. Dublán y Lozano, *Legislación mexicana*, 3:pp. 25–28.

44.   Urías, "Escandón," in Cardoso, ed., *Formación de la burguesía,* pp. 38–40.

45.   *Memoria de Hacienda 1870,* p. 142.

46.   *Memoria de Hacienda 1870,* p. 154; Dublán y Lozano, *Legislación mexicana,* 3:pp. 124–26. For an excellent picture of how this was viewed by agiotistas, see Walker, "Martínez del Río," pp. 292–93.

47.   Prior to January 1836, the creditors holding pre- and post-Independence paper were awarded one-sixteenth *(la media octava parte)* of the customs and toll collections. In the boom year of 1830–31 when customs duties reached $ 8,483,006, creditors of the internal debt received $ 435,930 (5 percent). *Memoria de Hacienda 1870,* pp. 108, 154.

48.   *Memoria de Hacienda 1870,* pp. 153–54.

49.   Bazant, *Church Wealth,* pp. 28–29.

50.   Walker, "Martínez del Río," pp. 183; Barker, *French Experience,* pp. 60–61.

51.   Walker, "Martínez del Río," pp. 294–95.

52.   Randall, *Real del Monte,* pp. 194–95.

53.   Dublán y Lozano, *Legislación mexicana,* 3:pp. 260–65, 459, 535, 591–92, 662–63; 4:pp. 24–25, 62–66; Bazant, *Church Wealth,* p. 24. For a thorough analysis of the "bank" and the tobacco monopoly, see David W. Walker, "Business as Usual: The Empresa del tabaco in Mexico, 1837–44," *Hispanic American Historical Review,* 64 (1984) pp. 675–705.

54.   Dublán y Lozano, *Legislación mexicana,* 3:pp. 352, 359–61. The government pledged to set aside 100 million acres in Texas, Chihuahua, Nuevo México, Sonora, and Alta California.

55.   Casasús, *Historia deuda,* pp. 113, 132, 137, 165–71, 245–308; Jan Bazant, *Historia de la deuda exterior de México (1823–1946)* (Mexico: El Colegio de México, 1968), pp. 51, 56, 58–59.

56.   As for example with the tobacco bonds, see Walker, "Martínez del Río," pp. 320–50.

57.   Rosa María Meyer Cosío, "Empresarios, Crédito y Especulación (1820–1850)," paper given at "Coloquio sobre el crédito y las finanzas en México, 1800–1930," Mexico City, December 1984, p. 5.

58.   Walker, "Martínez del Río," pp. 295–298.

59.   Frances Calderón de la Barca, *Life in Mexico,* ed. Howard and Marion Fisher (Garden City, N. Y.: Doubleday and Company, 1964), pp. 554 and 745, n. 13.

60.   Pedro Ansoateguí to Gregorio José Martínez del Río, Mexico City, July 4, 1840, as quoted in Walker, "Martínez del Río," p. 293.

61.   Rosa María Meyer Cosío, "Los Béistegui, Especuladores y Mineros, 1830–1869," in Cardoso, ed., *Formación de la burguesía,* p. 112.

62.   Walker, "Martínez del Río," p. 302.

63.   *Ibid.*, pp. 298–99. For another view, see Walker, "Empresa del tabaco," p. 698.

64.   Urías, "Escandón," in Cardoso, ed., *Formación de la burguesía*, p. 44; Manning-MacKintosh Papers, Folder 95, Wallet 1, Benson Latin American Collection, University of Texas, Austin, for lists of duties owed and by whom for 1842–1844; Walker, "Martínez del Río," p. 309.

65.   Urías, "Escandón," in Cardoso, ed., *Formación de la burguesía*, pp. 25–56; Bazant, *Church Wealth*, pp. 86–87; Calderón de la Barca, *Life in Mexico*, pp. 508, 694, n. 22, and 718, n. 9; Platt, "Finanzas británicas," p. 245.

66.   Walker, "Martínez del Río," pp. 305–6; Walker, "Empresa del tabaco," pp. 699–702.

67.   Bazant, *Church Wealth*, p. 24; Calderón de la Barca, *Life in Mexico*, p. 508.

68.   Walker, "Martínez del Río," pp. 293–95, 306–7.

69.   Walker, "Martínez del Río," pp. 307–12.

70.   Walker, "Martínez del Río," pp. 309–12.

71.   Tomás Murphy, *Memoria sobre deuda* (París: Imprenta d'Ad. Blondeau, 1848), pp. 9–31; Bazant, *Deuda*, pp. 58–60; Casasús, *Historia deuda*, pp. 257–63. Bazant speculates that Santa Anna's government had to support Lizardi in order to maintain Mexico's credit rating after Murphy had aired his complaints in public, but adds that nevertheless Lizardi did profit from the deal.

72.   Hubert Howe Bancroft, *History of Mexico*, 5: pp. 239, 246, n. 58; Bazant, *Church Wealth*, pp. 25, 27–28.

73.   Urías, "Escandón," in Cardoso, ed., *Formación de la burguesía*, p. 43.

74.   José Pablo Martínez del Río to Gregorio José Martínez del Río, March 9, 1843, as quoted in Walker, "Martínez del Río," pp. 312–14.

75.   Walker, "Martínez del Río," pp. 179–83.

76.   Guillermo Prieto, *Memorias de mis tiempos* (Mexico: Editorial Patría, 1969), p. 363.

77.   Walker, "Martínez del Río," pp. 186–88.

78.   Urías, "Escandón," in Cardoso, ed., *Formación de la burguesía*, pp. 41–42; Walker, "Martínez del Río," pp. 215–16. Curiously Walker makes no mention of the Fresnillo investment.

79.   Jan Bazant, *Estudio sobre la productividad de la industria algodonera mexicana en 1843–1845*, p. 314, as cited in Dawn Keremitsis, *La Industria textil mexicana en el siglo XIX* (Mexico: Secretaría de Educación Pública, 1973), pp. 38–39; Pedro Ansoateguí to Gregorio José Martínez del Río, July 20, 1840, as quoted in Walker, "Martínez del Río," p. 249.

80.   Guillermo Beato, "La Casa Martínez del Río: Del comercio co-

lonial a la industria fabril, 1829–1864," in Cardoso, ed., *Formación de la burguesía*, pp. 70–78.

81. Potash, *Banco*, p. 152.
82. Urías, "Escandón," in Cardoso, ed., *Formación de la burguesía*, p. 44.
83. Potash, *Banco*, p. 151.
84. Valadés, José C. *Alamán: Estadista e historiador* (Mexico: Antigua Libería Robredo, 1938), pp. 395–99, 408–11. On the other hand, Alamán's participation guaranteed a certain lack of cooperation from prominent federalists like Juan Álvarez.
85. *Memoria de Hacienda 1870*, p. 239.
86. Walker, "Martínez del Río," p. 280.
87. Walker, "Martínez del Río," pp. 281–82.
88. Walker, "Martínez del Río," pp. 269–71.
89. Walker, "Martínez del Río," p. 272.
90. Walker, "Martínez del Río," pp. 261–68.
91. Kicza, *Colonial Entrepreneurs*, Appendix, pp. 245–52.
92. Walker, "Martínez del Río," p. 60.
93. Fanny Calderón de la Barca, *Life in Mexico*, p. 550; Oyarzábal Salcedo, "Mier y Terán," in Cardoso, ed., *Formación de la burguesía*, pp. 142–59.
94. Walker, "Martínez del Río," pp. 60–61.
95. Walker, "Martínez del Río," pp. 60–62.
96. Walker, "Martínez del Río," pp. 101–3, 199, 200, 239.
97. Now known as Pentecost Sunday.
98. Walker, "Martínez del Río," pp. 226–27.
99. Calderón de la Barca, *Life in Mexico*, pp. 268–74, 454–60.
100. Prieto, *Memorias de mis tiempos*, pp. 359–62.
101. Walker, "Martínez del Río," p. 326.
102. Dublán y Lozano, *Legislación mexicana*, 5:pp. 7, 23–25, 29–32; *Memoria de Hacienda 1870*, pp. 266–67.
103. Frank N. Samponaro, "Mariano Paredes y el movimiento monarquista mexicano en 1846," in *Historia Mexicana*, 32 (1982): 39–47.
104. Guillermo Prieto, *Memorias de mis tiempos*, pp. 377–78.
105. Vázquez, "Primeros tropiezos," pp. 31–33; Hale, *Liberalism*, pp. 29–30; Samponaro, "The Political Role of the Army in Mexico 1821–1848," unpublished Ph. D. dissertation, State University of New York at Stony Brook, May 1974, pp. 322–24.
106. Walker, "Martínez del Río," pp. 317–18; *Memoria de Hacienda 1870*, pp. 276, 278.
107. The Active Bonds were converted at 90 percent of face value; the deferred and debentures at 60 percent. The government issued an extra $ 10,676,590 in bonds which it sold to Escandón and MacKintosh for $ 200,000 cash and some credits. Thomas R. Lill, *The National Debt*

of Mexico: History and Present Status (New York: Searle, Nichols and Lill, 1919), p. 92, and Turlington, *Foreign Creditors*, pp. 92–93.

108.   Dublán y Lozano, *Legislación mexicana*, 5: pp. 169–71.

109.   Dublán y Lozano, *Legislación mexicana*, 5: pp. 175–77. José Fernando Ramírez asserts that the taxes were repealed because of bribes paid to Treasury Minister Antonio Haro y Tamariz. See José Fernando Ramírez, *Mexico during the War with the United States*, ed. Walter V. Scholes and trans. Elliott B. Scherr (Columbia, Missouri: University of Missouri Press, 1950), p. 90.

110.   Bazant, *Church Wealth*, pp. 25, 27–28.

111.   Bazant, *Church Wealth*, p. 29; Jan Bazant, *Antonio Haro y Tamariz y sus aventuras políticas 1811–1869* (Mexico: El Colegio de México, 1985), pp. 48–50. For Bazant's explanation of Haro's resignation, see pp. 50–51.

112.   *Memoria de Hacienda 1870*, p. 258.

113.   Dublán y Lozano, *Legislación mexicana*, 5: pp. 7–8, 23–25.

114.   Manuel Rivera Cambas, *Historia antigua y moderna de Jalapa y de las revoluciones del estado de Veracruz*, 4 (Mexico: Cumplido, 1870), p. 703.

115.   Michael Costeloe, "Church-State financial negotiations in Mexico during the American War, 1846–47," *Revista de historia de América* 60 (1965), pp. 99–102; Dublán y Lozano, *Legislación mexicana*, 5: pp. 240–242.

116.   Ramírez, *Mexico during War*, p. 93.

117.   See Michael Costeloe, "The Mexican Church and the Rebellion of the *Polkos*," in *Hispanic American Historical Review*, 46 (1966): pp. 170–78. Also Ramírez, *Mexico during War*, pp. 104–7. Ramírez claims that the Vicar Capitular Juan Manuel Irisarri paid for the revolt and that the rebels had $ 93,000 left over after expenses. He blames the Church for the loss of Veracruz (p. 113) and claims a noticeable decline in respect for religion following the incident (p. 114). For more on Irisarri, see Walker, "Martínez del Río," pp. 163–64.

118.   Walker, "Martínez del Río," pp. 318–19; Meyer Cosío, "Empresarios," p. 8.

119.   Meyer Cosío, "Empresarios," p. 9.

120.   Oyarzábal Salcedo, "Mier y Terán," in Cardoso, ed., *Formación de la burguesía*, pp. 147–48.

121.   Ramírez, *Mexico during War*, p. 148.

122.   Juan José del Corral, *Breve Reseña sobre el estado de la hacienda y del que se llama crédito público, o sea exposición de los males y reseña de la república que la han llevado y siguen conduciendo las maniobras de los agiotistas y de los males empleados, 28 Octubre 1848*, pp. 29–30 as quoted in Bazant, *Church Wealth*, p. 32. Bazant

says that Corral exaggerated, but adds (p. 33) that his opinion was widely held.

123.   Michael P. Costeloe, *Church and State in Independent Mexico: A Study of the Patronage Debate 1821–1857* (London: Royal Historical Society, 1978), pp. 161–62.

124.   George L. Rives, *The United States and Mexico, 1821–1848* (New York: Scribner's, 1913) 2: pp. 495–96, 505–06, 510. For more on this, see Barbara A. Tenenbaum, "Neither a borrower nor a lender be: Financial Constraints and the Treaty of Guadalupe Hidalgo," in Papers Presented at a Conference on Mexicans and Mexican-Americans in the Nineteenth Century," May 1984, University of California, Irvine, forthcoming.

125.   Pedro Ansoateguí to Gregorio José Martínez del Río, November 27, 1847, as quoted in Walker, "Martínez del Río," pp. 319–20.

Chapter 3

1.   See Dennis Berge, "A Mexican Dilemma: The Mexico City Ayuntamiento and the Question of Loyalty, 1846–1848," in *The Hispanic American Historical Review* 50 (1970) pp. 229–56.

2.   *Memoria de Hacienda 1870*, pp. 280–81.

3.   Agustín Cue Canovas, *Historia Social y Económica de México 1521–1854* (Mexico: Editorial F. Trillas, S.A., 1963), p. 407.

4.   The Bustamante account, *Cuadro histórico*, appeared in 1823–1832. The Zavala work, *Ensayo histórico de las revoluciones de Méjico desde 1808 hasta 1830*, 2 vols., appeared in 1831–1832; the Mora history, *Méjico y sus revoluciones*, 3 vols., Paris, 1836. For more on their impact see Hale, *Liberalism*, pp. 22–27, and Reyes Heroles, *El Liberalismo Mexicano*, 2, pp. 255–86. For evidence of the complication of definition, see Moisés González Navarro, "Tipología del liberalismo mexicano," in *Historia Mexicana*, 32 (1982) pp. 201–05.

5.   See Reyes Heroles, ed., *Obras de Mariano Otero* (Mexico: UNAM, 1967), and his *El Liberalismo Mexicano*, 2, pp. 89–140. For a sample of the feelings of other liberals about Otero, see Ramírez, *Mexico during War*, pp. 47–48. As for influence–peddling, see Walker, "Martínez del Río," pp. 326–30.

6.   Hale, *Liberalism*, pp. 17–19, 27–31, 213–14, 244; Valadés, *Alamán*, chapter 11.

7.   Prieto, *Memorias*, pp. 378–79.

8.   *Memoria de Hacienda 1870*, p. 277.

9.   *Memoria de Hacienda 1852*, chart D.

10.   *Memoria de Hacienda 1850*, chart opposite p. 12.

11.   Rivera Cambas, *Historia de Jalapa* 4, pp. 197–98; Thomas Ewing Cotner, *The Military and Political Career of José Joaquín de Herrera*, (Austin: Institute of Latin American Studies, University of Texas, 1949) pp. 198–99.

12.   The previous low figure was $ 11,656,479 in 1829–30.

13.   *Memoria de Hacienda 1870*, pp. 314–15.

14.   *Memoria de Hacienda 1870*, pp. 310–11; Juan Antonio Mateos, ed., *Historia parlamentaria de los congresos mexicanos* (Mexico, 1877–1912) 23:713–18. *Representación que elevaron al Supremo Gobierno algunos proprietarios de fincas urbanas en esta capital sobre contribuciones* (Mexico, 1849), p. 10.

15.   *El Siglo XIX*, April 9, 1850, pp. 3–4; Manuel Payno, "Voto particular sobre proporcionar recursos al gobierno con que cubrir el deficiente," as appeared in *El Siglo XIX*, April 17, 1850, pp. 3–4; "Dictamen de la segunda comisión de hacienda sobre el acuerdo de la cámara de diputados relativos a contribuciones y recursos del gobierno" (Fagoaga, Esparza, Garza Flores), April 22, 1850 as appeared in *El Siglo XIX*, April 24, 1850, p. 1.

16.   *El Siglo XIX*, August 15, 1849, p. 2; Manuel Payno y Bustamante and Ignacio de la Barrera, March 30, 1848 as published in *El Universal*, August 16, 17, 18, 1849, p. 2; Bonifacio Gutiérrez, *Iniciativa que Bonifacio Gutiérrez dirigió a la augusta cámara de diputados para reestablecer en el distrito y territorios los impuestos indirectos*, September 29, 1849 (Mexico, 1849), pp. 10–64.

17.   Manuel Payno, *Esposición que el ministro de Hacienda dirige a las Cámaras sobre el estado de la Hacienda Pública en el presente año* (Mexico, July 1850), pp. 83, 97, 103. See for example, *El Siglo XIX*, September 2, 1850, p. 3. One example of the various defenses of the mining fund was printed in *El Siglo XIX*, September 1, 1850, pp. 2–3. The fund, which originated in colonial times, was reestablished under the republic on February 13, 1822. It supported a school of mining technology, scholarships for students, and other activities designed to promote the development of the science of mining. Its resources came from a surcharge on the price of mercury, but as mining output declined in the first half of the nineteenth century, the fund became the repository for a substantial amount of money.

18.   Valadés, *Alamán*, pp. 468–72; Niceto de Zamacois, *Historia de Méjico, desde sus tiempos más remotas hasta nuestras días, escrita en vista de todo lo que de irrecusable han dado a luz los más caracterizados historiadores*, t. 13, Barcelona, 1880, pp. 337–38.

19.   *El Monitor Republicano*, May 2, 1851, p. 3; *El Siglo XIX*, May 7, 1851, pp. 1–2.

20.   Mateos, *Historia parlamentaria*, XXIV, May 2, 1851, p. 369; *El*

Siglo XIX, May 18, 1851, pp. 1–2, May 19, 1851, p. 1; Guillermo Prieto, Ricardo Villaseñor, J. M. Manso Cevallos, *Manifestación de las opiniones y conducta de los individuos que formaron en la cámara de diputados* (Mexico, 1851), pp. 12–17; *El Monitor Republicano*, May 21, 1851, pp. 1 and 3; May 28, 1851, p. 1.

21. Voss, *Periphery*, pp. 109–16; Bancroft, *History of Mexico*, 5: pp. 572–75.

22. *Memoria del estado de Guanajuato 1850, 1851; Memoria del estado de Oaxaca 1852.*

23. Letter of José Gómez to Mariano Riva Palacio, Mariano Riva Palacio Papers, Folder 16, November 13, 1850, García Collection, Benson Latin American Collection, University of Texas, Austin, as cited in Clyde Gilbert Bushnell, "The Military and Political Career of Juan Álvarez, 1790–1867," (Ph. D. diss., University of Texas, June 1958), p. 236. Álvarez had not paid Gómez, his principal assistant, in four months. According to Berry, the same holds true for Oaxaca in 1850. See Charles Berry, *The Reform in Oaxaca* (Lincoln: University of Nebraska Press, 1981), p. 24.

24. *Memoria de Hacienda 1870*, pp. 351–52.

25. Echevarría, Alamán, Pasquel, Pimentel, "Dictamen de las comisiones primera y segunda de la cámara de diputados del congreso general, sobre del deficiente del erario federal," 26 de junio de 1851; *Documentos relativos a la Reunión en esta Capital de los Gobernadores de los Estados Convocados para proveer a las Exigencias del Erario Federal* (Mexico: J. M. Lara, 1851), pp. 41–52; *Memoria de Hacienda 1870*, p. 77; Macune, *Federación*, chapter 5.

26. Miguel González Avelar, *México en el umbral de la Reforma* (Mexico: Federación Editorial Mexicana, S.A. de C. U., 1973), pp. 68–69; *El Monitor Republicano*, June 3, 1851, p. 4; July 9, 1851, pp. 3–4.

27. *La Voz de Alianza*, July 1, 1851 (Guadalajara) as reprinted in *El Siglo XIX*, July 13, 1851, pp. 2–3; "Estracto de las observaciones de les Exmos. Sres. gobernadores de los Estados a la circular con que se les remitieron las iniciativas sobre recursos," *Reunión de gobernadores*, chart 2; "Esposición del secretarío del despacho de Hacienda é iniciativas que el Ministro de Hacienda ha dirigido a la cámara de diputados, leída en consejo de ministros con asistencia de los gobernadores de los estados en 17 de agosto de 1851," *Reunión de gobernadores*, pp. 19–27.

28. "Communicación al supremo gobierno . . . sobre la situación de la Hacienda Federal y renuncia del ministerio," *Reunión de gobernadores*, pp. 6–8, 20–41, 45–53.

29. Letter of Mariano Otero to José María Luis Mora, November 13, 1848, in Genaro García, ed., *Documentos inéditos o muy raros para la historia de México*, "Papeles inéditos y obras selectas del Doctor Mora" (Mexico: Bouret, 1906) 6: pp. 134–35.

30.   Letter of Valentín Gómez Farías to his sons, March 13, 1848, Farías's papers in the García Collection, Benson Latin American Collection, University of Texas, Austin, No. 2844.

31.   *The London Times*, August 17, 1849, p. 3; December 21, 1849, p. 5; Turlington, *Mexico and Foreign Creditors*, p. 97; Arrangoiz, *México desde 1808 hasta 1867*, pp. 402–403; Committee of Spanish American Bondholders, "Statement of Proceedings," as cited in Casasús, *Historia deuda*, p. 229; and as cited by Bazant, *Deuda*, pp. 70–71.

32.   Cotner, *Herrera*, pp. 214–215.

33.   Casasús, *Historia deuda*, p. 239.

34.   For precise figures see Manuel Payno, *México y sus cuestiones financieras con la Inglaterra, la España y la Francia* (Mexico, 1862), pp. 22–25; Bazant, *Deuda*, p. 71; and Thomas Lill, *National Debt of Mexico*, pp. 37–38.

35.   *Memoria de Hacienda 1870*, p. 367.

36.   Letter from Lucas Alamán to Mariano Riva Palacio, August 26, 1848, in Mariano Riva Palacio Archives, García Collection, Benson Latin American Collection, University of Texas, Austin, No. 2909. Riva Palacio had received loans in the past from Gregorio Mier y Terán for $ 70,000 (1839) and $ 30,000 (1842) in order to buy a hacienda at San Juan de Dios. However, just as the taking out of a mortgage from a bank in modern times does not make a homeowner into a partisan of banking interests, it does not necessarily follow that Riva Palacio should have considered himself indebted to Mier y Terán in any sense but financial. Oyarzábal Salcedo, "Mier y Terán," in Cardoso, ed., *Formación de la burguesía*, p. 149.

37.   Manuel Payno, *Historia de la deuda de México* (Mexico: Imprenta Económica, 1865), p. 15.

38.   *Espediente mandado imprimir por acuerdo de la cámara de senadores sobre que el gobierno informe a dicha cámara lo ocurrido en el negocio de los cinco millones de pesos que debió entregar la casa de los Sres. Manning y MacKintosh en créditos reconocidos* as appeared in *El Siglo XIX*, October 1–8, 20, 22–25, 1848, p. 1.

39.   *El Siglo XIX*, September 28, 1848, p. 1.

40.   *El Siglo XIX*, January 29, 1849, p. 4; January 31, 1849, p. 3; *El Heraldo*, January 29, 1849, as printed in *El Siglo XIX*, February 4, 1849, p. 2.

41.   Guillermo Beato, "Martínez del Río," in Cardoso, ed., *Formación de la burguesía*, pp. 68–69; Payno y Flores, *Cuestiones*, pp. 74–75; *El Siglo XIX*, February 8, 1849, p. 3. For a full history of the tobacco bonds, see Walker, "Martínez del Río," pp. 320–37.

42.   *El Heraldo*'s accusation against Piña y Cuevas might have been valid because the treasury minister received a $ 76,000 loan without security after his resignation from office. Cotner, *Herrera*, pp. 210–11.

43.   Mariano Otero, *Discurso pronunciado en la cámara de senadores contra el dictamen de las comisiones de hacienda y crédito público sobre la autorización de un millón y medio*, March 12, 1849, as printed in Jésus Reyes Heroles, ed., *Obras de Mariano Otero* 2: pp. 805, 808–11; and *El Siglo XIX*, March 15, 1849, p. 4; March 16, 1849, p. 1; March 22, 1849, p. 2; April 8, 1849, pp. 1 and 2.

44.   Muñoz Ledo Castillo, *Dictamen de la comisión del crédito público del senado*, May 15, 1849 (Mexico, 1849).

45.   *El Siglo XIX*, April 28, 1849, p. 3.

46.   Walker, "Martínez del Río," pp. 337–39.

47.   *Dictamen de la Comisión de Crédito Público de la cámara de diputados sobre arreglo de la deuda interior de la nación* (Mexico, 1849), pp. 26–27, 29, 31, 71.

48.   *Documentos relativos al arreglo de la deuda interior de la república mexicana, mandados imprimir de orden del supremo gobierno* (Mexico, 1851), pp. 18–19, 41–42, 46–47, 64–65.

49.   *Ibid.*, pp. 35, 41–42, 46–47; *Ley de 30 de noviembre de 1850, sobre el arreglo de la deuda interior de la república mexicana y reglamento acordado por el Gobierno para su ejecución*; Vicente Riva Palacio, ed., *México a través de los Siglos*, vol. 4 (Mexico City, publication date unknown), p. 747; Zamacois, *Historia de Méjico*, 13: p. 410.

50.   Walker, "Martínez del Río," p. 339.

51.   Manuel Payno, *Reseña sobre el estado de la Hacienda Pública* (Mexico, 1851), p. 1.

52.   José Ignacio Esteva, *Exposición que dirige al Exmo. Sr. Presidente de la República* (Mexico, 1851), pp. 25–27.

53.   *Ibid.*, pp. 8–10, 19–21, 25–27, 85–88, 91.

54.   *Memoria de Hacienda 1870*, pp. 336–37; *El Siglo XIX*, April 25, 1851, pp. 1–2.

55.   Martínez del Río Hermanos to Percy Doyle, Mexico City, April 19, 1851, FO 204–107:158 as cited in Walker, "Martínez del Río," p. 342.

56.   Percy Doyle to Lord Palmerston, Mexico City, October 5, 1851, FO 204–106:651 as cited in Walker, "Martínez del Río," p. 347.

57.   *Ibid.*, pp. 285–86; Manuel Payno, *Cuestiones*, pp. 143–49. The creditors involved included José Antonio Béistegui, Benito Maqua, and Muriel Hermanos who held $ 1,351,115 (44 percent) of the tobacco bonds.

58.   *Memoria de Hacienda 1870*, pp. 374, 376–77; Payno, *Cuestiones*, pp. 75–83, 149; Walker, "Martínez del Río," p. 346–51.

59.   Payno, *Cuestiones*, pp. 220–22, 224; *Acusación contra el ex-Ministro de Relaciones, José F. Ramírez por Bernardino Alcalde* (Mexico City, 1852); *Memoria de Hacienda 1870*, pp. 372–73.

60.   *Memoria de Hacienda 1870*, p. 367. Another reason that the gov-

government agreed to provide supplies and the syndicate would pay $ 600,000 at 6 percent.

3. Levasseur, March 31, 1853, in Díaz, trans., *Versión francesa*, p. 30; Bancroft, *History of Mexico*, 5: p. 622; *Memoria de Hacienda 1870*, p. 397; Richard A. Johnson, *The Mexican Revolution of Ayutla, 1854–1855* (Augustana Library Publications, No. 17. Rock Island, Illinois: Augustana Book Company, 1939), p. 12.

4. Levasseur, April 27, 1853, in Díaz, trans., *Versión francesa*, p. 31.

5. Arrangoiz, *México desde 1808 hasta 1867*, pp. 420–23.

6. Levasseur, April 29, 1853, in Díaz, trans., *Versión francesa*, pp. 37–38; Johnson, *Ayutla*, p. 15. For an interesting analysis of the relations between Alamán and Haro at this critical moment, see Bazant, *Haro y Tamariz*, pp. 65–66.

7. Levasseur, April 30, 1853, in Díaz, trans., *Versión francesa*, pp. 40–45; Barker, *French Experience*, pp. 141–42.

8. For a complete copy, see García Cantú, *Reacción Mexicana*, pp. 349–59; Levasseur, April 27, 1853, in Díaz, trans., *Versión francesa*, pp. 34–36. On issue of the press, see Gerald McGowan, *La prensa y el poder* (Mexico: El Colegio de México, 1978), chapters 1–4.

9. Dublán y Lozano, "Legislación mexicana," vol. 6, pp. 366–68, 395–96, 455, 525–26, as cited in Johnson, *Ayutla*, p. 16; *Memoria de Hacienda 1870*, pp. 395–96.

10. Dublán y Lozano, "Legislación mexicana," vol. 6, p. 416, as cited in Johnson, *Ayutla*, p. 21; *Memoria de Hacienda 1870*, p. 395.

11. For an excellent account of Haro y Tamariz's early years, see Bazant, *Haro y Tamariz*, pp. 15–52.

12. Levasseur, April 29, 1853, in Díaz, trans., *Versión francesa*, p. 38.

13. Antonio Haro y Tamariz, *Informe presentado al presidente por el ministro de hacienda* (Mexico, 1853), pp. 23–25.

14. Letter of Lucas Alamán to William H. Prescott, March 17, 1849, in the Massachusetts Historical Society Collection, "I have been in very bad health, afflicted with asthma or suffocation of the chest so that I cannot breathe." Although most books state that Alamán died of pleurisy, his symptoms could also be diagnosed as congestive heart disease.

15. Haro y Tamariz, *Informe*, pp. 1–9 and 27–30; Bazant, *Haro y Tamariz*, pp. 70–71.

16. Levasseur, April 27, 1853, in Díaz, trans., *Versión francesa*, p. 38.

17. This bank has never received the kind of study it deserves. For a brief summary, see José Antonio Bátiz Vázquez, "Aspectos financieros y monetarios (1821–1880)" in Ciro Cardoso, ed., *México en el siglo XIX:*

Historia económica y de la estructura social (Mexico: Editorial Nueva Imagen, 1980), pp. 177–78.

18. Haro y Tamariz, *Informe*, pp. 9–14.

19. Levasseur, July 18, 1853, in Díaz, trans., *Versión francesa*, p. 56; *El Universal*, July 30, 1853, pp. 1–2.

20. Alphonse Dano, September 1, 1853, in Díaz, trans., *Versión francesa*, p. 64; Bazant, *Haro y Tamariz*, p. 72.

21. Marcy to Gadsden, July 15, 1853, Dept. of State, Inst., Mex., XVI, no. 3, as cited in Garber, *Gadsden Treaty*, pp. 83–85.

22. Letter of Gadsden to Marcy, August 17, 1853, as cited in J. D. Manning, *Diplomatic Correspondence of the United States 1831–1860*, vol. 9 (Washington, D. C.: Carnegie Endowment for International Peace, 1937), p. 601.

23. Payno, *Cuestiones*, pp. 224–27.

24. Payno, *Cuestiones*, pp. 155–80; *Memoria de Hacienda 1870*, pp. 409–10.

25. Alberto María Carreño, *La diplomacia extraordinaria entre México y Estados Unidos, 1787–1947*, 2 (Mexico: Editorial Jus, 1951) pp. 97–99, 104, 106; Angel Calderón was the husband of the highly observant Fanny Calderón de la Barca.

26. Walker, "Martínez del Río," p. 352.

27. Garber, *Gadsden Purchase*, pp. 103–4.

28. Letter of Gadsden to Marcy, July 11, 1855, Dept. of State, Des., Mex., XIX Unofficial, and January 2, 1854, Marcy Papers, 46, as cited in Garber, *Gadsden Treaty*, pp. 106–7.

29. *Memoria de Hacienda 1870*, pp. 411–12, 415–16, and Pedro F. de la Garza, "Comprobantes se pagó de contribuciones directados por Casimiro Gómez Farías," March 4, 1854. Matamoros, Valentín Gómez Farías Papers, García Collection, Benson Latin American Collection, University of Texas, 3534.

30. Johnson, *Ayutla*, pp. 19–20.

31. Johnson, *Ayutla*, p. 41; Anselmo de la Portilla, *Historia de la Revolución de México Contra la Dictadura del General Santa–Ana, 1853–1855* (Mexico, 1856), pp. 38–45.

32. Portilla, *Historia Revolución*, appendices, pp. li–lxvi.

33. Francisco López Cámara, *La Estructura Económica y Social de México en la época de la Reforma* (Mexico, Siglo Veintiuno Editores, S. A., 1967), pp. 148–49.

34. *El Universal*, August 4, 1849, p. 1 contained an advertisement for Guerrero as a land of opportunity for cotton manufacturing, but Guerrero remains isolated and underdeveloped to this day. According to statistics published in 1968, Guerrero was the least industrialized state in

the nation. Moisés Ochoa Campos, *Historia del estado de Guerrero* (Mexico: Libreria Porrúa Hnos y Cia., 1968), p. 9.

35.   Letter of Juan Álvarez to Col. Ignacio Comonfort, May 17, 1854, Comonfort Papers, García Collection, Benson Latin American Collection, University of Texas.

36.   Portilla, *Historia Revolución,* pp. 153–164; see also Johnson, *Ayutla,* pp. 81–82.

37.   Comonfort and Hitchcock Agreement, November 7, 1854, Comonfort Papers, García Collection, Benson Latin American Collection, University of Texas; Portilla, *Historia Revolución,* pp. 152–53, p. 153, n. 2; Johnson, *Ayutla,* p. 55.

38.   *Cuentas de la Comisaría y Sub–Comisaría del Ejército Restaurador de la libertad que manifiestan los ingresos y egresos que han tenido en la fecha que mencionan* (Mexico, 1856).

39.   Alphonse Dano, September 1, 1853, in Díaz, trans., *Versión francesa,* p. 64–65.

40.   Tariff collections in August and September amounted to only $ 80,523 and $ 109,965, respectively, and contraband continued unabated. *El Siglo XIX,* October 6, 1853; *El Universal,* October 28, 1853, pp. 2–3.

41.   Walker, "Martínez del Río," pp. 89–90, 354.

42.   Manuel Olasagarre, *Informe que por orden de Su Alteza Serenísima presenta al supremo gobierno sobre el estado de la hacienda pública y sus reformas* (Mexico, 1855), 12ff.

43.   Johnson, *Ayutla,* p. 68.

44.   Olasagarre, *Informe,* pp. 35–37. Some observers even doubted Olasagarre's basic honesty. For example, French Minister Alexis de Gabriac was certain that Olasagarre had enriched himself as treasury minister and quoted three–time Treasury Minister Joaquín Parrés who commented, "When I entered (the government) for the first time as Treasury Minister (January 30, 1854), I found in the strongbox 14 *reales* of counterfeit money; the second time (January 18, 1855), I found $ 700, but this time it would be very difficult to distinguish the real from the false." Alexis de Gabriac, January 25, 1855, in Díaz, trans., *Versión francesa,* p. 162.

45.   *Memoria de Hacienda 1870,* p. 412.

46.   The original Compañía Arrendataria del Estanco del Tabaco was composed of Manuel de Lizardi and Cayetano Rubio. A few months later, they sold 17 (out of 100) shares to Béistegui. Still later Manuel Escandón, Garuste, Labadie and Company, Pedro del Valle and Miguel Bringas joined. See Meyer Cosío, "Los Béistegui," in Cardoso, ed., *Formación de la burguesía,* p. 130.

47.   *Memoria de Hacienda 1870,* p. 412.

48.   This figure for monopolies in 1853–54 does not include collec-

tions for the lottery, official paper, or salt. Olasagarre never supplied the actual totals by area, and indeed it is difficult to know how he arrived at $ 6,304,532 for state contributions.

49. For more on this see Carmen Blázquez, *Miguel Lerdo de Tejada: un liberal veracruzano en la política nacional* (Mexico: El Colegio de México, 1978), pp. 62–70. Apparently the Lerdo family had known Santa Anna in Jalapa.

50. Portilla, *Historia Revolución*, pp. 79–83.

51. Garber, *Gadsden Treaty*, pp. 137–40.

52. *El Siglo XIX*, July 25, 1854, as quoted in Riva Palacio, *México a través de los Siglos*, 4: pp. 841–42. Arrangoiz paid himself a hefty commission of $ 68,390.

53. Martínez del Río Hermanos must have supplied cash and credits since it received less than the face value of the loan. After the fall of the Santanista administration, the Álvarez government jailed Olasagarre. Olasagarre, ed., *Cuenta corriente de los fondos de la Mesilla en Nueva York al cargo del Escmo. Sr. Francisco de Arrangoiz* (Mexico, 1854), p. 67.

54. Manuel Olasagarre, *Manifestación que M. J. Olasagarre hace del ingreso y egreso de la tesorería, durante la época que desempeñó el ministerio* (Guadalajara, 1856), 9ff.

55. M. Olasagarre, *Manifestación*, pp. 4, 9ff.

56. Oyarzábal Salcedo, "Mier y Terán," in Cardoso, ed., *Formación de la burguesía*, p. 159.

57. Beato, "Martínez del Río," in Cardoso, ed., *Formación de la burguesía*, p. 90.

58. Chapman, *Ferrocarril mexicano*, pp. 46–48.

59. In 1840, Miraflores was worth $ 250,000; in 1854 its value had more than doubled. Even with large outputs, in 1854, Miraflores turned out only 7 percent of Mexican textiles for that year. See Walker, "Martínez del Río," chapter 6, pp. 248–87; Beato, "Martínez del Río," in Cardoso, ed., *Formación de la burguesía*, pp. 57–107; Keremitsis, *La industria textil*, pp. 71–76.

60. *Cuentas del ejercito restaurador.*

61. Gadsden to Marcy, July 11, 1855, Dept. of State, Des. Mex., Vol. 19, unofficial as cited in Garber, *Gadsden Treaty*, p. 154.

62. From December 19, 1854 to July 9, 1855, drafts were written by the Mexican government on the money in the U. S. to Howland and Aspinwall ($1,500,000 U.S. total), and to Hargous brothers. One draft of $650,000 (U.S.) was sold for $256,000 (U.S.). Gadsden felt that some drafts went for 70 percent maximum and 50 percent regularly, and that bankers profited $1,000,000 (U.S.) from the deal. Senate Ex. Docs (821) 34 Cong., 1 & 2 Sess, XII, No. 8; Lettsom to Clarendon 8/2/55, FO Mex.,

vol. 279 no. 46; Gadsden to Marcy, June 5, 1855, Dept of State Des., Mex., vol. 19, private as cited in Garber, *Gadsden Treaty*, pp. 155–56.

63.   Letter of Gadsden to Marcy, July 11, 1855, Dept. of State, Des., Mex., vol. 19, unofficial, as cited in Garber, *Gadsden Treaty*, p. 166. If Gadsden had not been representing the United States, it is possible that Santa Anna would have remained in power longer despite President Franklin Pierce's unwillingness to disturb precarious regional harmony in the United States. See Garber, *Gadsden Treaty*, p. 181.

64.   de Gabriac, January 25, 1855, and May 2, 1855, in Díaz, trans., *Versión francesa*, pp. 161, 177.

65.   Johnson, *Ayutla*, pp. 90–91.

66.   Letter of Gadsden to Marcy, July 3, 1855, Dept. of State, Des., Mex., 19: no. 66, as cited in Garber, *Gadsden Treaty*, p. 155.

67.   Casasús, *Historia deuda*, p. 287; Johnson, *Ayutla*, p. 95.

68.   de Gabriac, January 25, 1855, in Díaz, trans., *Versión francesa*, p. 161.

69.   de Gabriac, June 23, 1855, in Díaz, trans., *Versión francesa*, pp. 185–86. Mexico also levied a forced loan on its citizens. Manuel Olmedo, José de Jesús Pliego, Leandro Mendez, Angel Sobrino, and Juan Hernández Renedo paid $ 20,000 each. On February 1, 1855, there was a forced loan of $ 48,300 levied on Guadalajara of which $ 5,450 was supplied by the Church. *El Universal*, February 13, 1855, pp. 2–3.

70.   de Gabriac, June 23, 1855, in Díaz, trans., *Versión francesa*, pp. 185–86.

71.   Johnson, *Ayutla*, pp. 70, 93.

72.   de Gabriac, May 15, 1855, in Díaz, trans., *Versión francesa*, pp. 181–83.

Chapter 5

1.   Richard N. Sinkin, *The Mexican Reform, 1855–1876: A Study of Liberal Nation–Building* (Austin: Institute of Latin American Studies, University of Texas, 1979), chapter 4.

2.   Walter F. Scholes, *Mexican Politics during the Juárez Regime, 1855–1872* (Columbia, Missouri: University of Missouri Press, 1957), p. 22.

3.   Sinkin, *Reform*, pp. 46–54. According to his calculations, 42 percent of Reform leaders were lawyers, nearly twice the percentage of the next highest group, the military.

4.   Portilla, *Historia Revolución*, p. 261. Many Mexicans regarded Vidaurri as an opportunist. See Zamacois, *Historia de Méjico*, 14, pp. 40–41. For an excellent analysis of these revolts see Bazant, *Haro y Tamariz*, pp. 77–93.

5. Doblado had often acted on his own. During the Mexican–American War, as governor of Guanajuato, Doblado refused to send any of his troops to the national army, claiming that they were needed in their home state. In 1848, he vehemently opposed the signing of the Treaty of Guadalupe Hidalgo and the ending of the war. Indeed, he staged a small revolt against the treaty and allied briefly with Mariano Paredes and Padre Jarauta against the Herrera government. William John Ross, "The Role of Manuel Doblado in the Mexican Reform Movement, 1855–1860," unpublished Ph. D. dissertation, University of Texas, August 1967, pp. 33–35.

6. de Gabriac, August 25, 1855, in Díaz, trans., *Versión francesa*, pp. 195–96; Johnson, *Ayutla*, pp. 105–106.

7. de Gabriac, September 5 and 26, 1855, in Díaz, trans., *Versión francesa*, pp. 200, 206; Zamacois, *Historia de Méjico*, 14, p. 74.

8. *Memoria de Hacienda 1855–56*, pp. 36–37; de Gabriac, October 24, 1855, in Díaz, trans., *Versión francesa*, pp. 216; Bazant, *Haro y Tamariz*, p. 94.

9. de Gabriac, November 20, 1855, in Díaz, trans., *Versión francesa*, pp. 226; Benito Gómez Farías to his brother Casimiro, April 7, 1854, in Valentín Gómez Farías Papers, García Collection, Benson Latin American Collection, University of Texas, Austin, no. 3653.

10. Letter of Gadsden to Marcy, November 25, 1855, Department of State, Des., Mex., vol. 19, no. 77, as cited in Garber, *Gadsden Treaty*, pp. 169–70.

11. Bancroft, *History of Mexico*, 5: p. 677; Berry, *Oaxaca*, p. 30.

12. *Memoria de Hacienda 1870*, p. 435.

13. Edmundo O'Gorman, *Breve Historia de las divisiones territoriales de México* (Mexico: Editorial Porrúa, S. A., 1966), pp. 121–26; Francisco Zarco, ed., *Historia del Congreso Constituyente* (Mexico: Fondo de cultura económica, 1956), pp. 209–27, 260–65. Sinkin argues that events from 1857–1867 produced the trend toward centralism in the Restored Republic. Sinkin, *Reform*, chapter 5. However, the *Organic Provisional Statute* and the *Constitution of 1857* certainly laid significant groundwork in that direction.

14. Guillermo Prieto, *Circular del ministro de hacienda a los gobernadores de los estados* (Mexico, 1855), pp. 8–15; Zamacois, *Historia de Méjico*, 14: p. 103.

15. "Proyecto de préstamo," Fondo Bustamante 50, num. 54, Archives of the National Museum of Anthropology, Mexico City. Ildefonso López, "Préstamo patriótico," October 15, 1855, Fondo Bustamante 50, num. 25, Archives of the National Museum of Anthropology, Mexico City.

16. *Memoria de Hacienda 1855–56*, p. 8; *Memoria de Hacienda 1870*, p. 436. The customs paid off $ 2,116,124 in debts during this period.

17. *Memoria de Hacienda 1855–56*, pp. 7, 17–18.

18. Letter of Carlos J. Furber to Manuel I. Madrid, January 20, 1856, Manuel I. Madrid Papers, García Collection, Benson Latin American Collection, University of Texas, Austin.

19. Dublán and Lozano, *Legislación mexicana*, 7: pp. 566–70. Apparently moneylenders often pushed for ownership of the tobacco monopoly, only to find it unprofitable. See Walker, "Empresa del tabaco," pp. 698–704.

20. *Memoria de Hacienda 1855–56*, pp. 17, 35–37.

21. *Ibid.*, cuenta general, p. 3, and pp. 22–23. Payno lists a "floating debt" of $ 2,116,124.

22. Dublán and Lozano, *Legislación mexicana*, 8: pp. 42–94.

23. *Memoria de Hacienda 1855–56*, pp. 43–53. The government made some money at the outset by selling what little tobacco and other necessities it possessed for $ 813,238. It should be remembered that Payno was a close friend of Manuel Escandón.

24. Indeed, Comonfort negotiated with Lizardi for a $ 300,000 loan. Casasús, *Historia deuda*, pp. 288–89, 296; *Memoria de Hacienda 1855–56*, pp. 56–60.

25. The history of the Jecker, Torre Company is profoundly intertwined with the history of Mexico in the next decade. During the course of its transactions, it became a major holder of the French debt and so would become deeply involved in the French diplomatic settlement. At the end of 1855, for reasons not altogether clear, the firm dissolved, but Juan B. Jecker continued to be an important speculator and his loan to the Zuloaga government in 1858 would serve as one of the rationales for the French intervention into Mexico. de Gabriac, March 2 and March 18, 1856, in Díaz, trans., *Versión francesa*, pp. 253–54, 257; Barker, *French Experience*, chapter 6, and Huerta, "de la Torre," in Cardoso, ed., *Formación de la burguesía*, pp. 164–74.

26. Garber, *Gadsden Treaty*, pp. 170–71.

27. For a full account of this revolt, see Bazant, *Haro y Tamariz*, pp. 105–38.

28. Of course, as Bazant rightly points out, Labastida probably took one position in public and another in private. Bazant, *Haro y Tamariz*, pp. 121–22. See also de Gabriac, February 1, 1856, in Díaz, trans., *Versión francesa*, pp. 250–52; Rivera Cambas, *Jalapa* 4, pp. 623–47; Portilla, *Historia revolución*, pp. 257–335.

29. de Gabriac, March 7, 1856, in Díaz, trans., *Versión francesa*, pp. 254–56.

30. In his treasury report for December 1855 to May 1856, Manuel Payno commented that the Puebla revolt "should have necessitated a multitude of ruinous contracts, excessive bonuses for providing cash

promptly, and claims upon many years of income in the future" as if it didn't. But he says nothing to prove that somehow this time the government found itself some ingenious way of avoiding the inevitable. In fact, the rest of the report is a testimony to precisely what he denies. See *Memoria de Hacienda 1855–1856*, pp. 10–11, 22; de Gabriac, March 7, 1856, in Díaz, trans., *Versión francesa*, p. 255; Rivera Cambas, *Jalapa* 4, p. 595; Bazant, *Haro y Tamariz*, pp. 124–25.

31.   de Gabriac, March 7, 1856, in Díaz, trans., *Versión francesa*, pp. 254–56; Portilla, *Historia revolución*, pp. 279–313. Bazant's verson is somewhat different, see Bazant, *Haro y Tamariz*, pp. 125–33.

32.   Portilla, *Historia revolución*, pp. 304–13.

33.   de Gabriac, April 1, 1856, in Díaz, trans., *Versión francesa*, p. 265.

34.   Letter from Bishop Pelagio Labastida y Dávalos to Governor Mariano Riva Palacio, April 24, 1856, in Mariano Riva Palacio Archives, García Collection, Benson Latin American Collection, University of Texas, Austin, no. 5900; Rivera Cambas, *Jalapa* 4, p. 660.

35.   *Memoria de Hacienda 1855*, "Cuenta general," p. 4; *Memoria de Hacienda 1870*, pp. 438–39.

36.   Robert J. Knowlton, *Church Property and the Mexican Reform 1856–1910* (DeKalb: Northern Illinois University Press, 1976), appendix I, pp. 225–38.

37.   Bazant, *Church Wealth*, pp. 12–13.

38.   Knowlton, *Church Property*, appendix I, pp. 225–38. On p. 229, n. 14, Knowlton identifies Y. O. as Manuel Payno. I have accepted Olvera's authorship based on the initials. See also Jacqueline Covo, *Las Ideas de la Reforma en México (1855–1861)* (Mexico: UNAM, 1983), p. 418, n. 109.

39.   Sinkin, *Reform*, chapter 3; Bazant, *Church Wealth*, conclusion.

40.   According to Blázquez, Lerdo's father, Juan Antonio, had been a member of the Veracruz Municipal Council in 1820 and had authored various pamphlets on problems between the port and the city and on the need for prohibiting trade in foreign wheat. Lerdo's elder brother Francisco served on the Jalapa Municipal Council in 1841. Francisco Lerdo believed in a mix of trade and industry and requested funds to build a fountain to supply water power for the four cotton factories on the northern end of the city. In 1846 Francisco became the head official at the customshouse of Mazatlán. Blázquez, *Lerdo*, pp. 5–16.

41.   Robert Potash has discovered that Lerdo misread British trade statistics and used the figures for commerce with all of Latin America as that for the interchange with Mexico alone. Thus British exports to Mexico from 1840–1846 were $ 2,298,605, not $ 11,749,525 as Lerdo had listed it. See Robert A. Potash, "El Comercio Exterior de México de

Miguel Lerdo de Tejada: un error estadístico," *Trimestre Económico*, 20 (1953) pp. 474–79.

42.   Carmen Blázquez, *Lerdo*, pp. 5–18, 61; Bazant, *Church Wealth*, pp. 68–74.

43.   Blázquez, *Lerdo*, pp. 58–60; Lilía Díaz, "El liberalismo militante," in *Historia General de México*, vol. 3 (Mexico: El Colegio de México, 1976), p. 92.

44.   Blázquez, *Lerdo*, pp. 22–57, 80. It is important to keep Lerdo's connections with the French community in mind when using such newspapers as *Le Trait d'Union* as a source. As it was written by his French friends, its assessment of his activities was hardly impartial. See Covo, *Las ideas*, chapter 7, pp. 391–468.

45.   The moneylenders did not, as some authors claim, see railroads in only symbolic terms as "a type of good luck charm the possession of which might straighten out all evils," but as a very practical way of helping their products reach larger markets. The selection of route proposals for the Mexico City–Veracruz railway line clearly demonstrates that sort of mentality. The Escandón family insisted on a Cordoba–Orizaba route, which was much more difficult to build, because it would run near their Cocolapan textile factory. Enrique Florescano and María del Rosario Lanzagorta, "Política económica," in *La economía mexicana en la época de Juárez* (Mexico: Secretaría de industria y comercio, 1972), pp. 104–05.

46.   *Memoria de Hacienda 1855*, pp. 33–34; *Memoria de Hacienda 1870*, pp. 435–36.

47.   *Memoria de Hacienda 1857*, pp. 7–9.

48.   The Assembly decreed that purchasers of royal property could make a down payment of 12 percent within fourteen days and could pay the rest in equal parts over the next twelve years using paper money issued by the treasury to pay for the property. Afterwards the government agency handling the transaction presumably burned the notes, thus retiring the debts as the property was sold. This discussion derives from a reading of the following works: J. F. Bosher, *French Finances 1770–1795* (Cambridge: Cambridge University Press, 1970), chapter 14; John McManners, *The French Revolution and the Church* (New York: Harper and Row, 1970), pp. 24–79; Marcel Marion, *La Vente des biens nationaux pendant la révolution . . .* (Geneva: Slatkine–Megariotis Reprints, 1974), pp. 12–110; Jacques Godechot, *Les institutions de la France sous la Révolution et l'émpire* (Paris: Presses Universitaires de France, 1968), pp. 160–207.

49.   This discussion derives from information and analysis presented in the following works: Francisco Simón Segura, *La Desamortización Española del Siglo XIX* (Madrid: Ministerio de Hacienda, Instituto

de Estudios Fiscales, 1973); J. M. Sánchez, *Reform and reaction: the politico–religious background of the Spanish civil war* (Chapel Hill: University of North Carolina Press, 1964), pp. 11–30. Note: the final expropriation in 1855 affected municipal and rural property much more than that owned by the clergy.

50. Bazant, *Church Wealth*, p. 1.

51. "Ley de Desamortización de Bienes Civiles y Eclesiásticos" (Mexico, 1856), article 32 and p. 5.

52. Francisco Zarco, *Historia del Congreso*, I, pp. 423–35.

53. Knowlton, *Church Property*, pp. 29–36; Berry, *Oaxaca*, pp. 138–43.

54. See Bazant, *Church Wealth*, pp. 41–134 and conclusion. Bazant rightly distinguishes between urban property which was purchased by many buyers of various social classes and a small number of rural estates which were bought by a few wealthy merchants and industrialists. For figures on the value of clerical property and the governmental income derived from its sale, see Knowlton, *Church Property*, appendices II and III.

55. Knowlton, *Church Property*, p. 45; *Memoria de Hacienda 1857*, p. 11.

56. Knowlton, *Church Property*, pp. 36–49.

57. Sinkin, *Reform*, chapter 5.

58. Chapman, *Ferrocarril mexicano*, pp. 50–163. According to Chapman, the Escandón family sold all of its holdings in the railroad between 1877–1910, and the government sold its shares in 1881 (p. 103).

59. Knowlton, *Church Property*, pp. 75–86.

60. Alphonse Dubois de Saligny, July 17, 1861, in Díaz, trans., *Versión francesa*, 2, p. 260.

Conclusion

1. Voss, *Periphery*, chapter 5.

2. Sinkin, *Reform*, pp. 37–39.

3. See Walker, "Empresa de tabaco," pp. 703–05; Meyer Cosío, "Empresarios."

4. See Huerta, "Isidoro de la Torre"; Meyer Cosío, "Béistegui"; Mario Cerutti, "Patricio Milmo, empresario regiomontaño del siglo XIX"; and Roberto C. Hernández Elizondo, "Comercio e industria textil en Nuevo León, 1852– 1890," in Cardoso, ed., *Formación de la burguesía*, pp. 168–74, 110–29, 231–66, and 267–86, respectively.

5. The financial aspects of the empire, particularly those other than the Jecker loans, merit serious study.

6. John Womack, Jr., *Zapata and the Mexican Revolution* (New York: Alfred Knopf, 1969), p. 16.

Bibliography

Primary Sources

Manuscripts

Great Britain
    Public Record Office (London)
    Foreign Office Papers: FO 50, 1824–30, 1848–57
Mexico
    Archivo del ex–ayuntamiento de México
    Archivo del ex–ayuntamiento de Puebla
    Archivo general de la nación
    Archivo del museo nacional de Antropología
        Fondo Bustamante 50
    Archivo nacional de Hacienda
    Biblioteca de Banco de México
    Biblioteca de México
        Basave Collection
    Biblioteca Nacional de México
        Lafragua Collection
    Centro de estudios históricos (Fundación cultural de Condumex)
    Hemeroteca Nacional de México
United States
    Harvard University
        Houghton Manuscript Collection
            De Radepont Papers
        Law School Library
        Widener Library
    Massachusetts Historical Society
        Letters to William Prescott
    University of California, Berkeley
        Bancroft Library
            Documents of the French Foreign Ministry, 1848–
                1853 (copies of Abraham Nasatier)

Baring Papers (copies of manuscripts of the Public
Archive, Ottawa, Canada)
University of San Francisco
Sutro Pamphlet Collection
University of Texas, Austin
Nettie Lee Benson Latin American Collection
Genero García Manuscript Collection
Papers of Lucas Alamán
Papers of Ignacio Comonfort
Papers of Valentín Gómez Farías
Papers of Manuel I. Madrid
Papers of Manning and MacKintosh
Papers of Mariano Paredes y Arrillaga
Papers of Mariano Riva Palacio

Printed Documents

Alcalde, Bernardino, *Acusación presentada contra el ex–ministro de Relaciones, José Fernando Ramírez.* Guanajuato, 1852.
———, *Apuntes para servir a la historia de las convenciones diplomáticas celebradas por el ministro de Relaciones D. José Fernando Ramírez en el año 1851.* Mexico, 1852.
———, *Observaciones hechas sobre documento 4 de la memoria de José Fernando Ramírez.* Mexico, May 14, 1852.
Anonymous, *Los millones de la Mesilla y sus misterios.* Mexico, 1855.
Archivo Mexicano. *Actas de las sesiones de las cámaras. Despacho diario de los ministerios, sucesos notables, documentos oficiales importantes, y rectificación de hechos oficiales.* Vol. 1–2, Mexico, 1852.
Ayuntamiento de la ciudad de México, "Esposición de los individuos que compusieron el ayuntamiento próximo pasado hacen al público en respuesta al informe de Lucas Alamán," Mexico, 1849.
———, "Informe dado por el Ayuntamiento de esta capital a la comisión de la cámara de diputados encargada de los aranceles y presupuestos y relativo a varios puntos de administración municipal," Mexico, 1849.
———, *Memoria de la corporación municipal que funcionó en el año 1851.* Mexico, 1852.
———, *Representación de la Ayuntamiento. February 29, 1852.* Mexico, 1852.
———, "Representación hecha por el ayuntamiento contra el dictamen de la comisión de aranceles y presupuestos," Mexico, 1849.
Bocanegra, José María, Exposición documentada leyó en la cámara de

diputados el día 19 de noviembre de 1833, a consecuencia del acuerdo de la misma del día 16 del propio mes, sobre dar cuenta con los contratos celebrados en los tres últimos meses. Mexico, 1833.

Boves, Crescencío, *Discurso pronunciado por Boves en la cámara de diputados sobre el ruidoso negocio de L. S. Hargous.* Mexico, 1849.

Cámara de diputados, *Comisión de crédito público de la cámara de diputados sobre el arreglo de la deuda inglesa.* Mexico, 1850.

————, *Dictamen de la comisión de crédito público de la cámara de diputados sobre el arreglo de la deuda interior de la nación.* Mexico, 1849.

————, *Dictamen de la comisión primera y segunda de hacienda de la cámara de diputados del Congreso General, sobre consignaciones de fondos para la deuda interior y recursos con que cubrir el deficiente del erario federal, leído en la sesión de 26 de junio 1851 e impresó.* Mexico, 1851.

————, *Dictamen de la mayoría de la comisión de crédito público de la cámara de diputados, voto particular y documentos relativos al arreglo de la deuda interior de la República.* Mexico, 1850.

————, *Dictamen de la mayoría de la comisiones unidas de diputados sobre la baja de aranceles.* Mexico, April 23, 1852.

————, *Manifiesto que hacen al público los contadores mayores de Hacienda y Crédito Público de todo lo ocurridó en la cámara de diputados del ultimo Congreso, sobre la suspensión del ejercicio de sus empleos por 3 meses, que injustamente se acordó en la sesión de 5 de septiembre de 1849.* Mexico, 1849.

————, *Manifiesto de las opiniones y conducta de los individuos que formaron en la cámara de diputados la última comisión para conceder recursos al gobierno, investiéndolo de facultades extraordinarios.* Mexico, 1851.

Cámara de Diputados (ed.), *Los Presidentes de México ante la Nación, 1821–1966,* 2 vols. Mexico, 1966.

Cámara de Senadores, *Dictamen de la comisión de crédito público de la senado sobre la deuda interior.* Mexico, 1850.

————, *Dictamen de la comisión de crédito público de la cámara de senadores.* Mexico, 1849.

————, *Dictamen de la comisión especial del senado sobre el proyecto relativo a nivelar los ingresos con los egresos de la Hacienda Pública.* Mexico, 1849.

————, *Dictamen de la comisión especial sobre Tehuantepec del senado.* Mexico, March 24, 1851.

————, *Dictamen de la primera comisión de hacienda del Senado sobre el contrato de armamento celebrado por Ignacio Loperena.* Mexico, 1850.

————, *Segunda dictamen de las comisiones de crédito público y segunda de Hacienda de senado en el negocio sobre arreglo de la deuda interior.* Mexico, 1850.

Cambio de la administración. Mexico, 1851.

Carbajal, Francisco, *Discursos sobre propiedad de los empleos. Un plan general de reformas de oficinas.* Mexico, Septiembre, 1848.

Corral, Juan José del, *Breve reseña sobre el estado de la hacienda y del que se llama crédito público.* Mexico, 1848.

————, *Exposición acerca de los perjuicios que ha causado al erario de la República y a su administración el agiotage sobre sus fondos y reflexiones sobre los medios de remediar aquellos males.* Mexico, 1834.

Cuentas de la Comisaría y Sub–Comisaría del Ejército Restaurador de la libertad que manifiestan los ingresos y egresos que han tenido en la fecha que mencionan. Mexico, 1856.

"Decreto de José Joaquín de Herrera sobre una iniciativa para la consolidación de la deuda de empleados y de todos los créditos contra el erario que no tengan consignado un fondo especial para su pago." Mexico, 1848.

"Decreto de 14 de Junio de 1848," in *Documentos relativos al arreglo de la deuda interior de la República Mexicana mandados imprimir de orden del supremo gobierno.* Mexico, 1851.

"Directorio para la exacción y contabilidad de las contribuciones directas." Mexico, 1853.

Documentos relativos al arreglo de la deuda interior de la República Mexicana, mandados imprimir de orden del supremo gobierno. Mexico, 1851.

Documentos relativos a la reunión . . . de los Gobernadores de los Estados. Mexico, 1851.

Dublán, M., and J. M. Lozano, *Legislación mexicana o colección completa de las disposiciones legislativas espedidas desde la independencia de la República.* Vols. 1–6. Mexico: Imprenta del Comercio, 1876–1912.

Echevarría, Alamán, Pasquel, Pimentel, "Dictamen de los comisiones primera y segunda de la cámara de diputados del congreso general, sobre consignación de fondos para la deuda interior y recursos con que cubrir el deficiente del erario federal." Mexico, June 26, 1851.

Un empleado, *Reflexiones sobre partida doble.* Mexico, 1850.

Escandón, Manuel, Breve exposición al público sobre el negocio del camino de fierro entre Veracruz y México. Mexico, 1858.

Esparza, Marcos, "Iniciativa del gobierno para el arrendamiento de las aduanas maritimas, con el fin de nivelar los gastos mas indispensables de la administración con los ingresos de la hacienda pública." Mexico, 1852.

Esteva, José Ignacio, *Exposición que dirige al exmo. sr. presidente.* Mexico, 1851.

"Exposición que los acreedores al fondo dotal de mineral llevan a la cámara de diputados." Mexico, 1849.

Fonseca, J. Urbano, *Dimisión del Ministerio.* Mexico, 1852.

Gutiérrez, Bonifacio, *Iniciativa que dirigió a la augusta cámara de diputados sobre restablecer los impuestos indirectos.* Mexico, 1849.

Haro y Tamariz, Antonio de, *Informe presentado al escmo. sr. presidente de la República, por el ministro de hacienda, sobre los puntos de que en el se trata.* Mexico, D. F., 1853.

Junta de Crédito Público, *Inventario de titulos de la deuda interior que en cumplimiento del artículo sesto del reglamento de la ley de 19 de mayo último, se entregaron a la sección liquidadora para los efectos que dicho artículo previene.* Mexico, 1852.

————, *Noticia del crédito activo del Erario Nacional.* Mexico, 1852.

Larrainzar, Manuel, *Análisis del dictamen de la comisión de negocios estraordinarios del senado de Tehuantepec.* Washington, D. C., November 25, 1852.

Lerdo de Tejada, Miguel, *Carta a gobernadores.* Mexico, 1856.

"Ley de 19 de Mayo de 1852 sobre la deuda interior y reglamento acordado por el gobierno para su ejecución." Mexico, 1852.

"Ley de 30 de noviembre de 1850, sobre el arreglo de la deuda interior de la República Mexicana, y reglamento del gobierno para su ejecución." Mexico, 1850.

"Ley penal para los empleados de Hacienda." Mexico, 1853.

"Ley del 14 de junio de 1848, sobre el arreglo de la Hacienda."

"Ley de Desamortización de Bienes Civiles y Eclesiásticos." Mexico, 1856.

Mateos, Juan Antonio, ed., *Historia parlamentaria de los congresos mexicanos.* Vol. 21–25, Mexico: V. S. Reyes, 1877–1912.

Memoria del estado de Guanajuato 1850, 1851.

Memoria del estado de Michoacán 1829.

Memoria del estado de Oaxaca 1852.

Memoria de Hacienda 1826, 1827, 1828, 1829, 1830, 1831, 1832, 1833, 1835, 1836/37, 1838, 1839, 1840, 1841, 1844, 1845, 1848/49, 1849/50, 1850/51, 1851/52, 1855/56, 1857, 1870.

Moro, Gaetano, *Communication between the Atlantic and the Pacific.* New York, 1852.

Múgica y Osorio, Juan. *Ley para el arreglo de la hacienda.* Puebla, 1849.

Munguía, Clemente de Jesús, "Manifiesto dirige a la nación mexicana," Morelia, 1851.

Muñoz Ledo, Castillo, *Dictamen de la comisión del crédito público del senado.* Mexico, May 15, 1849.

Murphy, Thomas, *Memoria sobre deuda.* Paris, 1848.

Ocampo, Melchor, *Mis quince días de Ministro.* Mexico, 1856.

Olasagarre, Manuel, ed., *Cuenta corriente de los fondos de la Mesilla en Nueva York al cargo del Escmo. Sr. Francisco de Arrangoiz.* Mexico, 1854.

———, *Cuenta de la percepción, distribución e inversión de los diez millones de pesos que produjó el tratado de la Mesilla, celebrado por el gobierno supremo de la República con el de los Estados–Unidos de America, en 13 de diciembre de 1853.* Mexico, 1856.

Olasagarre, Manuel, *Informe que por orden de Su Alteza Serenísima presenta al supremo gobierno sobre el estado de la hacienda pública y sus reformas.* Mexico, 1855.

———, *Manifestación que M. J. Olasagarre hace del ingreso y egreso de la tesorería, durante la época que desempeñó el ministerio.* Guadalajara, 1856.

Ordoñez, Juan, *Refutación al proyecto para el arreglo del ejército de Arista.* November 30, 1848. Mexico, 1848.

Oriundos Mexicanos, *Cuarta parte sobre la consolidación de la República Mexicana.* Mexico, 1851.

———, *Quinta parte sobre la consolidación de la República Mexicana.* Mexico, 1851.

———, *Tercera parte sobre la consolidación de la República Mexicana.* Mexico, 1851.

Palacio, Ricardo, *Cortes de caja y estado general de la cuenta de la comisaría de guerra de la división Comonfort.* Mexico, 1855.

Partido progreso democrático, "Exposición a Santa Ana," March 18, 1853. Mexico, 1853.

Payno y Flores, Manuel, *Cuestión del día. Reflexiones sobre la hacienda pública y el crédito escritos con motivo del proyecto presentado al supremo gobierno para la formación de un banco nacional, y el arrendamiento o administración de las rentas.* Mexico, 1853.

———, *La deuda interior de Mexico.* Mexico, 1865.

———, *Esposición que el Ministro de hacienda dirige a las cámaras al darles una cuenta sobre el estado del país.* Mexico, 1850.

———, *Esposición que el Ministro de Hacienda dirige a las cámaras sobre el estado de la Hacienda Publica en el presente año.* July 1850. Mexico, 1850.

———, *Historia de la deuda de México.* Mexico, 1866.

———, *México y sus cuestiones financieras con la Inglaterra, la España y la Francia.* Mexico, 1862.

———, *Proyectos de arreglo de los gastos de la Hacienda Pública y contribuciones para cubrirlos.* Mexico, 1848.

————, *Reseña sobre el estado de los principales ramos de la hacienda pública.* Mexico, 1851.

Payno, Arriaga, Herrera, *Dictamen de la Secretaría de Hacienda a la cámara de diputados.* August 1849. Mexico, 1849.

Piña y Cuevas, Manuel, *Esposición del Exmo. Sr. Ministro de Hacienda a la cámara de diputados sobre la urgencia de cubrir el deficiente, y medios de verificarlo.* February 14, 1849. Mexico, 1849.

————, *Esposición e iniciativas del Ministerio de Hacienda al congreso general sobre consignación de fondos para la deuda interior y recursos con que cubrir el deficiente del erario federal.* Mexico, 1851.

Presupuestos de los gastos que en un mes hace el tesorería y comisaría general y las oficinas recaudadoras. September 7, 1850. Mexico, 1850.

Prieto, Guillermo, *Circular del ministro de Hacienda, a los gobernadores de los estados.* Mexico, 1855.

————, *Indicaciones sobre el origen, vicisitudes y estado que guardan actualmente las rentas generales de la federación mexicana.* Mexico, 1850.

————, *Informe con que el secretario de hacienda dió cuenta en junta de servir ministros acerca del negocio relativo a la emisión de los bonos Lizardi e incidente del mismo.* Mexico, 1855.

————, *Informes leídos en la cámara de diputados por el Secretario de Hacienda sobre el estado que guarda el erario público y sobre las últimas operaciones practicadas en las deuda exterior y interior de la república mexicana.* Mexico, 1852.

————, *Instrucción que deja Prieto sobre los negocios pendientes en la secretaría que estuvo a su cargo a sucesor J. María Urquidi.* Mexico, 1853.

Prieto; Villaseñor; Manso Cevallos, *Manifestación de las opiniones y conducta de los individuos que formaron en la cámara de diputados.* Mexico, 1851.

Redactores del [sic] *Universal* y de otras periódicos, "Protesta contra la presidencia del señor General D. Mariano Arista." Guadalajara, 1850.

Reflexiones a la exposición del Excmo. Sr. Ministro de Hacienda, don Ignacio Esteva sobre el alza de prohibiciones. Mexico, 1851.

"Reglamento para el establecimiento de las colonias militares de Tehuantepec." Mexico, November 1851.

Remite a la 2a. sección del Ministerio de Hacienda razón de los créditos presentados en este mes de diciembre–enero, 1852–53. (Legajo 2000. Ramo de gobernación, AGN.)

Representación que elevaron al Supremo Gobierno algunos propietarios de fincas en esta capital sobre contribuciones. Mexico, 1849.

Robertson, William Parrish, *The Foreign Debt of Mexico.* London, 1850.

Segunda esposición que dirige de la suprema corte sobre la reposición del fondo judicial. Mexico, 1851.

Suárez Iriarte, Francisco, *Defensa pronunciada el 21 de marzo, 1850 a acusación de agosto 1848 de los crimenes de sedición contra el gobierno de Querétaro.* Mexico, 1850.

Supreme Corte de Justicia, *Sentencias absolutorias pronunciadas en la causa que se promovió contra Pedro F. del Castillo.* Mexico, 1849.

TePaske, John, with the collaboration of José and Mari Luz Hernández Palomo, *La Real Hacienda de Nueva España; La real caja de México (1576–1816).* Mexico: Departamento de Investigaciones Históricas Seminario de Historia Económica. Colección Científica. Fuentes. (Historia Económica de México) Vol. 41, 1976.

TePaske, John, "Sumario General de Carta Cuenta de Veracruz," unpublished Xerox copy supplied by the author.

Tornel, José Maria, *Voto particular sobre el negocio de Tehuantepec del Tornel, individuo de la comisión especial del senado.* December 30, 1852. Mexico, 1852.

Unzueta, Juan Antonio,"Informe respecto de los contratos sobre anticipación de derechos que celebró la administración de Anastasio Bustamante." Mexico, 1830.

V. C., *Ligera reseña de los partidos, facciones y otros males que agobian en la República Mexicana.* Mexico, 1851.

Varios Mexicanos, *Consideraciones sobre la situación política y social.* Mexico, 1847.

Willie, Robert C., *México. Noticia sobre su hacienda pública bajo el gobierno español y después de la independencia.* Mexico, 1845.

Yañez, Mariano, *Iniciativa elevada a la augusta cámara de diputados por el Exmo. Sr. Ministerio de Hacienda . . . en 2 de Mayo de 1851.* Mexico, 1851.

Contemporary Accounts

Alamán, Lucas, *Documentos Diversos, Inéditos, y muy raros.* 4 vols. Mexico, Editorial Jus, 1947.

———, *Historia de Méjico desde los primeros movimientos que prepararon su independencia en el año de 1808, hasta la época presente.* 5 vols. Mexico, 1849–52.

Arrangoiz, Francisco de Paula de, *México desde 1808 hasta 1867.* Madrid, 1872.

Bustamante, Carlos María de, *Cuadro histórico.* Mexico: Empresas Editoriales, 1953.

Calderón de la Barca, Frances E., *Life in Mexico: The Letters of Fanny*

Calderón de la Barca, ed. Howard T. Fisher and Marion Hall Fisher. Garden City: Doubleday Books, 1966.

Cuevas, Luis Gonzaga, *El Porvenir de México,* ed. Francisco Cuevas Cancino. Mexico: Editorial Jus, 1954.

Díaz, Lilia, ed. *Versión francesa de México. Informes diplomáticos, 1853–1857,* 4 vols. Mexico: El Colegio de México, 1963–67.

Fonseca, Fabián and Carlos de Urrutia, *Historia General de Real Hacienda,* 6 vols. Mexico, 1845–1853.

García, Genaro, ed. *Documentos inéditos o muy raros para la historia de México,* "Gobiernos de Álvarez y Comonfort según el archivo del general Doblado," vol. 31. Mexico: Viuda de Bouret, 1910.

de la Granja, Juan, *Epistolario.* Mexico: Talleres gráficos del museo nacional de arqueología, historia y ethnografía, 1937.

Hernández Rodríguez, Rosaura, ed. *Ignacio Comonfort, trayectoria y documentos.* Mexico: UNAM, 1967.

Lerdo de Tejada, Miguel, *Comercio exterior de México desde la Conquista hasta hoy.* Mexico: Banco Nacional de Comercio Exterior, 1967.

———, *Cuadro sinóptico de la República Mexicana en 1856 formado en vista de los últimos datos oficiales y otras noticias fidedignas.* Mexico, 1856.

López de Santa Anna, Antonio, *Mi historia militar y política, 1810–1874.* Mexico: Viuda de C. Bouret, 1905.

Manning, J. D. ed. *Diplomatic correspondence of the United States, 1831–1860,* vols. 8 and 9, Mexico. Washington, D. C.: Carnegie Endowment for International Peace, 1937.

Mayer, Brantz, *Mexico as it was and as it is.* New York, 1844.

Mora, José María Luis, *México y sus revoluciones,* 3 vols., 2nd ed. Mexico: Editorial Porrúa Hmns., 1950.

———, *Papeles inéditos y obras selectas del Doctor Mora,* ed. Genero García, *Documentos inéditos o muy raros para la historia,* vol. 6. Mexico: Bouret, 1906.

Otero, Mariano, *Obras,* ed. Jesus Reyes Heroles. Mexico City: Editorial Porrúa Hmns., 1967.

Payno y Flores, Manuel, *Artículos y Narraciones.* Francisco Monterde, ed. Mexico: UNAM, 1945.

———, *La Reforma Social en España y México. Apuntes históricos y principales leyes sobre desamortización de bienes eclesiásticos.* Mexico: Imprenta Universitaria, 1958.

de la Portilla, Anselmo, *Historia de la revolución de México contra la dictadura del general Santa Ana, 1853–1855.* Mexico, 1856.

———, *Méjico en 1856 y 1857. Gobierno del General Comonfort.* New York, 1858.

Prieto, Guillermo, *Memorias de mis tiempos, 1840 a 1853.* Mexico: Editorial Patria, 1969.

——, *Viajes de orden suprema por Fidel.* Años 1853–1855. Mexico, 1857.

Ramírez, José Fernando, *Mexico during the War with the United States.* ed. Walter V. Scholes; trans., Elliot B. Scherr. Columbia: University of Missouri Press, 1950.

Robertson, William Parish, *A Visit to Mexico,* 2 vols. London, 1853.

Suárez y Navarro, *Historia de México y del general Santa Ana,* 2 vols. Mexico, 1851.

Thompson, Waddy, *Recollections of Mexico.* New York, 1846.

Tornel y Mendivil, José María, *Breve reseña histórica de los acontecimientos más notables de la nación mexicana desde el año 1821 hasta nuestros días.* Mexico, 1852.

von Humboldt, Alexander, *Ensayo Político sobre el reino de la Nueva España.* Mexico: Editorial Porrúa, 1973.

Wilson, Robert Anderson, *Mexico and its Religion.* New York, 1855.

Zarco, Francisco, ed. *Historia del Congreso Estraordinario Constituyente de 1856 y 1857,* 2 vols. Mexico, 1857.

Zavala, Lorenzo, *Albores de la República.* Mexico: Empresas Editoriales, S. A., 1949.

——, *Ensayo histórico de las revoluciones de México, desde 1808 hasta 1830.* Mexico: Empresas Editoriales, 1950.

Contemporary Periodicals

Anales de Fomento. Mexico, 1854.
La Aurora del Sur. Chilpancingo, Guerrero, 1851.
Las Cosquillas. 1852.
El Heraldo. 1849.
El Libro del Pueblo. Puebla, 1849.
The London Times. 1848–1851.
El Monitor Republicano. 1848–1853, 1855–1856.
El Siglo XIX. 1848–1857.
El Tío Nonilla. 1849–1850.
El Universal. 1848–1855.

Secondary Sources

Aguilar Monteverde, Alonso, *Dialéctica de la Económia Mexicana del colonialismo al imperialismo.* Mexico: Editorial Nuestro Tiempo, S. A., 1972.

Alperovich, M. S., *Historia de la Independencia de México (1810–1824)*, trans. Adolfo Sanchez Vázquez. Mexico: Editorial Grijalba, S. A., 1967.

Amaral, Samuel, "Public Expenditure Financing in the Colonial Treasury: An Analysis of the Real Caja de Buenos Aires Accounts, 1789–91," *Hispanic American Historical Review* 64(1984):287–95 and commentaries by Javier Cuenca, John TePaske, Herbert Klein, John Fisher, and Tulio Halperin Donghi, pp. 297–322.

Anna, Timothy E., *The Fall of the Royal Government in Mexico City*. Lincoln: University of Nebraska Press, 1978.

———, "The Finances of Mexico City During the War of Independence," *Journal of Latin American Studies* 4(1972):55–75.

———, "The Role of Agustín de Iturbide: A Reappraisal," *Journal of Latin American Studies* 17(1985):79–110.

Archer, Christon, *The Army in Bourbon Mexico*. Albuquerque: University of New Mexico Press, 1977.

———, "Bourbon Finance and Military Policy in New Spain, 1759–1812," *The Americas* 37(1980):315–50.

Archivo General de la Nación, *Homenaje a D. Valentín Gómez Farías (1781–1858)*. Mexico: Talleres gráficos de la nación, 1933.

Arcila Farías, Eduardo, *Reformas económicas del siglo XVIII en Nueva España*. Mexico: Secretaría de Educación Pública, no. 117, 1974.

Ardant, G., "Financial Policy and Economic Infrastructure of Modern States and Nations," in Charles Tilly, ed., *The Formation of National States in Western Europe*. Princeton: Princeton University Press, 1975, pp. 164–242.

Arnáiz y Freg, Arturo, "Estudio Biográfico del Doctor en Teología y Licenciado en Derecho Civil Don José María Luis Mora," *El Doctor José María Luis Mora, 1794–1850*. Homenaje de la Universidad National de México al Reformador Ilustre. Mexico: UNAM, 1934.

———, "Prologo," in José María Luis Mora, *Ensayos, Ideas, y Retratos*. Biblioteca del Estudiante Universitario, no. 25. Mexico: UNAM, 1941.

Bancroft, Hubert Howe, *History of Mexico*, vol. V. San Francisco: A. L. Bancroft and Company, 1885.

Barbier, Jacques, "Peninsular Finance and Colonial Trade: The Dilemma of Charles IV's Spain," *Journal of Latin American Studies* 12(1980): 21–37.

Barbier, Jacques and Herbert S. Klein, "The Madrid Treasury 1784–1807," *Journal of Economic History* 41(1981):315–39.

Barker, Nancy Nichols, *The French Experience in Mexico, 1821–1861: A History of Constant Misunderstanding*. Chapel Hill: University of North Carolina Press, 1979.

Bauer, Arnold J., "The Church in the Economy of Spanish America: Censos and Depósitos in the Eighteenth and Nineteenth Centuries," *Hispanic American Historical Review,* 63(1983):707–33.

Baur, John E., "The Evolution of a Mexican Foreign Trade Policy, 1821–1828," *The Americas* 19(1963):225–62.

Bazant, Jan, *Alienation of Church Wealth in Mexico. Social and Economic Aspects of the Liberal Revolution 1856–1875,* trans. M. Costeloe. Cambridge: Cambridge University Press, 1971.

——, *Antonio Haro y Tamariz y sus aventuras políticas 1811–1869.* Mexico: El Colegio de México, 1985.

——, *A Concise History of Mexico from Hidalgo to Cardenas.* London: Cambridge University Press, 1977.

——, "The Division of Some Mexican *Haciendas* during the Liberal Revolution, 1856–1862," *Journal of Latin American Studies* 3(1971): 25–37.

——, *Historia de la deuda exterior de México (1823–1946).* Mexico: El Colegio de México, 1968.

Benson, Nettie Lee, *La deputación provincial y el federalismo mexicano.* Mexico: El Colegio de México, 1955.

——, ed. *Mexico and the Spanish Cortes, 1810–1822: Eight Essays.* Austin: University of Texas Press, 1966.

——, "The Plan of Casa Mata," *Hispanic American Historical Review* 25(1954):45–56.

Berge, Dennis E., "A Mexican Dilemma: The Mexico City Ayuntamiento and the Question of Loyalty, 1846–1848," *Hispanic American Historical Review* 50(1970):227–56.

Berry, Charles, *The Reform in Oaxaca.* Lincoln: University of Nebraska Press, 1981.

Bitar Letayf, Marcelo, "La vida económica de México y sus proyecciones." Tesis UNAM–Escuela Nacional de Económia, Mexico, 1964.

Blázquez, Carmen, *Miguel Lerdo de Tejada, un liberal veracruzano en la política nacional.* Mexico: El Colegio de México, 1978.

Bobb, Bernard, *The Viceregency of Antonio María Bucareli in New Spain.* Austin: University of Texas Press, 1962.

Bosher, J. F., *French Finances 1770–1795.* Cambridge: Cambridge University Press, 1970.

Brading, David A., *Miners and Merchants in Bourbon Mexico 1763–1810.* Cambridge: Cambridge University Press, 1971.

Bravo Ugarte, José, *Diócesis y Obispos de la Iglesia Mexicana.* Colección México Heroico no. 39. Mexico: Editorial Jus, 1965.

——, *Periodistas y Periódicos Mexicanos.* Mexico: Editorial Jus, 1966.

Broussard, Ray, "Ignacio Comonfort and his contribution to the Mexican reform 1855–1857," unpublished Ph.D. dissertation. University of Texas, 1959.

Burgin, Miron, *The Economic Aspects of Argentine Federalism 1820–1852*. New York: Russell & Russell, 1971.

Bushnell, Clyde Gilbert, "The military and political career of Juan Álvarez, 1790–1867," unpublished Ph.D. dissertation. University of Texas, 1958.

Bushnell, David, *The Santander Regime in Gran Colombia*. Newark, Delaware: University of Delaware Press, 1954.

Busto, Emiliano, *La Administración pública*. Mexico, 1889.

———, *Estadística de la República Mexicana*, 3 vols. Mexico, 1880.

Calderón, Franciso R., et al., "La vida económica," in Daniel Cosío Villegas, ed., *Historia Moderna de México. El Porfiriato*. Mexico: Editorial Hermes, 1965.

———, "La vida económica," in Daniel Cosío Villegas, ed., *Historia Moderna de México. La República Restaurada*. Mexico: Editorial Hermes, 1973.

Callahan, James Morton, *American Foreign Policy in Mexican Relations*. New York: Macmillan Company, 1932.

Callcott, Wilfrid Hardy, *Church and State in Mexico, 1822–1857*. Durham, North Carolina: Duke University Press, 1926.

———, *Santa Anna: The Story of an Enigma Who Once Was Mexico*. Norman: University of Oklahoma Press, 1936.

Cardoso, Ciro F. S., ed., *Formación y desarrollo de la burguesía en México. Siglo XIX*. Mexico: Siglo Vientiuno Editores, 1978.

———, ed., *México en el siglo XIX (1821–1910). Historia económica y de la estructura social*. Mexico: Editorial Nueva Imagen, 1980.

Carmagnani, Marcello, "Finanzas y Estado en Mexico, 1820–1880," *Ibero–Amerikanisches Archiv* 9(1983):279–317.

———, "Regionalism and the Central Government of Mexico During the Nineteenth Century," presented at the Woodrow Wilson International Center for Scholars, Smithsonian Institution, Washington, D. C., July 25, 1984.

Carreño, Alberto María, *La diplomacia extraordinaria entre México y Estados Unidos, 1789–1947*. Mexico: Editorial Jus, 1951.

Carrión, Anselmo, *Historia de la ciudad de Puebla de los Ángeles*. Puebla, 1896–1897.

Cásarez de Garibay, Rubén, "Spanish–Mexican Diplomatic Antecedents to the French Intervention in Mexico 1836–1862," unpublished Master's thesis, University of Texas, 1957.

Casasús, Joaquín D., *Historia de la deuda contraída en Londres con un apéndice sobre el estado actual de la hacienda pública*. Mexico, 1885.

Chapman, John Gresham, *La construcción del ferrocarril mexicano (1837–1880)*. Mexico: Secretaria de Educación Pública, Sep–Setentas, no. 209, 1975.

Charlton, Agnes, "Ignacio Comonfort and the Mexican Constitution 1857," unpublished Master's thesis, University of Texas, 1927.

Christelow, Allan, "Great Britain and the Trades from Cádiz and Lisbon to Spanish America and Brazil, 1759–1783," *Hispanic American Historical Review* 27(1947):1–29.

Coatsworth, John H., "Obstacles to Economic Growth in Nineteenth Century Mexico," *American Historical Review* 83:80–100.

Collier, Simon, *Ideas and politics of Chilean Independence 1808–1833*. London: Cambridge University Press, 1967.

Cosío Villegas, Daniel, *La Cuestión Arancelaria en México*, III. Historia de la política aduanal. Mexico: Centro mexicano de estudios económicos, 1932.

Costeloe, Michael, "Church–State financial negotiations in Mexico during the American War, 1846–1847," *Revista de historia de América* 60(1965):91–123.

———, *Church and State in Independent Mexico*. London: Royal Historical Society, 1978.

———, *Church Wealth in Mexico*. Cambridge: Cambridge University Press, 1967.

———, "The Mexican Church and the Rebellion of the *Polkos*," *Hispanic American Historical Review* 46(1966):170–78.

———, *La Primera República Federal de México (1824–1835)*. Mexico: Fondo de cultura económica, 1975.

Cotner, Thomas Ewing, "Diplomatic relations between the United States and Mexico concerning a Tehuantepec transit route 1823–1860," unpublished Master's thesis, University of Texas, 1939.

———, *The Military and Political Career of José Joaquín de Herrera, 1792–1854*. Austin: Institute of Latin American Studies, University of Texas, 1949.

Court, W. H. B., *A Concise Economic History of Britain from 1750 to Recent Times*. Cambridge: Cambridge University Press, 1954.

Covo, Jacqueline, "Los clubes políticos en la revolución de Ayutla," *Historia Mexicana* 28(1978):438–55.

———, *Las ideas de la Reforma en México*. Mexico: UNAM, 1983.

Cross, Harry E., "Living Standards in Rural Nineteenth–Century Mexico: Zacatecas 1820–80," *Journal of Latin American Studies* 10(1978): 1–19.

Cué Cánovas, Agustín, *Historia social y económica de México 1521–1854*. Mexico: Editorial F. Trillas, S. A., 1963.

Cuevas, Mariano, *Historia de la Iglesia en México*, Vol. 5. Mexico: Ediciones Cervantes, 1947.

Cumberland, Charles C., *Mexico: The Struggle for Modernity*. New York: Oxford University Press, 1968.

Deas, Malcolm, "The Fiscal Problem of Nineteenth–Century Colombia," *Journal of Latin American Studies* 14(1982):287–328.

Decorme, S. J., Gerardo, *Historia de la Compañía de Jesús en la República Mexicana durante el Siglo XIX*. Guadalajara, Tip. "El Regional," 1914–.

Díaz, Lilia, "El liberalismo militante," in *Historia General de México*, Vol. 3. Mexico: El Colegio de México, 1976.

Díaz y Díaz, Fernando, *Caudillos y caciques: Antonio López de Santa Anna y Juan Álvarez*. Mexico: El Colegio de México, 1972.

———, *Santa Anna y Juan Álvarez: Fuente a Fuente*. Mexico: Secretaría de Educación Pública, 1972.

Diccionario Porrúa de historia, biográfia, y geográfia de México. Mexico: Editorial Porrúa, S. A., 1966.

di Tella, Torcuato S., "The Dangerous Classes in Early Nineteenth Century Mexico," *Journal of Latin American Studies* 6(1974):79–105.

Domínguez, Miguel, *La erección del Estado de Guerrero. Antecedentes Históricos*. Mexico: Secretaría de Educación Pública, 1949.

Fisher, John, "Imperial 'Free Trade' and the Hispanic Economy, 1778–1796," *Journal of Latin American Studies* 13(1981):21–56.

———, "The Imperial Response to 'Free Trade': Spanish Imports from Spanish America, 1778–1796," *Journal of Latin American Studies* 17(1985):35–78.

Flores Caballero, Romeo, *Counterrevolution, The Role of the Spaniards in the Independence of Mexico, 1804–1838*, trans., Jaime Rodríguez O. Lincoln: University of Nebraska Press, 1974.

Florescano, Enrique, *Precios del maíz y crisis agrícolas en México 1708–1810*. Mexico: El Colegio de México, 1969.

Florescano, Enrique, and Isabel Gil Sánchez, "La época de las reformas borbónicas y el crecimiento económico, 1750–1808," in *Historia General de Mexico*, Vol. 2. Mexico: El Colegio de México, 1976.

Florescano, Enrique, and María del Rosario Lanzagorta, "Política económica. Antecedentes y consecuencias," in *La económia mexicana en la época de Juárez*. Mexico: Secretaria de Educación Pública, 1976.

Florstedt, Robert F., "Mora contra Bustamante," *Historia Mexicana* 12(1962/63):28–52.

———, "Mora y la génesis del liberalismo burgués," *Historia Mexicana* 11(1961/62):207–23.

Fraser, Donald J., "La Política de desamortización en las comunidades indígenas, 1856–1872," *Historia Mexicana* 21(1972):615–32.

Furtado, Celso, *The Economic Growth of Brazil.* Berkeley: University of California Press, 1965.

Garber, Paul Neff, *The Gadsden Treaty.* Gloucester, Massachusetts: P. Smith, 1959.

García, Clara, "Sociedad, crédito, y cofradía en la Nueva España. El caso de Nuestra Señora de Aránzazu," *Historias* 3(1983):53–68.

García Cantú, Gastón, *El Pensamiento de la Reacción Mexicana. Historia documental 1810–1962.* Mexico: Empresas Editoriales, S. A., 1965.

Godechot, Jacques, *Les institutions de la France sous la Révolution et l'émpire.* Paris: Presses Universitaires de France, 1968.

González Avelar, Miguel, *México en el Umbral de la Reforma.* Mexico: Federación Editorial Mexicana, S. A. de C. V., 1971.

González Navarro, Moisés, *Anatomía del Poder en México (1848–1853).* Mexico: El Colegio de México, 1977.

———, "Tipología del Liberalismo Mexicano," *Historia Mexicana* 32 (1982):198–225.

———, "La venganza del Sur," *Historia Mexicana* 21(1972):677–92.

Gootenberg, Paul, "Merchants, Foreigners, and the State in Post–Independence Peru." unpublished Ph.D. dissertation, University of Chicago, 1985.

Graham, Richard, *Britain and the Onset of Modernization in Brazil 1850–1914.* Cambridge: Cambridge University Press, 1972.

Greer, Viola Ann, "Santiago Vidaurri, Cacique of Northern Mexico: His Relationship to Benito Juárez," unpublished Master's thesis, University of Texas, 1949.

Gurría Lacroix, Jorge, *Las Ideas monárquicas de don Lucas Alamán.* Mexico: Instituto de Historia, 1951.

Hale, Charles A., *Mexican Liberalism in the Age of Mora, 1821–1853.* New Haven: Yale University Press, 1968.

Halperin Donghi, Tulio, *The Aftermath of Revolution in Latin America,* trans., J. Bunsen. New York: Harper & Row, 1973.

———, *Guerra y Finanzas en los Origenes del Estado Argentino (1791–1850).* Buenos Aires: Editorial Belgrano, 1982.

Hamill, Hugh M., Jr., *The Hidalgo Revolt. Prelude to Mexican Independence.* Gainesville: University of Florida Press, 1966.

Hammond, Bray, *Banks and Politics in America from the Revolution to the Civil War.* Princeton: Princeton University Press, 1967.

Hamnett, Brian R., "Anastasio Bustamante y la guerra de independencia 1810–1821," *Historia Mexicana* 28(1979):515–45.

———, "The Appropriation of Mexican Church Wealth by the Spanish Bourbon Government—the 'Consolidación de Vales Reales,' 1805–1809," *Journal of Latin American Studies* 19(1969):85–113.

———, "The Economic and Social Dimension of the Revolution of Independence in Mexico, 1800–1824," *Ibero–Amerikanisches Archiv* 6(1980):1–27.

———, "Mexico's Royalist Coalition: the Response to Revolution 1808–1821," *Journal of Latin American Studies* 12(1980):55–86.

———, *Politics and Trade in Southern Mexico 1750–1821.* Cambridge: Cambridge University Press, 1971.

———, *Revolución y contrarevolución en México y el Perú. (Liberalismo, realeza y separatismo 1800–1824).* Mexico: Fondo de cultura económica, 1978.

———, "Royalist Counterinsurgency and the Continuity of Rebellion: Guanajuato and Michoacán, 1813–1820," *Hispanic American Historical Review* 62(1982):19–48.

Hanighen, Frank C., *Santa Anna, the Napoleon of the West.* New York: Coward–McCann, 1934.

Haring, Clarence, *The Spanish Empire in America.* New York: Harcourt, Brace & World, 1963.

Harris, Charles H., III, *A Mexican Family Empire. The Latifundio of the Sánchez Navarro Family 1765–1867.* Austin: University of Texas Press, 1975.

Hawtrey, R. G., *Economic Aspects of Sovereignty,* 2nd ed., New York: Longsman, Green and Company, 1930.

Herr, Richard, *The 18th Century Revolution in Spain.* Princeton: Princeton University Press, 1958.

Hidy, Ralph W., *The House of Baring in American Trade and Finance. English Merchant Bankers at Work, 1763–1861.* Cambridge, Massachusetts: Harvard University Press, 1949.

Hofstadter, Richard, *The Idea of a Party System. The Rise of a Legitimate Opposition in the United States, 1780–1840.* Berkeley: University of California Press, 1972.

Hutchinson, Cecil Alan, "The asiatic cholera epidemic of 1833 in Mexico," *Bulletin of the History of Medicine* 32(1958):1–23.

———, "Valentín Gómez Farías: A Biographical Study," unpublished Ph.D. dissertation, University of Texas, 1948.

Iimura, "The Financial Relationship between the Mexican Federal Government and the States: 1825–1828," M.A. thesis, University of Texas.

Imlah, Albert H., "British Balance of Payments and Export of Capital, 1816–1913," *Economic History Review,* 2nd series, 5(1952): 208–39.

Jenks, Leland Hamilton, *The Migration of British Capital to 1875.* New York: Knopf, 1927.

Johnson, Richard A., *The Mexican Revolution of Ayutla, 1854–55.*

Augustana Library Publications, no. 17. Rock Island, Illinois: Augustana Book Company, 1939.

Kaufmann, William W., *British Policy and the Independence of Latin America 1804–1828*. Connecticut: Archon Books, 1967.

Kenwood, A. G., and A. L. Laugheed, *The Growth of the International Economy 1820–1960*. London: Allen & Unwin, 1971.

Keremitsis, Dawn, *La industria textil mexicana en el siglo XIX*. Mexico: Secretaría de Educación Pública, 1973.

Kicza, John E., *Colonial Entrepreneurs: Families and Business in Bourbon Mexico City*. Albuquerque: University of New Mexico Press, 1983.

Klein, Herbert S., "Structure and Profitability of Royal Finance in the Viceroyalty of the Río de la Plata in 1790," *Hispanic American Historical Review* 53(1973):440–69.

Knapp, Frank G., Jr., "Parliamentary Government and the Mexican Constitution of 1857: A Forgotten Phase of Mexican Political History," *Hispanic American Historical Review* 33(1953):65–87.

Knowlton, Robert J., *Church Property and the Mexican Reform 1856–1910*. DeKalb: Northern Illinois Press, 1976.

———, "La individualización de la propiedad corporativa civil en el siglo XIX—notas sobre Jalisco," *Historia Mexicana* 28(1978):24–61.

———, "Some practical effects of clerical opposition to the Mexican Reform, 1856–1860," *Hispanic American Historical Review* 45 (1965):246–56.

Lacerte, Robert K., "Great Britain and Mexico in the Age of Juárez, 1854–1876," unpublished Ph.D. dissertation, Case Western Reserve University, September 1971.

Ladd, Doris M., *The Mexican Nobility at Independence 1780–1826*. Austin: Institute of Latin American Studies, University of Texas, 1976.

Landes, David S., *Bankers and Pashas*. New York: Harper Torchbooks, 1969.

Latourette, Kenneth Scott, *The Nineteenth Century in Europe: Background and the Roman Catholic Phase*. Westport, Connecticut: Greenwood Press, 1965.

Lavrin, Asunción, "Mexican Nunneries from 1835–1860," *The Americas* 28(1972):288–310.

———, "Problems and Policies in the Administration of Nunneries in Mexico 1800–1835," *The Americas* 28(1971):57–77.

———, "The role of the nunneries in the economy of New Spain in the eighteenth century," *Hispanic American Historical Review* 46 (1966):371–93.

Levin, Jonathan V., *The Export Economies: Their Pattern and Devel-*

opment in Historical Perspective. Cambridge: Harvard University Press, 1960.

Liehr, Reinhard, "La deuda exterior de México y los 'merchant bankers' británicos 1821–1860," *Ibero–Amerikanisches Archiv* 9(1983): 415–39.

Lill, Thomas R., *National Debt of Mexico, history and present status.* New York: Searle, Nichols and Hill, 1919.

Lindley, Richard, *Haciendas and Economic Development: Guadalajara, Mexico at Independence.* Austin: University of Texas Press, 1983.

Liss, Peggy K., *Mexico Under Spain 1521–1556: Society and the Origins of Nationality.* Chicago: University of Chicago Press, 1975.

López Camara, Francisco, *La estructura económica y social de México en la época de la Reforma.* Mexico: Siglo Vientiuno Editores, S. A., 1967.

López Gallo, Manuel, *Economía y política en la historia de México.* Mexico: Ediciones Solidaridad, 1965.

Lynn, Vela Leatrice, "The Political Career of Teodosio Lares, 1844–1867," unpublished Ph.D. dissertation, University of Texas, 1961.

McAlister, Lyle N., *The "Fuero Militar" in New Spain 1764–1800.* Gainesville: University of Florida Press, 1957.

McCaleb, Walter F., *The Public Finances of Mexico.* New York: Harper Brothers, 1921.

McGowan, Gerald L., *La prensa y el poder.* Mexico: El Colegio de México, 1978.

McGreevey, William Paul, *An Economic History of Colombia 1845–1930.* Cambridge: Cambridge University Press, 1971.

Mack, Raymond, "Constitutional Centralism in Mexico—A Study of the Constitutions of 1836 and 1843." M.A. thesis, University of Texas, 1949.

McLean, Malcolm D., *Vida y obra de Guillermo Prieto.* Mexico: El Colegio de México, 1960.

McManners, John, *The French Revolution and the Church.* New York: Harper and Row, 1970.

Macune, Charles William, Jr., *El estado de México y la federación mexicana, 1823–1835.* Mexico: Fondo de cultura económica, 1978.

———, "The impact of Federalism on Mexican Church–State Relations, 1824–1835: The Case of the State of Mexico," *The Americas* 40(1983):505–29.

Maisel, Jay Max, "Origins and Development of Mexican Antipathy to the South, 1821–1867," unpublished Ph.D. dissertation, University of Texas, June 1955.

Marion, Marcel, *La Vente des biens nationaux pendant la révolution*. . . Geneva: Slatkine–Megariotis Reprints, 1974.

Márquez Montiel, S. J., Joaquín, *Hombres ilustres de Puebla*, 2 vols. Mexico: Editorial Jus, 1952.

Mateos, José María, *Historia de la masonería en México desde 1806 hasta 1884*. Mexico, 1884.

Mayo, John, "The Impatient Lion: Britain's 'official mind' and Latin America in the 1850s," *Ibero–Amerikanisches Archiv* 9(1983): 197–223.

Meyer, Michael C., and William Sherman, *The Course of Mexican History*, 2nd ed. New York: Oxford University Press, 1983.

Meyer Cosío, Rosa María, "Empresarios, Crédito y Especulación (1820–1850)," paper given at Seminario de la historia de la bancaría en México, 1984.

Morales, María Dolores, "Estructura urbana y distribución de la propriedad en la ciudad de Mexico en 1813," *Historia Mexicana* 25(1975):363–402.

Moreno, Daniel, *Hombres de la reforma*. Mexico: B. Costa–Amic, Ed., 1961.

Morgan, Iwan, "French Policy in Spanish America: 1830–48," *Journal of Latin American Studies* 10(1978):309–28.

Moses, Bernard, *The Railway Revolution in Mexico*. San Francisco: Berkeley Press, 1895.

Muñoz y Pérez, Daniel, *El General Don Juan Álvarez*. Mexico: Editorial Academia Literaria, 1959.

Ochoa Campos, Moisés, *Historia del Estado de Guerrero*. Mexico: Librería Porrúa Hmns., 1968.

O'Gorman, Edmundo, *Breve historia de las divisiones territoriales*. Mexico: Editorial Porrúa, 1937.

———, *La supervivencia política Novo–Hispana (reflexiones sobre el monarquismo mexicano)*. Mexico: Editorial Porrúa, 1969.

Olliff, Donathon C. *Reforma Mexico and the United States: A Search for Alternatives to Annexation, 1854–1861*. University, Ala.: University of Alabama Press, 1981.

Parkes, Henry Bamford, *A History of Mexico*. Boston: Houghton Mifflin Publishing Company, 1966.

Pastor y Carreto, Luis G., *Presidentes poblanos, ensayo histórico crítico y biográfico*. Mexico: Costa–Amic, 1965.

Peñafiel, Antonio, *Ciudades coloniales y capitales de la república mexicana: Estado de Guerrero*. Mexico: Imprenta de la Secretaria de fomento, 1908.

Pendle, George, *History of Latin America*. London: Penguin Books, 1976.

Platt, D. C. M., *The Cinderella Service: British Consuls since 1825.* London: Longman, 1971.

——, *Finance, Trade, and Politics in British Foreign Policy, 1815–1914.* Oxford: Clarendon Press, 1968.

——, "Finanzas británicas en México (1821–1867)," *Historia Mexicana* 32(1982):226–61.

——, *Latin America and British Trade, 1806–1914.* New York: Barnes and Noble, 1973.

Potash, Robert A., *Mexican Government and Industrial Development in the Republic: The Banco de Avío.* Amherst: University of Massachusetts Press, 1983.

——, "El Comercio Exterior de México de Miguel Lerdo de Tejada: un error estadístico," *Trimestre Económico* 20(1953):474–79.

Powell, T. G., "Priests and Peasants in Central Mexico: Social Conflict during 'La Reforma' " *Hispanic American Historical Review* 57(1977):298–313.

Priestley, Herbert Ingram, *José de Gálvez, Visitor–General of New Spain (1765–1771).* Berkeley: University of California Press, 1916.

Randall, Laura, *Comparative Economic History of Latin America, vol 1: Mexico.* Ann Arbor: University Microfilms International, 1977.

Randall, Robert, *The Real del Monte: A British Mining Venture in Mexico.* Austin: University of Texas Press, 1972.

Reyes Heroles, Jesús, *El Liberalismo mexicano,* 3 vols. Mexico: UNAM, 1961.

Ríos, E. M. de los, *Liberales ilustres mexicanos de la Reforma y la intervención.* Mexico, 1890.

Riva Palacio, Vicente, ed., *México a través de los siglos,* 5 vols. Mexico and Barcelona, 1887–1889.

Rivera Cambas, Manuel, *Los gobernantes de México,* 2 vols. Mexico, 1872–73.

——, *Historia antigua y moderna de Jalapa y de las revoluciones del estado de Veracruz,* IV. Mexico, 1871.

Rives, George L., *The United States and Mexico, 1821–1848,* Vol. 2. New York: Scribner's, 1913.

Robertson, Frank Delbert, "The Military and Political Career of Mariano Paredes y Arrillaga, 1797–1849," unpublished Ph.D. dissertation, University of Texas, 1955.

Robertson, William Spence, "The French Intervention in Mexico in 1838," *Hispanic American Historical Review* 24(1944):222–52.

——, *Iturbide of Mexico.* Durham, North Carolina: Duke University Press, 1952.

Rodríguez O., Jaime, "Down from Colonialism: Mexico's Nineteenth

Century Crisis," lecture presented May 28, 1980, University of California, Irvine.

———, *The Emergence of Spanish America: Vicente Rocafuerte and Spanish Americanism 1808–1832*. Berkeley: University of California Press, 1975.

———, "Oposición a Bustamante," *Historia Mexicana* 20(1970):189–234.

Ross, William John, III, "The Role of Manuel Doblado in the Mexican Reform Movement, 1855–1860," Ph.D. dissertation, University of Texas, August, 1967.

Ruiz Castañeda, María del Carmen, *Periodismo Político de la Reforma en la Ciudad de México, 1854–1861*. Mexico: Editorial Tradición, S. A., 1964.

Salvucci, Linda K., "Costumbres viejas, 'hombres nuevos': José de Gálvez y la burocracia fiscal novohispana (1754–1800)," *Historia Mexicana*, 33(1983):224–64.

Samponaro, Frank N., "Mariano Paredes y el movimiento monarquista mexicano en 1846," *Historia Mexicana* 32(1952):39–54.

———, "The Political Role of the Army in Mexico 1821–1848," unpublished Ph.D. dissertation, State University of New York at Stony Brook, May 1974.

———, "Santa Anna and the Abortive Anti–Federalist Revolt of 1833 in Mexico," *The Americas* 40(1983):95–107.

Sánchez, J. M., *Reform and reaction: the politico–religious background of the Spanish Civil War*. Chapel Hill: University of North Carolina Press, 1964.

Sarrailh, Jean, *L'Espagne éclairée de la seconde moitié du XVIIIième siècle*. Paris: Klinekieck, 1954.

Scholes, Walter F., *Mexican Politics during the Juárez Regime, 1855–1872*. Columbia: University of Missouri Press, 1957.

Shearer, Ernest C., "Border Diplomatic Relations between the United States and Mexico, 1848–1860." Ph.D. dissertation, University of Texas, 1939.

Sheils, W. E., "Church and State in the first decade of Mexican independence," *Catholic Historical Review* 28(1942):206–28.

Sierra, Justo, *The Political Evolution of the Mexican People*. trans. C. Ramsdell. Austin: University of Texas Press, 1969.

Silva Herzog, Jesús, *El Pensamiento económico, social, y político de México 1810–1964*. Mexico: Fondo de cultura económica, 1947.

Simón Segura, Francisco, *La Desamortización Española del Siglo XIX*. Madrid: Instituto de Estudios Fiscales, Ministro de Hacienda, 1973.

Sims, Harold D., *La expulsión de los Españoles de México (1821–28)*. Mexico: Fondo de cultura económica, 1974.

Singletary, Otis A., *The Mexican War*. Chicago: University of Chicago Press, 1960.

Sinkin, Richard N., *The Mexican Reform, 1855–1876: A Study of Liberal Nation–Building*. Austin: Institute of Latin American Studies, University of Texas, 1979.

Smith, Robert, "The Institution of the Consulado in New Spain," *Hispanic American Historical Review* 24(1944):61–83.

———, "Sales Taxes in New Spain," *Hispanic American Historical Review* 28(1948):2–37.

———, "Shipping in the Port of Vera Cruz 1790–1821," *Hispanic American Historical Review* 23(1943):5–20.

Stevens, Donald F., "Instability in Mexico from Independence to the War of the Reforma." Ph.D. dissertation, University of Chicago, 1984.

Stone, Irving, "The Composition and Distribution of British Investment in Latin America." Ph.D. dissertation, Columbia University, 1962.

Tenenbaum, Barbara A., "Development and Sovereignty, Intellectuals and the Second Empire," paper given at the VI Conference of Mexican and United States Historians, Chicago, Illinois, September 1981.

———, "Merchants, Money, and Mischief: The British in Mexico, 1821–1862," *The Americas* 35(1979):317–39.

———, "Neither a borrower nor a lender be: Financial Constraints and the Treaty of Guadalupe Hidalgo," in *Papers presented at a Conference on Mexicans and Mexican Americans in the Nineteenth Century*, May 1984, University of California, Irvine, forthcoming.

Toro, Alfonso, *Dos Constituyentes del Año de 1824. Biografías de Don Miguel Ramos Arizpe y Don Lorenzo Zavala*. Mexico: Museo Nacional, 1925.

Turlington, Edgar, *Mexico and her Foreign Creditors*. New York: Columbia University Press, 1930.

Tutino, John, "Creole Mexico: Spanish Elites, Haciendas, and Indian towns." Ph.D. dissertation, University of Texas, 1976.

Valadés, José C., *Alamán, estadista e historiador*. Mexico: Antigua Librería Robredo, 1938.

———, *Melchor Ocampo: Reformador de Mexico*. Mexico: Editorial Patria, S. A., 1954.

Vázquez, Josefina Z., "Los primeros tropiezos," in *Historia General de México*, Vol. 3. Mexico: El Colegio de México, 1977.

Velasco, Alfonso Luis, *Geográfia y estadística de la República Mexicana*, Vol. 10, "Guerrero." Mexico: Secretaría de Fomento, 1892.

Velázquez, María del Carmen, *El estado de guerra en Nueva España 1760–1808*. Mexico: El Colegio de México, 1950.

Villers, M. Guadalupe, *Hacienda Pública de los estados mexicanos*, 2 vols. Mexico: Tip. de la oficina impresora de estampillas, 1911.

Voss, Stuart F., *On the Periphery of Nineteenth Century Mexico*. Tucson: University of Arizona Press, 1982.

Walker, David Wayne, "Business as Usual: the Empresa del Tabaco in Mexico, 1837–1844," *Hispanic American Historical Review* 64 (1984):675–706.

———, "Kinship, Business and Politics: The Martínez del Río Family in Mexico, 1824–1864." Ph.D. dissertation, University of Chicago, August 1981.

Wheat, Raymond C., *Francisco Zarco: El Portavoz Liberal de la Reforma*. Antonia Castro Leal, trans. Mexico: Editorial Porrúa, 1957.

Williams, Judith Blow, *British Commercial Policy and Trade Expansion*. Oxford: Clarendon Press, 1972.

Womack, John, Jr.,"The Mexican Economy During the Revolution, 1910–1920: Historiography and Analysis," *Marxist Perspectives* 1(1978):80–122.

———, *Zapata and the Mexican Revolution*. New York: Knopf, 1969.

Zamacois, Niceto de, *Historia de Méjico, desde sus tiempos más remotas hasta nuestros días, escrita en vista de todo lo que de irrecusable han dado a luz los más caracterizados historia dores. . .*, Vols. 13 and 14. Barcelona, 1880.

Index